Everything DiSC® Manual

Mark Scullard, Ph.D.

Dabney Baum, Ed.D.

WILEY

Library of Congress Cataloging-in-Publication Data

Scullard, Mark.
    Everything DiSC manual / Mark Scullard, Dabney Baum.
        pages cm
    Includes bibliographical references and index.
    ISBN 978-1-119-08067-1 (pbk.)
    1. Personality tests.   2. Personality assessment.   3. Personality and emotions.   4. Personality and occupation.
I. Baum, Dabney, date. II. Title.
        BF698.5.S396 2015
        155.2'83—dc23
                                                                                            2014046109

Printed in the United States of America
PB Printing   10 9 8 7 6 5 4 3

Contents

List of Tables

List of Figures

Preface

The DISC model was first proposed by William Marston in 1928, but it wasn't until the 1970s when the first explicit measure of this model was made widely available for general use. Although elements of Marston's original model have been retained in the current manifestation of DiSC® (i.e., *Everything DiSC*®), many aspects of the theory have evolved to better reflect contemporary psychological measurement and theory. Today, *Everything DiSC* is used in a wide range of industries to address needs such as leadership development, management training, sales training, conflict management, and team building.

The *Everything DiSC* offering includes, but is not limited to, assessments, profiles, and facilitation kits. *Assessment* refers to the measurement of the DiSC model, which is available only in an online format. *Profile* refers to the PDF report that is generated for the respondent so that he or she can view the results of the assessment. *Facilitation kit* refers to a collection of materials (e.g., videos, PowerPoint® slides, scripts) available to help practitioners conduct classroom training. This *Manual* is chiefly designed to discuss the assessment portion of the *Everything DiSC* offering.

The *Everything DiSC* offering is separated into six application areas, each of which addresses a different topic. These applications are *Workplace, Management, Sales, Productive Conflict, Work of Leaders,* and *363 for Leaders.* Sections of the assessment do vary across these applications, but the core assessment of DiSC style is the same in all six. This *Manual* discusses the research behind the assessment of DiSC style as well as the research associated with each of the specific applications.

CHAPTER 1

DiSC Overview and Theory

The Purpose of Everything DiSC

Everything DiSC® is a personal development assessment that measures an individual's tendencies and priorities. It is designed to support an individual's understanding of his or her work-related behaviors, the behaviors of others, and how to apply this knowledge in work situations.

Unlike many other personality assessments, the *Everything DiSC* assessment is written for a nontechnical, general audience, rather than for a clinical, industrial-organizational, or academic audience. The assessment does not assume any previous training in psychological theory. Although it is possible for a respondent to understand his or her profile without the assistance of a trained professional, experience suggests that the instrument is far more engaging and impactful if the respondent has the insight and support of such a professional. The feedback in the profile is written to be neutral in tone, and although there are sections that explore the respondent's potential shortcomings, efforts were made to eliminate feedback that might be psychologically sensitive or threatening in nature.

The ultimate goal of *Everything DiSC* is to take wisdom about interpersonal dynamics that has been developed through psychological research and theory and help people use this knowledge to improve their relationships and performance in a variety of diverse contexts.

The DiSC Model

The foundation of DiSC® was first described by William Moulton Marston in his 1928 book, *Emotions of Normal People.* Marston identified what he called four "primary emotions" and associated behavioral responses, which today we know as Dominance (D), Influence (i), Steadiness (S), and Conscientiousness (C). Since Marston's time, the theoretical understanding of this model has grown to include developments in contemporary psychology. As well, the measurement of this model has evolved substantially since the earliest attempts to assess DISC over 40 years ago. The *Everything DiSC* assessment uses the circle, or circumplex, as illustrated in Figure 1.1, as an intuitive way to represent this model. Although all points around the circle are equally meaningful and interpretable, the basic DiSC model describes four specific styles.

Dominance: direct, strong-willed, and forceful

Influence: sociable, talkative, and lively

Steadiness: gentle, accommodating, and soft-hearted

Conscientiousness: private, analytical, and logical

The Two Dimensions Behind DiSC

Although DiSC describes four styles, the model is at its core two-dimensional. These two dimensions reflect fundamental aspects of human nature and can be viewed as independent constructs, as shown in Figure 1.2. The first dimension is visualized with a vertical axis that runs from fast-paced at the top to moderate-paced at the bottom. This dimension is conceptually similar to the constructs of surgency (Norman, 1963) and potency

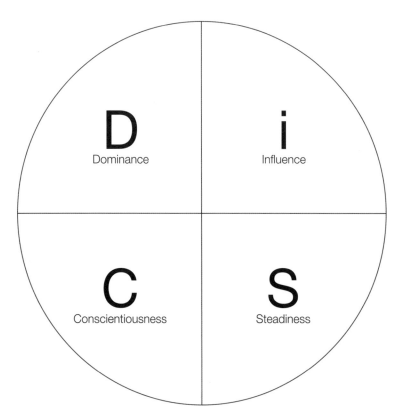

Figure 1.1 The Basic Everything DiSC Model

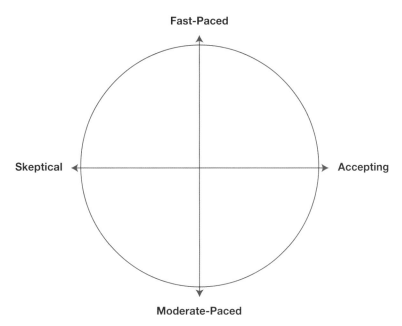

Figure 1.2 The Two Dimensions of DiSC

(Goldberg, 1981). It describes a person's outward activity level, where a person scoring toward the top of this dimension is expected to display a high level of outward energy/ activity and to be outspoken and assertive. This construct has conceptual overlap with Gray's (1987) postulation of a neurobiological system referred to as the *behavioral activation system*, in which influencing or assertive behavior is activated in response to perceived rewards.

In contrast, a person scoring toward the bottom of this dimension is expected to demonstrate a lower level of outward energy/activity (i.e., more internal, reflective behavior), and show less assertiveness. He or she is also expected to be thoughtful and careful and less comfortable taking risks. There are people who are quick and assertive in their reactions to the environment, but people whose dots are located on the lower half of the DiSC map tend to be slower and more contemplative in their reactions. This construct has some, although not complete, conceptual overlap with Gray's (1987) *behavioral inhibition system*, in which avoidant behavior is activated in response to perceived threats.

The second dimension, the horizontal axis, ranges from skeptical on the left to accepting on the right. People who fall toward the left side of this continuum are expected to be more questioning and cynical in nature. They are more likely to be outwardly or inwardly challenging of others. People who fall toward the right side of this continuum are expected to be more trusting and receptive to others. They are more likely to show outward signs of friendliness and empathy. This dimension is conceptually similar to the construct of agreeableness (McCrae & Costa, 2010). Those who are highly agreeable place a priority on cooperation and social harmony, whereas those who are less agreeable show less concern for cooperation and social harmony.

Unlike the more common representation of traits as a one-dimensional continuum, the DiSC model examines the interaction of two independent continua. As such, style descriptions include traits associated with two continua and the resulting interaction between those two traits. As a point of comparison, the interpretation of a one-dimensional trait may describe someone who scores high on the moderate—fast-paced dimension (i.e., faster pace) as "assertive, adventurous, and bold." In the DiSC model, this person is simultaneously measured on a second dimension, and this is also included in the interpretation. Therefore, if the individual scores high on the moderate—fast-paced dimension but also low on the skeptical—accepting dimension (i.e., more skeptical), the individual may read an interpretation that looks like "direct, outspoken, and forceful."

The DiSC Quadrants

These two dimensions create four quadrants, as shown in Figure 1.3. Each of these four quadrants has been labeled to describe the typical characteristics of people who have the corresponding placement on both axes. For example, people who fall toward the top of the vertical axis (fast-paced) and the left of the horizontal axis (skeptical), tend to be forceful, direct, and demanding. As a consequence, this quadrant has been labeled Dominance (D). The remaining three quadrants are labeled Influence (i), Steadiness (S), and Conscientiousness (C).

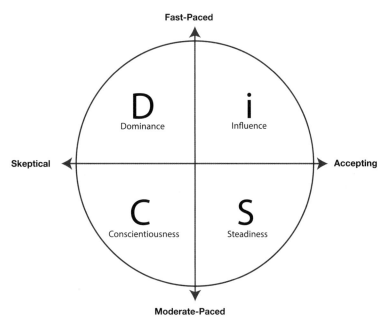

Figure 1.3 The Four Quadrants

In the same way that any individual can be measured on any two independent dimensions, a person can be placed within the two-dimensional *Everything DiSC* map. This placement represents a *style*. A style is a set of typical response patterns that are expected from a person. However, that doesn't mean that a person can only exhibit that pattern. For instance, an individual who has been assessed and located in the D quadrant will demonstrate more dominant behaviors and preferences than the average person, but will also, from time to time, show behaviors and preferences that are associated with the other three quadrants.

The Twelve Everything DiSC Styles

The two-dimensional *Everything DiSC* map can also be split into twelve segments rather than four quadrants, as shown in Figure 1.4. This allows for finer differentiation among the different locations with the map. In the *Everything DiSC* reports, these segments are referred to as styles.

Some of the styles (i.e., segments) have a single letter designation and others have a double letter designation. The single letters simply refer to the traditional D, i, S, and C

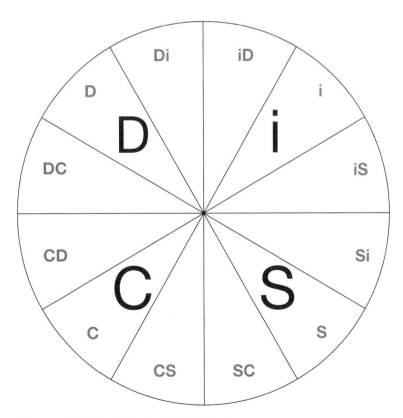

Figure 1.4 The Twelve DiSC Styles

locations on the circular map. Those styles with two letters fall between the single letter styles but are no less "pure" or inherently meaningful than the single letter styles. The Di style is often described as a combination of the D and i styles, but it is equally true (and false) that the D style is the combination of the DC and Di styles. The Di style does share characteristics with the D style, but each contains characteristics that the other does not. DiSC styles that are adjacent to each other on the *Everything DiSC* map will have more in common, and those that are across from each other on the map will be theoretically opposite.

Note that in the *Everything DiSC* assessment, there is a difference between the twelve styles (used for interpretation of results) and the eight scales (used for measurement). When respondents take the assessment, they are scored on eight scales that form a circle around the DiSC model. These scales are Di, i, iS, S, SC, C, CD, and D. These scales are used to calculate placement within the model, but are not reported to respondents in the profile (although they are presented for review in the *Supplement for Facilitators*). When respondents receive their profile, they are told the one style (out of twelve) that is the most descriptive of them. The twelve styles are described below. Because styles are often confused, styles that share two letters are grouped together and contrasted. The conceptual descriptions below can also be applied to the eight scales of *Everything DiSC.*

Dominance/Influence (Di or iD) Styles: Fast-Paced. The Di and iD styles are positioned in the middle of the skeptical—accepting dimension, but toward the top of the moderate—fast-paced dimension. One of the adjectives that best captures the nature of this style is *dynamic.* The qualities that are captured in these styles point to an individual who has a bias toward action. People who fall in this location on the map describe themselves as adventurous and bold. They are also more likely than the average person to identify themselves as enterprising or entrepreneurial. They typically have a combination of self-confidence and social poise that can be described as magnetic or inspiring. The Di style is accurately described as convincing and daring, while the iD style is accurately described as animated and inspiring. Overall, these styles both contain two major conceptual elements: (1) being bold and (2) having a bias toward action.

Influence (i) Style: Fast-Paced/Accepting. In the top right of the *Everything DiSC* map is the i style. Statistically speaking, the two items that best capture the nature of this style are, "I am lively" and "I am extremely outgoing." Conceptually, this style describes people who both have high energy and are very interpersonally positive. Consequently, they are frequently described as enthusiastic and high-spirited. Behaviorally, they are quicker than the average person to seek out new social opportunities and are generally highly talkative. Overall, this style contains two major conceptual elements: (1) being highly sociable and (2) being lively.

Influence/Steadiness (iS or Si) Style: Accepting. The iS and Si styles are positioned in the middle of the moderate—fast-paced dimension, but to the right of the skeptical—accepting dimension. This suggests that people who fall in this location of the map are positive, but not to the extremes of being highly enthusiastic, or, on the other hand, being extremely gentle. One of the adjectives that statistically best captures the essence of these styles is *cheerful.* In general, people who fall in these segments of the map tend to be trusting and to see the best in others. They are more likely than the average person to rate themselves as compassionate and welcoming. The iS style is accurately described as upbeat and lighthearted, while the Si style is accurately described as supportive and agreeable. Overall, these styles contain two major conceptual elements: (1) being positive and (2) showing empathy.

Steadiness (S) Style: Moderate-Paced/Accepting. In the bottom right of the *Everything DiSC* map is the S style. The adjective *gentle* represents one of the most unifying themes of this style. People fall in this region of the map because they are both interpersonally warm and have a lower level of outward energy. As a consequence, they frequently describe themselves as calm, peaceful, or even-tempered. Likewise, because of a slower pace and a more accepting nature, people who fall in this region of the map measure as more patient and accommodating than the average person. They show a great deal of concern for the feelings of the people around them. Overall, this style contains two major conceptual elements: (1) being pleasantly calm and (2) being accommodating of others.

Steadiness/Conscientiousness (SC or CS) Style: Moderate-Paced. The SC and CS styles are positioned in the middle of the skeptical—accepting dimension, but toward the bottom of the moderate—fast-paced dimension. As such, people who fall in this location on the *Everything DiSC* map tend to be less prone to action and more likely to deliberate on their options. They tend to be careful in their decision making and describe their pace as steady and step-by-step. Compared to the average person, they show less outward energy. This style is also associated with a degree of passivity. Statistically, the item that measures most centrally to this region of the map is, "I am soft-spoken." People in this location often prefer to work behind the scenes or let others take control. The SC style is accurately described as modest and unassuming, while the CS style is accurately described as quiet and self-controlled. Overall, these styles contain two major conceptual elements: (1) being cautious and (2) showing passivity.

Conscientiousness (C) Style: Moderate-Paced/Skeptical. In the bottom left of the *Everything DiSC* map is the C style. The overarching theme in this style is best captured by the adjective *analytical.* Statistically, the item that measures most centrally to this style is, "I prefer a quiet, analytical environment." People who fall in this location on the map are more reserved than the average person and are more likely to keep to themselves. Because people who measure in this style are both cautious and skeptical, they often come across as interpersonally restrained. They are also more likely to be skeptical of emotional displays in favor of a reflective, logical approach to decision making. Likewise, they describe themselves as being systematic and having a strong focus on accuracy. Overall, this style contains three major conceptual elements: (1) being analytical, (2) being precise, and (3) being private.

Conscientiousness/Dominance (CD or DC) Style: Skeptical. The CD style is positioned in the middle of the moderate—fast-paced dimension, but to the left of the skeptical—accepting dimension. This indicates that people who fall in this location of the map are more skeptical than the average person, but not to the extremes of being either highly aggressive or highly withdrawn. The word *challenging* is frequently used to describe these individuals, as they commonly challenge both ideas and other people. People in this location tend to describe themselves as highly logical and as strong critical thinkers. To this point, the item that is statistically most central to the measurement of this style is, "I quickly get irritated by illogical people." As this item suggests, they are prone to show little sympathy or patience for people who do not meet up to their standards. Likewise, because they may not engage in social niceties, they are frequently perceived as being cynical or interpersonally guarded. The CD style is accurately described as unsentimental and matter-of-fact, while the DC style is accurately described as resolute and strong-willed. Overall, these styles contain two major conceptual elements: (1) being skeptical and (2) being irritable or prone to frustration.

Dominance (D) Style: Fast-Paced/Skeptical. As the label suggests, the most concise way to describe people who fall in this style is dominant. Individuals with the D style are typically described as direct, result-oriented, firm, strong-willed, and forceful. They are more likely than others to display aggressive behavior and push vigorously for their opinions and goals. Likewise, people with this style are likely to seek control over situations and other people through force, showing less concern for the preferences of others. Because they are both skeptical and fast-paced, they typically demonstrate a high amount of drive and less patience for people and situations that do not conform to their goals, beliefs, or preferences. As a consequence, they are quicker than the average person to show irritation or become argumentative. Similarly, they tend to be direct, if not blunt, with their opinions. Finally, people who fall in this style are more likely to describe themselves as strong-willed, tough-minded, and competitive. Overall, this style contains two major conceptual elements: (1) being forceful and (2) being direct.

Connection to Other Models and Psychometric Theory

Interpersonal Circumplex

Interpersonal psychology started with Neo-Freudian therapist Harry Stack Sullivan, who believed that a person's behavior is not simply driven by situational demands or by internal motivations; rather, it is driven by the bi-directional influence that exists between the person and another individual within the context of a relationship (Sullivan, 2013). Behavior is almost always bi-directional (reflecting the mutual influence two individuals have on one another) rather than unidirectional. Thus, Sullivan believed that to understand human behavior fully, one also had to understand the interpersonal context in which it was manifested. Like Marston, Sullivan never operationalized his concepts by creating an assessment. Timothy Leary (1957) and his colleagues, interested in operationalizing Sullivan's concepts, started by observing the interaction patterns that occurred among individuals in group psychotherapy.

Leary discovered that the two dimensions of power and affiliation could explain most of the interaction patterns he observed. In other words, the dynamics of the interpersonal interaction was primarily one of negotiating power—"you are more (or less) powerful than me"—and affiliation—"this is going to be a close (or distant) relationship." Furthermore, Leary and his colleagues discovered that if they mapped all the interpersonal variables they observed on these two dimensions, the interpersonal variables formed a continuous circle around these two dimensions. Stated another way, each of the interpersonal variables represented a unique combination of power and affiliation, the two underlying dimensions. In the example shown in Figure 1.5, Variable 1 (for example, Aggressive) would represent equal combinations of a high need for control with a low need for affiliation, and Variable 2 (for example, Talkative) would represent equal combinations of a high need for control with a high need for affiliation.

Figure 1.5 is a highly simplified version of the actual Interpersonal Circumplex. A circumplex is built from two orthogonal (i.e., perpendicular) underlying dimensions, or axes, that together define a set of variables with a very specific ordering along the circumference (Guttman, 1954). The circumplex is not the same as a four-quadrant model, nor is it necessarily implied when variables are represented within a circle.

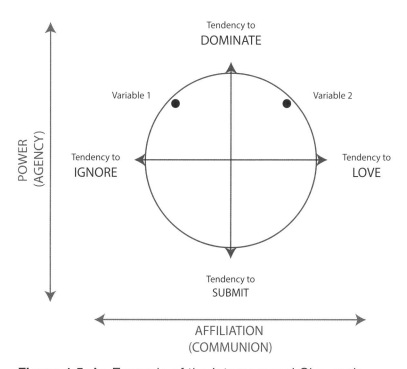

Figure 1.5 An Example of the Interpersonal Circumplex

Leary and his associates created the first measure of the Interpersonal Circumplex, the *Interpersonal Check List* (Laforge & Suczek, 1955). Since then, many more circumplex-based instruments have been built for the assessment of interpersonal behavior: *Structural Analysis of Social Behavior* (Benjamin, 1996), *Check List of Interpersonal Transactions* (Kiesler, 1987), *Impact Measure Inventory: IIA* (Kiesler & Schmidt, 1991), and *Interpersonal Adjective Scales* (Wiggins, 1995). The Interpersonal Circumplex has proven itself over time to be a very robust model of personality.

The Interpersonal Circumplex model has substantial conceptual overlap with the *Everything DiSC* model, with most differences springing from the intended audience for the model. Users of the Interpersonal Circumplex usually come from an academic or clinical background. End-users (e.g., classroom participants) of the DiSC model are typically members of the broader workforce and usually do not have a background in psychology. As such, the DiSC model deliberately begins by describing each location within the circle in neutral terms. For instance, the far left location on the circle is described as skeptical, questioning, and matter-of-fact. All of these adjectives statistically map to this space. Within Interpersonal Circumplex models, this same location is often described as contrary, resentful, stubborn, and suspicious (Conte & Plutchik, 1981), adjectives that also statistically map to this space. Research on a variant of the Interpersonal Circumplex, called the Interpersonal Problems Circumplex, suggests that all locations within the circle can be linked with distinct interpersonal problems. For instance, assuming the top of the circle is 0 degrees, the far right location of the circle (at 90 degrees) can be associated with behavior that is "overly nurturant." The very top, right location on the circle (at 45 degrees) can be associated with behavior that is intrusive or exhibitionistic (Alden, Wiggins, & Pincus, 1990). Likewise, each location on the map can be associated with behavior that is adaptive or healthy. When presenting information in the *Everything DiSC Profile,* most descriptions are designed to be neutral in tone, but certain sections report the less adaptive behavior associated with a given location, and other sections report the more adaptive behavior.

Another noticeable difference between the Interpersonal Circumplex model and the *Everything DiSC* model is the location of the dominance—submissiveness axis. Within the Interpersonal model, the axis is completely vertical. Within the *Everything DiSC* model, the axis is shifted 45 degrees counterclockwise, running from the top left corner to the lower right. This difference, however, is more an issue of terminology than it is of conceptual disagreement. For instance, within the Interpersonal model, the top of the vertical axis is described as assured, assuming control, and assertive. This is conceptually very similar to how the top of the circle is described in the *Everything DiSC* model. The term "dominance" in the *Everything DiSC* model is reserved for behavior that is more forceful and demanding. Within the Interpersonal model, this same location is often described as "dictating," "dominating," "competing," or "aggressive" (Myllyniemi, 1997; Strong et al., 1988).

The California Psychological Inventory

The *California Psychological Inventory*™ (CPI™) is a measure of personality that has a long history in academic and clinical psychology (Gough & Bradley, 1996). It contains 20 primary scales that measure a diverse range of interpersonal and intrapersonal differences. In an attempt to provide a broad overview of respondents' personalities, the 434 items of the CPI were factor analyzed (Gough & Bradley, 1996). These analyses ultimately produced three dimensions, two of which have conceptual overlap with the two dimensions in the *Everything DiSC* model.

The first dimension (v1) is labeled Externality versus Internality and measures a construct that covers such traits as expressiveness, self-confidence, participative inclinations, extraversion, assertiveness, and vigorous entry into the interpersonal world (Gough & Bradley, 1996). Conceptually, therefore, this dimension is very similar to the vertical moderate—fast-paced dimension in the DiSC model.

The second CPI dimension (v2) is labeled Norm-favoring versus Norm-doubting and measures a construct that covers such traits as rule questioning, unconventional behavior, lack of conformity, self-indulgence, rebelliousness, lack of trust in others, adventurousness, and cynicism. This dimension does have meaningful conceptual overlap with the horizontal skeptical—accepting dimension of DiSC, with some exceptions. Most notably, the skeptical—accepting dimension of DiSC does not measure reckless or self-indulgent behavior, nor does it measure adventurous behavior. On the other hand, the skeptical—accepting dimension does measure a cynical, nonconforming attitude.

The CPI uses v1 and v2 to create a 2x2 grid on which respondents are located with a dot, which is very similar to the method used to present a respondent's DiSC style. As well, each quadrant is labeled (alpha, beta, delta, and gamma) and described in a manner that is similar to the style descriptions in the *Everything DiSC Profile*.

The Five-Factor Model of Personality

The Five-Factor Model of Personality (FFM; also known as The Big Five) represents an attempt to describe individual differences in a manner that is simultaneously as comprehensive as possible and as succinct as possible. Research from a variety of sources (largely factor analytical) repeatedly suggests that five main factors can capture much of the diversity that is typically observed in personality (McCrae & Costa, 2010). These factors are Extraversion (E), Agreeableness (A), Conscientiousness (C), Openness to Experience (O), and Neuroticism (N).

Conceptually, the *Everything DiSC* model is expected to be meaningfully correlated with two of the FFM factors: Extraversion and Agreeableness. Despite the similarity in name, "Conscientiousness" in the DiSC model is not expected to have a strong relationship with "Conscientiousness" in the FFM. In DiSC, Conscientiousness is discussed and measured as a disposition that is analytical and reserved. In the FFM, Conscientiousness is discussed and measured as a disposition characterized by planning and organizing behavior, as well as "purposeful, strong-willed, and determined" behavior (McCrae & Costa, 2010).

The Extraversion factor within the FFM is expected to run diagonally through the DiSC model, roughly at a 45-degree angle through the i quadrant in the upper right-hand corner and through the C quadrant in the lower left-hand corner, as shown in Figure 1.6.

An analysis of 760 responses to both the DiSC assessment and the NEO™-PI-3 (a well-respected measure of the FFM) (McCrae & Costa, 2010) was used to explore the relationship between these models. (See Table B.1 for demographics.) As part of this exercise, scores on the moderate—fast-paced (i.e., vertical) dimension and the skeptical—accepting (i.e., horizontal) dimension of DiSC were calculated for each respondent. (Note that these dimension scores are for research purposes only and are not reported in the *Everything DiSC Profile.*) The results showed that the Extraversion scale of the NEO-PI-3 had meaningful correlations between both the moderate—fast-paced dimension and the skeptical—accepting dimension of DiSC (.57 and .52, respectively). When the six subscales (i.e., facets) of the Extraversion scale were examined, it was discovered that the moderate—fast-paced dimension had its strongest correlations with the Assertiveness and Activity subscales and its weakest correlations with the Warmth and Positive Emotions subscales. On the other hand, the skeptical—accepting dimension had its strongest correlations with the Positive Emotions and Warmth subscales and its weakest correlations with the Assertiveness and Activity subscales. This suggests that the two dimensions of DiSC both correlate with Extraversion, but that they both tap into different aspects of Extraversion. This is not surprising given that the two DiSC dimensions are conceptually independent and in this sample had a non-significant correlation of only .02.

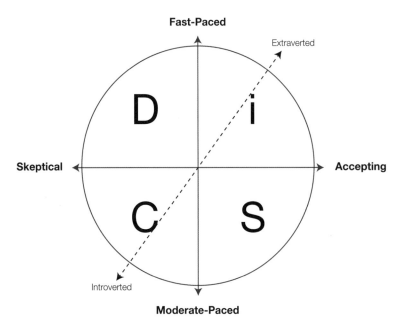

Figure 1.6 Relationship Between the DiSC Model and Extraversion

Agreeableness within the FFM has clear conceptual overlap with the skeptical—accepting dimension of DiSC, especially to the degree that it measures cooperative, empathetic behavior. To the degree that Agreeableness measures acquiescent or humble behavior, it is more similar to the dominant—submissive axis in the *Everything DiSC* model (i.e., the axis that runs diagonally from the D quadrant in the upper left-hand corner to the S quadrant in the lower right-hand corner). Analyses on the sample described above suggest that the skeptical—accepting dimension correlates meaningfully with Agreeableness ($r = .56$), but also with the moderate—fast-paced dimension ($r = -.46$). Analyzing the subscales of the Agreeableness scale on the NEO-PI-3, the aspects of Agreeableness that correlated negatively and strongly with the moderate—fast-paced dimension were Compliance and Modesty. Three of the subscales (Trust, Altruism, and Tender-mindedness), however, had near-zero correlations with the moderate—fast-paced dimension. On the other hand, the skeptical—accepting dimension had significant correlations with all six of the Agreeableness subscales, most notably Trust, Altruism, and Compliance.

An exploratory factor analysis was conducted on the 30 subscales of the NEO-PI-3 using the sample mentioned above. Using both a scree test and Kaiser Criterion (Bandalos & Boehm-Kaufman, 2008), five factors were extracted. Three of these factors appeared to have interpretations identical to the descriptions of Conscientiousness, Neuroticism, and Openness to Experience. The other two factors, however, appeared to be a combination of the Extraversion and Agreeableness subscales. One of these factors was marked by assertiveness and activity, and is labeled here as Surgency. The other factor was marked by warmth and altruism, and is labeled here as Positivity. These two factors were the second and third factors extracted, respectively. Table 1.1 shows the subscales, which had their highest loading on either of these two scales.

The Surgency and Positivity factors bear a striking resemblance to the moderate—fast-paced dimension and the skeptical—accepting dimension in the DiSC model, respectively. The correlation between the Surgency factor and the moderate—fast-paced dimension was .77. The correlation between the Positivity factor and the skeptical—accepting dimension was .69. These results suggest that the *Everything DiSC* model does measure some of the core constructs addressed by the FFM, but the organization and presentation of these constructs may be slightly different.

NEO Inventories: Professional Manual (McCrae & Costa, 2010) presents a series of 10 circumplexes, each of which contain two dimensions of the FFM arranged perpendicularly with a circle. The resulting four quadrants are referred to as *personality styles*. The circumplex labeled Style of Interaction contains Extraversion on the vertical axis and Agreeableness on the horizontal axis. This model strongly resembles the DiSC model. For instance, respondents plotted in the upper right-hand corner (+E, +A) are described similarly to the i style, whereas those plotted in the lower right-hand corner (+E, −A) are described similarly, although not identically, to the S style.

Table 1.1 NEO-PI-3 Subscales Loading on the Surgency and Positivity Factors

Surgency	Positivity
Assertiveness (E)	Warmth (E)
Activity (E)	Altruism (A)
Modesty* (A)	Positive Emotions (E)
Compliance* (A)	Gregariousness (E)
Excitement Seeking (E)	Trust (A)
Straightforwardness* (A)	Tender-mindedness (A)
	Openness to Feelings (O)

Note: Letters in parentheses indicate the original factor to which the subscale was assigned: (E)xtraversion, (A)greeableness, or (O)penness. Subscales are arranged from those with the highest loading on the factor to those with the lowest. Asterisks indicate a negative loading.

Hofstee, de Raad, and Goldberg (1992) conducted a similar exercise using data from an FFM assessment. Their analysis created 10 circumplex models pairing different dimensions of the FFM. Of interest here is the pairing of the Agreeable (A) and Extraversion (E) dimensions. The results showed adjectives such as forceful, bossy, domineering, and devious mapped to the +E/−A quadrant. Adjectives such as merry, friendly, happy-go-lucky, and enthusiastic mapped to the +E/+A quadrant. Adjectives such as humble, modest, naïve, and submissive mapped to the −E/+A quadrant. Adjectives such as aloof, skeptical, unfriendly, and joyless mapped to the −E/−A quadrant. Although not an exact fit with the DiSC model, this pattern of adjective mapping is consistent with the D, i, S, and C quadrants of the DiSC model. Additional research on the relationship between the NEO-PI-3 and the *Everything DiSC* assessment is included in Chapter 4 of this *Manual.*

The Myers-Briggs Type Indicator

The *Myers-Briggs Type Indicator®* (MBTI®) (Myers, McCaulley, Quenk, & Hammer, 1998) is a measure of personality that includes four primary scales: Extraversion—Introversion (E-I), Sensing—Intuiting (S-N), Thinking—Feeling (T-F), and Judging—Perceiving (J-P). Similar to DiSC, this instrument is often used for developmental purposes, helping groups of people better understand themselves and those around them. Two of the four MBTI continua share conceptual overlap with the *Everything DiSC* model: E-I and T-F. As discussed earlier, the E-I continuum is expected to run diagonally through the i quadrant in the upper right-hand corner of the DiSC model (extraversion), down through the C quadrant in the lower left-hand corner (introversion). The T-F continuum measures decision making from more objective, logical, and fact-based (thinking) to more subjective, values-driven, and empathetic (feeling). This is conceptually similar to the skeptical—accepting dimension in DiSC. The skeptical—accepting dimension does not purport to measure objectivity/subjectivity, but it does measure an element of emotional detachment as well as a comfort with more tender, so-called "touchy-feely" emotions.

The relationship between the DiSC model and the MBTI model had been explored in a study that used a previous version of the DiSC assessment and is described here only to elucidate this theoretical relationship. The study asked 209 participants to complete a DiSC assessment and an MBTI assessment (see Table B.1 for demographics). The data showed that the I-E scale had a −.66 correlation with the moderate—fast-paced dimension and a −.38 with the skeptical—accepting dimension. In line with DiSC theory, the I-E scale had a −.75 correlation with the i scale and a .73 correlation with the C scale. This suggests that the I-E scale does run diagonally through the i and C quadrants of DiSC rather than vertically or horizontally.

The T-F scale had a .48 correlation with the skeptical—accepting dimension and a .01 correlation with the moderate—fast-paced dimension. These results suggest that there exists a moderate relationship between T-F and skeptical—accepting constructs.

A theoretical diagram of the relationship between the MBTI and DiSC models was constructed using the DiSC dimensions and style scores, as shown in Figure 1.7.

The research further suggests that the DiSC model does not meaningfully measure constructs such as structure (J-P) or abstractness (S-N), as none of the correlations between the S-N and J-P scales and the two DiSC dimensions was above .27. Further, the MBTI model does not meaningfully measure constructs such as dominance—submissiveness.

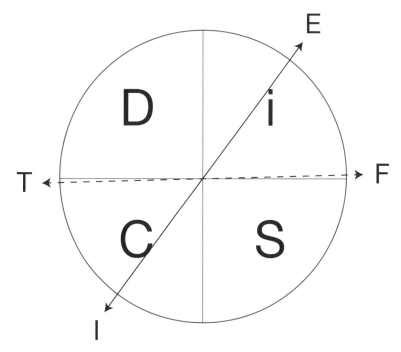

Figure 1.7 The Theoretical Relationship Between the MBTI and DiSC Models

CHAPTER 2

Methodology of Development

Previous Assessments Measuring the DiSC Model

In 1979, the original *Personal Profile System* (PPS) (Wiley, 2011) was created by John Geier. This assessment presented the respondent with 24 sets of four adjectives. Each adjective measured one of the four DiSC® scales: D, i, S, or C. Within each set, the respondent was instructed to choose one adjective that most described him or her and one that least described him or her. This forced-choice format was used to reduce social desirability in responding. For each scale, the number of "least" responses were subtracted from the number of "most" responses and a scale score was plotted. In 1994, the PPS was revised with new items to contain a total of 28 sets. An alternative version of the assessment was also created that used short phrases instead of adjectives. Today, this forced-choice assessment is known as *DiSC® Classic*.

In 2003, Inscape Publishing (now Wiley) released a measure of the DiSC model called *DiSC® Indra* (Cole & Tuzinski, 2003). This assessment presented the respondent with 150 adjectives (e.g., *warm, competitive*) and instructed the participant to indicate how frequently that adjective described him or her. These responses were used to measure the respondent on eight scales around the DiSC model—D, Di, i, iS, S, SC, C, CD. These scale scores, then, were used to locate an individual within the two-dimensional, circular DiSC model and plot him or her as a dot. More specifically, the eight scales were weighted according to their geometric placement on the vertical or horizontal DiSC dimensions. For instance, because the Di scale is conceptually located at the top of the vertical dimension, it was weighted as one for the vertical dimension. Because the CD scale is conceptually located in the exact middle of the vertical dimension, it was weighted as zero. This method of scoring is described in full by Wiggins, Phillips, and Trapnell (1989) and has been used by a variety of circumplex assessments (Kiesler & Schmidt, 2006; Ojanen, Gronroos, & Salmivalli, 2005).

In 2008, Inscape Publishing released the first version of the *Everything DiSC®* assessment. This assessment presented respondents with 79 adjectives and asked them to indicate how often each adjective describes them on a 5-point scale. As with the *Indra* assessment, respondents were scored on eight scales and these scales were used to locate the respondents within the *Everything DiSC* map.

Everything DiSC Technical Development

Rationale of Scale Construction

Researchers usually use one of three methods when constructing a self-report assessment: empirical scale construction, factorial scale construction, or rational scale construction. Empirical (keying) scale construction, also known as the criterion or external method, selects items that differentiate between predetermined groups (e.g., people diagnosed with major depression versus the general public). This method was used by the *Minnesota Multiphasic Personality Inventory®-2* (MMPI®-2) and the Occupational Scales of the *Strong Interest Inventory* (SII). Factorial scale construction, also known as the inductive or internal method, begins atheoretically with a large group of items that are then analyzed using any number of multivariate procedures to identify underlying themes or groupings. This method was used in the development of the Five-Factor Model of Personality, although not necessarily in the measurement of that model. Rational scale construction, also known as the intuitive, deductive, internal consistency, or theoretical method, starts with a conceptual model, and then items are created that are expected to measure that model. Data are then collected from a group of respondents and analyzed. Certain scales on the *California Psychological Inventory™* (CPI™) (e.g., Flexibility, Self-acceptance) and the SII (e.g., the General Occupational Themes) were developed using this method. Because the DiSC conceptual model predated the first DiSC assessment, this method is a good fit for assessments measuring that model. In fact, this method was used in the very first DiSC assessment and was again used in the construction of the *Everything DiSC* assessment.

The construction of the *Everything DiSC* scales broadly follows the scale construction process outlined in Furr (2011):

1.   articulate construct and context,

2.   choose response format and assemble initial item pool,

3.   collect data from respondents,

4.   examine psychometric properties and qualities, and

5.   create final scale.

This process is iterative in that developments at certain stages may send the researcher back to repeat earlier stages.

Generation of the Initial Item Pool

Existing data from the *DiSC Classic, DiSC Indra*, and the original *Everything DiSC* assessments were analyzed using factor analysis, multidimensional scaling analyses (MDS), reliability analyses, and basic correlation matrixes. Figure 2.1 shows an example from these analyses, as performed on a sample of the *DiSC Indra* data (see Table B.1 for demographics). The analysis shows that certain adjectives tend to cluster together (e.g., bold, daring, assertive) at a certain location in the two-dimensional circle (i.e., 90 degrees away from adjectives like warm and generous and 180 degrees away from adjectives like modest and conforming).

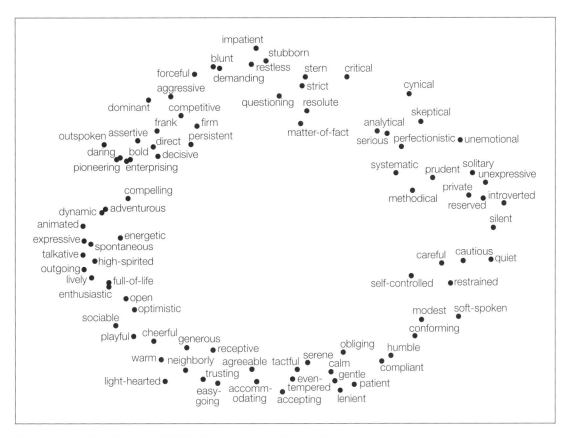

Figure 2.1 Preliminary MDS Map of an Existing Dataset
Note: Stress = .15307; RSQ = .91652; *N* = 811.

Ultimately, these preliminary analyses, combined with a review of research on related theoretical models (e.g., the interpersonal circumplex, the three vector scales of the *California Psychological Inventory*), were used to

- identify where DiSC-related constructs (e.g., directness, cautiousness) were located within the DiSC circle,

- identify how well different DiSC-related constructs fit within the two-dimensional, circular structure,

- identify which types of items best measured particular locations within the DiSC circle, and

- understand which constructs occupy similar locations on the DiSC circle.

This knowledge was used to guide the development of new items.

Three hundred and fifty-one new items were written to most precisely measure the DiSC model at eight points around the circle, starting at the very top and then in 45-degree increments. New items were written as statements (e.g., "I tend to see the best in people") instead of as adjectives (e.g., "trusting") as this allowed for the creation of a broader array of items. This flexibility was necessary to ensure that each location on the DiSC map could be precisely measured using items that were not too socially desirable or undesirable. For each statement, respondents were instructed to rate their level of agreement on a 5-point scale: strongly disagree, disagree, neutral, agree, and strongly agree. As will be discussed in Chapter 3, the intended reading level for all items was 8th grade or below. Items that might be considered intrusive or offensive were excluded from the item pool.

Pilot Test

A sample of 848 adults between the ages of 18 and 65 responded to the 351 items in the initial item pool, as well as basic demographic questions. The characteristics of this sample are included in Table B.1.

Item Evaluation

A number of criteria were used to select items for the beta version of the *Everything DiSC* assessment.

1. **Items should map to the appropriate location on the DiSC map.**

    Multidimensional scaling analyses were used to map items in two-dimensional space. As expected, conceptually similar items clustered together. Not all items that were expected to measure a given scale construct (e.g., Dominance for the D scale) clustered with other items addressing that construct. Further, not all items showed the appropriate relationship to constructs they were not intended to measure. For instance, a potential D item may have been much more distant from the cluster of Di items than expected under the DiSC theory. As a result, these items were removed as candidates for the beta version of the assessment.

2. **Items should contribute to high internal reliabilities of their assigned scale.**

    Internal reliability coefficients (Cronbach's alpha) were calculated with potential items that were expected to measure a given scale construct. Items that showed high item-total correlations were given preference over those that showed lower item-total correlations.

3. **Items should demonstrate appropriate correlations with their non-assigned scales.**

Using the results of the multidimensional scaling analyses described earlier, initial scale scores were calculated for the eight DiSC scales by averaging all promising items for a given scale. All items were then correlated to these eight scales. Within DiSC theory, certain relationships are specified among the scales and items. The correlation matrix was examined to evaluate these expected relationships against the actual relationships in the data.

4. **Items should not be endorsed too frequently or infrequently.**

Mean item responses were calculated for all items. Items that demonstrated moderate response rates (i.e., means close to the mean of all item means) were given preference over those that did not. More specifically, items with a mean response between 3 and 4 were preferred.

5. **Items should demonstrate variability across respondents.**

Standard deviations were calculated on all items. Items with lower standard deviations (i.e., below .7) were considered less desirable than other items.

6. **Scales should contain items that reflect the entire domain of constructs that are addressed at a given point on the DiSC map.**

Items that had been preliminarily assigned to a given scale were submitted to a series of principal components analyses, specifying anywhere from two to four components. This was done to identify major themes within that group of items. A panel of DiSC subject-matter experts evaluated the results and decided on the sub-constructs that would be included on each scale. For instance, it was determined that the D scale should contain items that measure both directness and forcefulness, as these are both part of the "Dominance" construct. Among the eight scales, seven were assigned two sub-constructs and one was assigned three sub-constructs, as shown in Table 2.1. Item selection, then, targeted items that would sufficiently measure each of the sub-constructs on each scale.

7. **Scale length should be kept to a minimum.**

Scales should contain items necessary to demonstrate evidence of strong reliability and validity, but additional items should be used sparingly.

Final Selection

After evaluating items on the seven criteria mentioned above, a total of 124 items were selected. Selected items were placed in two categories: base and extended. As will be

	Sub-constructs		
Scale	**1**	**2**	**3**
D	Directness	Forcefulness	
Di	Boldness	Action-bias	
i	Sociability	Liveliness	
iS	Positivity	Empathy	
S	Accommodation	Calmness	
SC	Cautiousness	Passivity	
C	Analysis	Precision	Reserve
CD	Skepticism	Irritability	

Table 2.1 Scale Sub-constructs

discussed in Chapter 3, base items are those items that would be administered to all test-takers, and extended items are those that are only administered to high-variance responders. There were a total of 78 base items and 46 extended items across the eight DiSC scales.

After 124 items had been selected, data were collected and analyses were conducted to examine the evidence for the reliability and validity of the assessment. These analyses are described in Chapter 4.

Standardization and Norming

As described in Table B.2, a sample of 26,703 was used for the final norming. This sample was taken from early users of the *Everything DiSC* assessment and was stratified to better represent the general U.S. population. Because certain demographic categories (e.g., ethnicity) are not represented equally in the general population (and consequently in the sample), analyses were conducted to examine scale differences based on these categories. These analyses are described in Chapter 5.

As with the previous *Everything DiSC* assessment, items assigned to a given scale were averaged and scales were standardized to have a mean of zero and standard deviation of one. The standardization of the eight scales ensured that the assignment of DiSC styles was roughly equal across the twelve styles. The *Everything DiSC* assessment has been translated into other languages where local norm groups are used to establish the optimal items and norms for each scale.

Item Translation

Everything DiSC was developed in the United States, and general guidelines to develop a text suitable for translation were applied, such as avoiding culturally specific expressions. The quality of the translation of the items was ensured through the application of a six-step process:

1. The items are translated by a professional translator from English (source language) to the target language. It is a general requirement that the translator's native language is the target language.

2. A second professional translator, also a native speaker of the target language, is tasked with back-translating the items from target language to source language.

3. The original items and the back-translated items are reviewed by three bilingual subject-matter experts.

4. In situations where there are differences in meaning/connotations between the source and the back-translation, this text is sent back to the first translator.

5. The translator assesses the differences and, when appropriate, states why a word should remain the same or substitutes it with a more suitable word to match the meaning of the original English item.

6. In situations where extra input is needed to aid the translation, the development team is contacted to establish the intended meaning/connotation of an item.

CHAPTER 3

Administration and Scoring of the Assessment

Appropriate Populations

The *Everything DiSC®* assessment has been developed and validated on adults 18 years or older and is appropriate for this population. It is a nonclinical assessment, designed to support personal development and professional relationships in a work setting. The assessment is expected to take 15–20 minutes to complete, although some applications (i.e., *Work of Leaders, 363 for Leaders*) will take longer. However, there is no time limit, making it possible for people requiring more time to complete the assessment without need of any special adaption or modification.

Readability tests were used to determine the ease and required reading comprehension level needed by a respondent to understand the assessment. These tests use the average number of syllables per word and the average number of words per sentence to determine a statistic designed to convey the reading level of the assessment. For the *Everything DiSC* assessment, the Flesch Reading Ease test was used (Kincaid, Fishburne, Rogers, & Chissom, 1975). This test uses a 100-point scale with higher scores indicating the increased ease of understanding the document. The formula for calculating the score is as follows:

$$206.835 - (1.015 \times \text{average sentence length}) - (84.6 \times \text{average syllables per word})$$

The DiSC® base items and product-specific items produced a score of 74.2, indicating that the assessment is understandable to most adult participants. The second readability test used was the Flesch-Kincaid Grade Level test (Kincaid et al., 1975). This test produces a U.S. school grade level using the following formula:

$$(0.39 \times \text{average sentence length}) + (11.8 \times \text{average syllables per word}) - 15.59$$

For the *Everything DiSC* items, the resulting grade level was 4.7.

Accessing the Everything DiSC Assessment

The *Everything DiSC* assessment is only available in an electronic, online format, and is hosted on EPIC (Wiley's secure assessment platform). Wiley offers this assessment through Authorized Partners who have received two days of training to facilitate the results of the assessment.

The Partner provides each respondent with an electronic access code. This access code is typically provided as a link embedded within an email that contains instructions on how to respond to the assessment. Respondents can also go directly to the EPIC website and enter their access code. After the code has been entered, the respondent receives instructions on how to take the assessment.

Responding to the Assessment

Respondents are given directions and examples for responding. The directions state the following:

> Please indicate the degree to which you agree with each of the following statements. Use the full range of response options to ensure the most accurate feedback. Click "Next" to begin.
>
> THIS IS NOT A TEST. There are no right or wrong answers. You cannot pass or fail. Completing this profile usually takes 15–20 minutes.

Respondents are then presented with a series of statements and asked to rate the degree to which they agree or disagree with that statement using a 5-point Likert scale, from strongly disagree to strongly agree. Sample statements include, "I am bold" and "I want things to be exact." If items are left incomplete, the respondent will receive an error message indicating that all items must be complete before proceeding. Once a respondent has started the assessment, he or she can exit the system at any time and continue it later if necessary. Additional item types may also be administered to the respondent, depending on the specific application that he or she has been assigned.

The Scales Within Everything DiSC

The two primary types of scales calculated in the *Everything DiSC* assessment are the DiSC scales and the priority scales, both of which can only be viewed in the *Supplement for Facilitators* report. Although most respondents will never see these scales directly, practitioners may choose to familiarize themselves with these scales so that they can (1) better understand the research behind the assessment and (2) further investigate a respondent's results and gain a deeper understanding of that individual.

The DiSC Scales

The DiSC scales measure eight equally spaced locations around the DiSC circle, as shown in Figure 3.1.

The basic description of the DiSC scales is provided in Table 3.1. (For a more in-depth description, see The Twelve Everything DiSC Styles section of Chapter 1.) The DiSC scales are the primary form of measurement within the *Everything DiSC* assessment and are used to determine an individual's dot placement and style assignment. They are composed of Likert items rated on a 5-point scale in which respondents are asked to indicate the degree to which they agree or disagree with a series of statements.

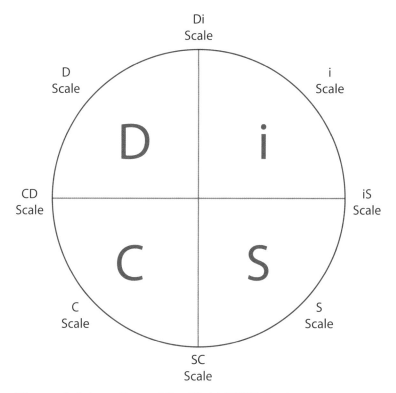

Figure 3.1 Location of the Eight DiSC Scales

Table 3.1 Description of the Eight DiSC Scales	
DiSC Scale	**Description**
D	The D scale measures a direct, forceful disposition using items such as, "I can be blunt" and "I am dominant."
Di	The Di scale measures a bold, active disposition using items such as, "I tend to be the first one to try new things" and "I am dynamic."
i	The i scale measures a sociable, lively disposition using items such as, "I love meeting new people" and "I tend to liven things up."
iS	The iS scale measures a positive, empathetic disposition using items such as, "I am naturally upbeat" and "I tend to see the best in people."
S	The S scale measures a calm, accommodating disposition using items such as, "I am gentle" and "I go out of my way to make sure I don't hurt anyone's feelings."
SC	The SC scale measures a cautious, passive disposition using items such as, "I tend to be soft-spoken" and "I spend more time listening than talking."
C	The C scale measures a private, analytical disposition using items such as, "I am analytical" and "I keep to myself."
CD	The CD scale measures a skeptical, impatient disposition using items such as, "Being skeptical is one of my strengths" and "I get impatient with incompetent people."

The Priority Scales

The priority scales are used much less extensively than the DiSC scales. The primary purpose of these scales is to let a respondent know that his or her results differ from the average person who shares the style. For instance, someone with the S style may show an unusually high level of enthusiasm given the prototypical calm disposition of the S style. In such a case, the respondent's report would contain shading that illustrates this distinction, as shown in Figure 3.2. This figure shows the eight priorities wrapped around the DiSC circle.

In comparison to the DiSC scales, the priority scales measure much more narrow constructs. For instance, the i DiSC scale measures a sociable, lively disposition. The priority scale of Enthusiasm measures only liveliness. These more narrow scales are used to interpret the respondent's results within a context that is most relevant to the respondent. In a management context, for instance, the priority scale on the left-hand side of the DiSC circle is Challenge. This helps the respondent understand that she is probably very challenging with her direct reports. In a sales context, the priority scale in this same location is

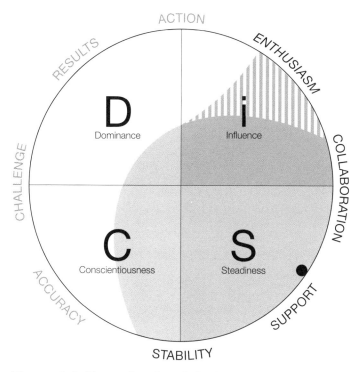

Figure 3.2 Example of an S Style with an Extra Priority

Competency. This helps the salesperson understand that he probably feels a strong need to highlight his competence when working with a customer.

The calculation of the priority scales is done in the same manner as the calculation of the DiSC scales. Although there are varying degrees of item overlap between a priority scale and a DiSC scale located at a given location on the DiSC map, each is measured separately.

In addition to the DiSC scales and priority scales, some *Everything DiSC* reports do contain additional scales. Specifically, the *Everything DiSC Work of Leaders®* report contains leadership continua, and the *Everything DiSC 363® for Leaders* report contains leadership performance scales. (For a complete list of the priorities used on the various DiSC reports, see Chapter 6.)

Adaptive Testing Procedures

Adaptive testing (AT) is used in the *Everything DiSC* assessment to increase the precision of style assignment. Generally speaking, an adaptive test (sometimes called a computerized adaptive test [CAT]) is one in which the assessment changes based on the respondent's previous answers. The two main benefits of AT are to (1) increase the precision of an assessment and (2) decrease the length of an assessment. Assessment designers can choose to focus on one of these benefits at the expense of the other.

On the *Everything DiSC* assessment, AT is used in two different ways. First, AT is used to increase the precision of the eight DiSC scales. Each respondent is required to answer 78 base items, each of which is used in the measurement of one of the eight DiSC scales. The variance among item responses within each of these scales is then calculated. If there is a scale on which the variance is above a predetermined threshold, the respondent is administered a set of additional items (e.g., extended items) that measure that same construct.

For instance, a respondent may respond to the base item, "I am mild-mannered" with a 2 and respond to the base item, "I am even-tempered" with a 5, even though both of these items are on the same DiSC scale (the S scale). If the variance in this respondent's responses on the S scale items is above a predetermined threshold, she will be administered a pre-set number of additional items. In practical terms, because this respondent was inconsistent in her responses to the items on the S DiSC scale, she is being asked additional questions to clarify the earlier responses.

As another example, Respondent 1 may receive 9 Di items in her assessment and Respondent 2 may receive 14 Di items in his assessment (i.e., 9 base items and 5 extended items). Both respondents, however, may still receive the same number of items on the D scale. In this manner, the *Everything DiSC* assessment mirrors assessments that offer alternative forms (e.g., form A and form B). In such cases, two respondents can take assessments that contain entirely different items and the resulting scores are considered to be comparable. It is important, however, to demonstrate that scale scores from the two versions are, in fact, equivalent. Table 3.2 shows the correlations between the base

Table 3.2 Correlations Between the Base and Extended Versions

Scale	r	Number of Items	
		Base	Extended
Di	.97	9	14
i	.96	7	12
iS	.96	9	14
S	.93	10	15
SC	.97	12	17
C	.92	11	19
CD	.95	12	20
D	.95	8	13

and extended scales on the assessment. These correlations range from .92 to .97, with a median of .96. Furthermore, the difficulty (i.e., endorsement frequency) of the base items is also comparable to the difficulty of the extended items. In a sample of 1,340 respondents, the average response on the base scales was 3.46 and the average response on extended scales was 3.41.

Respondents can receive extended items on any number of scales, but the average number of scales for which extended items are administered is 2.4 and the median is 2.0. Fewer than 1% of respondents receive more than 5 sets of extended items. Depending on the scale, the number of extended items ranges from 5 to 8, as shown in Table 3.2. Extended items are designed to mirror the base items on a given scale in terms of difficulty and meaning.

This method of AT allows the assessment to identify if sufficient information is present to estimate a scale score or if additional information is necessary. Practically speaking, the assessment is kept short for those who respond consistently to conceptually similar items. On the other hand, extra information is gathered from those who answer inconsistently to conceptually similar items. This methodology is shared with other adaptive testing assessments where the assessment is terminated not after the administration of a set number of items, but after a pre-set level of precision is met. As with other adaptive testing applications, the interpretation of a respondent's scores will be the same regardless of which specific items have been administered (Weiss, 2004).

On a technical note, this method of AT is most comparable to the two-stage strategy of adaptive testing (Weiss, 1974) in which an initial set of items is administered and then, depending on the respondent's responses, a second set of items is administered. This is among the simplest forms of adaptive testing. Item response theory-based adaptive testing methods were considered, but analyses suggested that, on any given scale, a roughly similar set of items would be chosen for all respondents regardless of their level on the measured trait. This is largely because the *Everything DiSC* items are polytomous (on a 5-point scale) and thus provide information at four points on the trait continuum. This is unlike most items that measure ability, which are dichotomous and provide information at only one level of the trait continuum. The analysis suggested that items that were the strongest at a specific trait level (theta) were generally the strongest at all levels (i.e., provided the most information from the pool of available items). Consequently, a more simple method of AT was deemed sufficient and had the added benefit of avoiding the intricacies associated with more complex AT strategies.

AT is used in a second way within the *Everything DiSC* assessment. For most respondents, there is a clear preference for one style over the other eleven. In cases where this preference is unclear, however, the system will administer clarifying questions. Here, the respondent is shown a set of two statements, each of which describes a different DiSC style. Based on the respondent's previous responses, both of these statements represent styles that are at least somewhat descriptive of the respondent. As a sample, one of the D style statements is, "I have a decisive, dominant style and tend to push strongly for my point of view." Unlike the typical *Everything DiSC* item, the statements in the clarifying items contain multiple descriptors. In this particular example, three constructs are included: decisiveness, dominance, and pushing strongly for one's opinions. The goal of these statements is to approximate the type of feedback that the respondent would receive in his or her report if that style were assigned to him or her. Figure 3.3 shows an example of one set of clarifying questions comparing the D and i styles. The respondent would receive the instructions, "Please read the descriptions at both ends of the continuum. Click the point on the line that best describes where you fall on the continuum."

Within a sample of 26,703 respondents, 6.5% received clarifying questions (see Table B.2 for demographics). Respondents who receive clarifying questions will receive five sets and their responses to these five sets will be used, along with their previous responses, to determine the most appropriate style assignment.

The flow chart shown in Figure 3.4 illustrates the *Everything DiSC* adaptive testing procedures, showing when extended and clarifying questions are administered.

Scoring

The eight DiSC scale scores are calculated by averaging the responses to all items assigned to a given scale. No items are reverse scored and no items are included on more than one DiSC scale. Before averaging scale items, however, each item is transformed. Using all 78 base items, a mean and standard deviation is calculated for each respondent. For each item, the mean is subtracted and the difference is divided by the standard deviation. This type of transformation is common in instruments that measure circumplex properties because all items in a circumplex assessment are balanced by conceptually opposite items (Locke, 2000; Soldz, Budman, Demby, & Merry, 1993; Wiggins, Steiger, & Gaelick, 1981). The transformation removes a general (conceptually irrelevant) factor from responses (Alden, Wiggins, & Pincus, 1990), which in the case of the *Everything DiSC* assessment is assumed to be response bias (e.g., acquiescence, responding toward the middle). The scores that result from this transformation are standardized to have a mean of zero and a standard deviation of one.

After the DiSC scales have been scored, style assignment is determined. Although the specifics of this algorithm are proprietary and confidential, a broad description of the process will be described here. The algorithm creates an Octant Score for each of eight locations around the DiSC circle, corresponding to the locations of the eight DiSC scales

I have a decisive, dominant style and tend to push strongly for my point of view.　　　　　　　I am outgoing, high-spirited, and tend to liven things up.

Figure 3.3 Example of a Set of Clarifying Questions

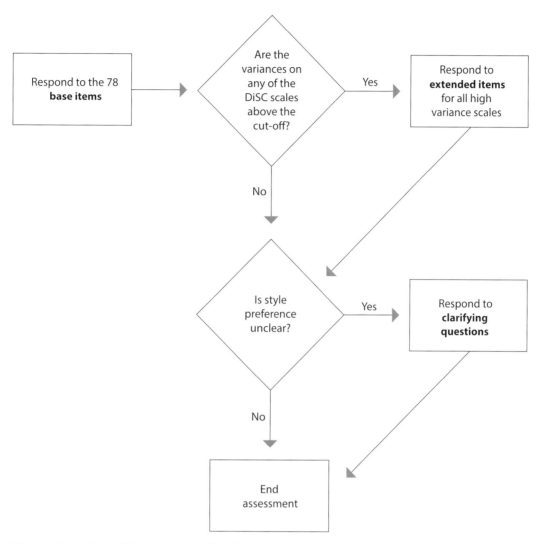

Figure 3.4 Flow Chart of Adaptive Testing Processes

(Di, i, iS, S, SC, C, CD, D). An Octant Score is the weighted average of a given DiSC scale score (weighted as 1) and the two scores of its adjacent DiSC scales (weighted as .5). For instance, the SC Octant Score is computed as follows:

$$\text{SC Scale Score} + [(\text{S Scale Score} \times .5) + (\text{C Scale Score} \times .5)] / 2$$

The resulting eight Octant Scores are compared, and the respondent is assigned a style that corresponds to the highest value. In cases where the two highest Octant Scores are very close in value, clarifying items are administered and those responses are used as an additional factor in determining style assignment. Note that the Octant Scores are created for computational purposes only and are never presented to respondents or administrators. Once style assignment is completed, the precise angle of the respondent's dot is determined by examining the relative magnitude of adjacent DiSC scale scores. Evidence for the reliability and validity of the scale scores and style assignments is included in Chapter 4.

The respondent's inclination (i.e., distance from the center of the circle) is also determined using the DiSC scale scores. In brief, the DiSC scale scores are used to calculate a vertical dimension score and a horizontal dimension score. From these two dimension scores, basic trigonometry can be used to determine the distance the respondent's location is from the center of the circle. The specific equations used in these calculations can be found in Wiggins, Phillips, and Trapnell (1989). For more information on how to interpret a respondent's inclination, see Chapter 8.

The *Everything DiSC* profiles also use priorities to help the respondent understand her pattern of results. Priority scale scores are calculated in the same manner as DiSC scale scores, as described earlier in this chapter. There are items that are used on both the DiSC scales and the priority scales. Unlike the items on the DiSC scales, however, some of the items on the priority scales are reverse scored.

The priorities included on each DiSC application (e.g., *Workplace, Sales, Management*) are different. Table 3.3 shows the priorities on the different DiSC applications. For more information on the development and validation of these priorities, see Chapter 6.

On the profile, the respondent is automatically assigned the three priorities that are closest to his or her dot on the DiSC circle. For instance, if a respondent has a dot in the D region on the *Workplace Profile*, he would receive the following priorities: Challenge, Results, and Action. For the respondent, the remaining five priority scale scores are analyzed. Scores that are above a pre-set threshold are identified as "extra priorities" and

Table 3.3 Priorities Listed by Everything DiSC Application

Angular Location	Closest Style	Workplace	Management	Sales	Productive Conflict	Work of Leaders/363
0	Di/iD	Action	Action	Action	Assertion	Pioneering
45	i	Enthusiasm	Encouragement	Enthusiasm	Expression	Energizing
90	iS/Si	Collaboration	Collaboration	Relationships	Reassurance	Affirming
135	S	Support	Support	Sincerity	Harmony	Inclusive
180	SC/CS	Stability	Reliability	Dependability	Stability	Humble
225	C	Accuracy	Objectivity	Quality	Objectivity	Deliberate
270	CD/DC	Challenge	Challenge	Competency	Justification	Resolute
315	D	Results	Drive	Results	Control	Commanding

are designated by diagonal shading on the respondent's DiSC map in the *Everything DiSC Profile.* A respondent may have a maximum of two extra priorities. In cases where three priority scale scores are above the threshold, only the two highest are assigned. In a sample of 57,648 respondents across all applications, a total of 32.6% of respondents received extra priorities. Within this group, 29.2% received one extra priority and 3.4% received two (see Table B.1 for demographics). No participants had three or more priority scale scores above the threshold. For more information on the interpretation of extra priorities, see Chapter 8.

CHAPTER 4

The DiSC Scales and Styles: Reliability and Validity

Reliability of the DiSC Scales and Styles

Internal Reliability of the Scales

Internal consistency evaluates the degree of correlation among questions that profess to measure the same thing. That is, each of the eight scales in the DiSC® model is measured using a series of different items (i.e., questions in the form of statements, such as, "I am direct," "I tend to take the lead," "I want things to be exact," "I am always cheerful"). Researchers recognize that if all of the items on a given scale (e.g., the D scale) are in fact measuring the same thing (e.g., Dominance), they should all correlate with each other to some degree. In other words, all of the items on a scale should be consistent with each other. A statistic called Cronbach's alpha is used to evaluate internal consistency.

Alpha coefficients were calculated for two samples—one with 752 respondents and one with 39,607 respondents. The demographics of these samples are included in Tables B.3 and B.5. The scales on the *Everything DiSC®* instruments demonstrate good-to-excellent internal consistency, as shown by the alpha values listed in Table 4.1. All reliabilities are well above .70, with a median of .87 ($N = 752$) and .83 ($N = 39,607$).

Test-Retest Reliability of the Scales

Stability refers to the assessment's ability to yield the same measurements over a period of time. This is generally tested by having the same people complete the assessment twice, with a suitable time interval between the two measurements (the so-called *test-retest.*) The results are then compared to determine how strongly they relate to each other (or correlate). If the traits being measured are considered to be stable, a reliable assessment should produce results that are quite similar between two different administrations.

Table 4.1 Internal Consistency of the Everything DiSC Scales

Scale	Number of Items	Cronbach's Alpha	Cronbach's Alpha
Di	9	.90	.85
i	7	.90	.88
iS	9	.86	.82
S	10	.87	.82
SC	12	.84	.86
C	11	.79	.80
CD	12	.87	.82
D	8	.88	.84
N		752	39,607

Stability can be quantified in the form of a *reliability coefficient,* the correlation between a group's initial scores on an instrument and their subsequent scores. Test-retest reliability coefficients generally range between 0 and +1. The closer that a correlation coefficient is to +1, the more stable the instrument is considered to be. Researchers generally use the following guidelines to help them interpret these test-retest reliability coefficients: coefficients above .70 are considered acceptable, and coefficients above .80 are considered very good (Streiner, 2003).

A sample of 599 respondents took the DiSC assessment twice with a two-week interval between testings. Test-retest correlations for the eight DiSC scales are shown in Table 4.2. The demographics of this sample are listed in Table B.4.

These data suggest that the DiSC scales are stable over repeated administrations. Consequently, test takers and test administrators should, on average, expect no more than small changes when the instrument is taken at different times. As the period between administrations increases, however, the divergent results of these administrations will become more and more noticeable.

Test-Retest Reliability of the Styles

A second examination of the test-retest reliability was performed by looking at the typical angle change between two testings over a two-week time period. To provide context, the DiSC map is broken into 360 degrees and each of the twelve styles occupies 30 degrees. All respondents are assigned an angle location on the DiSC map, which is then used to determine their DiSC style. All respondents who measure in the same predetermined 30-degree region will be assigned the same style, as shown in Figure 4.1.

Table 4.2 Scale Test-Retest Reliabilities

Scale	Reliability
Di	.86
i	.87
iS	.85
S	.86
SC	.88
C	.85
CD	.85
D	.86
N = 599	

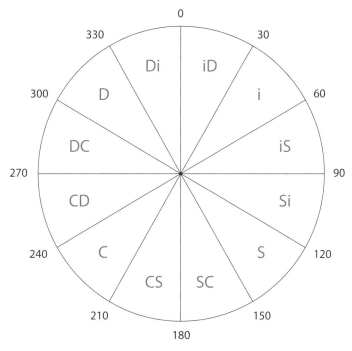

Figure 4.1 The Everything DiSC Map Broken Down by Degree

The typical angle change was calculated for a sample of 599 participants (see Table 4.3). The median angle change for all participants was 12 degrees. Thirty-three percent of participants had a change of 7 degrees or less. In addition, 66% of participants had a change of 19 degrees or less. Additionally, analyses were conducted to determine if those with longer vectors (i.e., greater inclination) showed greater consistency than those with shorter vectors

Table 4.3 Stability by Degree

	All	Short Vector	Long Vector
Median	12°	23°	10°
Mode	0°, 5°	0°	1°, 3°
33rd Percentile	7°	13°	6°
66th Percentile	19°	64°	15°
Percentage of Sample	100%	29%	71%

$N = 599$

(i.e., less inclination). Vectors were considered long if the respondent's dot placement was half the radius of the circle or longer. Dot placements that were less than half the radius of the circle were classified as short. As is consistent with the circumplex theory, participants who had short vectors showed more change between administrations than those with longer vectors.

The maximum possible amount of change for any respondent was 180 degrees and the largest amount of change of any actual respondent in the sample was 179 degrees. If angle placement were assigned randomly, researchers would expect the median change to be 90 degrees, substantially greater than the 12 degrees observed in the sample.

Evidence for the Validity of the DiSC Scales

Construct Validity of the Scales

Construct validity examines the validity of an assessment on a highly theoretical level. A *construct* is an abstract idea or concept (such as intelligence, dominance, or honesty) that is used to make sense of our experience. The Di scale of the *Everything DiSC* instruments, for example, measures a particular construct (i.e., the tendency to be bold, adventurous, and fast-paced). This "bold" construct, in turn, is theoretically related to a variety of other constructs. For instance, it is reasonable to assume that someone who is very bold will not be particularly cautious in nature. Thus, bold tendencies and cautious tendencies are theoretically linked in a negative manner. Consequently, if our measure of a bold tendency has high validity, people scoring high on the Di scale should score relatively low on a scale measuring cautiousness, such as the SC scale in DiSC. They should also score relatively high on scales measuring adventurousness, such as the Excitement Seeking scale of the NEO™-PI-3.

There are a variety of different ways to test construct validity. One aspect of construct validity asks if the internal structure of an assessment conforms to the theoretical structure of the domain being measured. Fittingly enough, Messick (1989) refers to this as "structure" within the validation context. Instruments like the *Everything DiSC* assessment propose an underlying model in which the scales have a specific relationship to each other. Researchers examine the actual, empirically derived relationships among the scales to see if they reflect the theoretical relationship proposed by the model.

Intercorrelations Between Scales

The DiSC model proposes that adjacent DiSC scales (e.g., Di and i) will have moderate correlations. These correlations should be positive and high, but considerably smaller than the internal reliabilities of the individual scales. For example, the correlation between the Di and i scales (.50) should be substantially lower than the internal reliabilities of the Di or i scales (both .90). On the other hand, scales that are theoretically opposite (e.g., i and C) should have strong negative correlations. Table 4.4 shows data obtained from a sample of 752 respondents who completed the *Everything DiSC* assessment. The correlations

Table 4.4 Scale Intercorrelations

	D	Di	i	iS	S	SC	C	CD
D	**.88**							
Di	.46	**.90**						
i	.14	.50	**.90**					
iS	−.37	.04	.47	**.86**				
S	−.69	−.31	.03	.57	**.87**			
SC	−.62	−.73	−.56	−.13	.34	**.84**		
C	−.19	−.43	−.70	−.49	−.18	.45	**.79**	
CD	.42	−.14	−.37	−.68	−.66	−.08	.26	**.87**

Note: Cronbach's alpha reliabilities are shown in bold along the diagonal, and the correlation coefficients among scales are shown within the body of the table. Correlation coefficients range from −1 to +1. A correlation of +1 indicates that two variables are perfectly positively correlated such that as one variable increases, the other variable increases by a proportional amount. A correlation of −1 indicates that two variables are perfectly negatively correlated, such that as one variable increases, the other variable decreases by a proportional amount. A correlation of 0 indicates that two variables are completely unrelated; $N = 752$, as shown in Table B.3.

among all eight scales conform to the proposed circumplex model. That is, moderate positive correlations are observed among adjacent scales and strong negative correlations are observed between opposite scales.

Because the *Everything DiSC* assessment model proposes that the eight scales are arranged as a circumplex, an even more strict set of statistical assumptions are required of the data. The patterns of correlations for a given scale are expected to be arranged in a particular order. As can be seen in Table 4.5, the strongest theorized correlation for a given scale is labeled r_1. The second strongest is labeled r_2, and so on. In this case, r_4 represents the correlation with a theoretically opposite scale. Consequently, r_4 should be a reasonably strong negative correlation. For each scale, we should observe the following relationship if the scales support a circumplex structure: $r_1 > r_2 > r_3 > r_4$.

Looking at Table 4.6, we do, in fact, observe a $r_1 > r_2 > r_3 > r_4$ pattern for each scale. In addition, we can examine the magnitude of these correlations in comparison to the theoretically expected magnitudes. The predicted magnitudes of r_1, r_2, r_3, and r_4 under a circumplex structure are listed in Table 4.6, as described by Wiggins (1995). The "actual"

Table 4.5 Expected Scale Intercorrelations

	D	Di	i	iS	S	SC	C	CD
D	1							
Di	r_1	1						
i	r_2	r_1	1					
iS	r_3	r_2	r_1	1				
S	r_4	r_3	r_2	r_1	1			
SC	r_3	r_4	r_3	r_2	r_1	1		
C	r_2	r_3	r_4	r_3	r_2	r_1	1	
CD	r_1	r_2	r_3	r_4	r_3	r_2	r_1	1

Table 4.6 Actual and Predicted Scale Relationships

r_1	>	r_2	>	r_3	>	r_4	
.45	>	−.11	>	−.46	>	−.69	Actual (median)
.42	>	.03	>	−.36	>	−.73	Predicted

r_x values are the median correlations for a given r_x. Although the actual and predicted values are not exactly the same (a near impossible standard for practical purposes), the magnitude of the actual and predicted correlation values is quite similar, thus providing additional support for the DiSC circumplex model and the ability of the *Everything DiSC* assessment to measure this model.

Multidimensional Scaling of Scales

A statistical technique called multidimensional scaling (MDS) also adds support to the DiSC model as a circumplex. This technique has two advantages. First, it allows for a visual inspection of the relationship among the eight scales. Second, this technique allows researchers to look at all of the scales simultaneously. In MDS, variables (e.g., scales) that are closer together have a stronger positive relationship. Variables that are farther apart are more dissimilar. The circumplex DiSC model predicts that the eight scales will be arranged in a circular format at equal intervals.

As can be seen in Figure 4.2, the scales are arranged in a way that is expected by the DiSC model. (Note that the original MDS rotation is presented below and this rotation is arbitrary.) Although the eight scales do not form a perfectly equidistant circle (as predicted by the model), this theoretical ideal is nearly impossible to obtain with actual data.

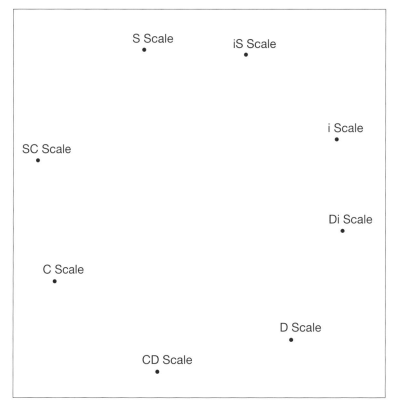

Figure 4.2 MDS Map of a Two-Dimensional Solution
Note: Stress = .01326; RSQ = .99825; *N* = 752.

The actual distance between the scales, however, is roughly equal, providing strong support for the model and its assessment.

As can be seen in Figure 4.2, all scales are closest to the scales that are theoretically adjacent to them in the model. For instance, the Di scale is closest to the D scale and i scale, as predicted by the model. In addition, scales that are theoretically opposite (e.g., i and C) are generally furthest away from each other on the plot. Consequently, this analysis adds strong support for the two-dimensional DiSC model and the ability of the *Everything DiSC* assessment to measure that model.

Additionally, the stress of the model is .01326 and the RSQ value is .99825. These values reflect the ability of a two-dimensional model to fit the data. Lower stress values are preferred (with a minimum of 0) and higher RSQ values are preferred (with a maximum of 1). Both of these values are almost ideal in the data, suggesting that a two-dimensional model fits the data exceptionally well.

Factor Analysis of Scales

To further explore the dimensionality of the model, a principal components factor analysis was performed on all eight scales using a varimax rotation. The resulting eigenvalues support the theoretical two-dimensional structure underlying the eight scales, as shown in Table 4.7. Only two components demonstrate eigenvalues above one, and both of these are well above one. Further, components 3 through 8 all have eigenvalues that decrease smoothly and are meaningfully below one. Consequently, regardless of whether we use

Table 4.7 Factor Analysis Eigenvalues

Component	Eigenvalues
1	3.10
2	2.95
3	0.60
4	0.38
5	0.37
6	0.31
7	0.23
8	0.04

N = 752

Kaiser Criterion or a scree plot method of determining the number of factors to extract (Bandalos & Boehm-Kaufman, 2008), the number of retained factors is two, as predicted by the model.

Factor Loadings and Angular Locations for the Eight DiSC Scales

The rotated factor loadings are listed in Table 4.8. (Note that the loadings were rotated such that the loadings reflect the original DiSC rotation.) The pattern of loadings was as expected for a circumplex model, as listed under the "Ideal Loadings" column. That is, with a circumplex model, some scales are expected to have high loadings on one component and near zero loadings on the other component (i.e., Di, iS, SC, and CD) and some scales would have moderately high loadings on both components (e.g., D, i, S, and C).

As an illustration, the i and C scales showed an opposing pattern of negative loadings (the C scale) and positive loadings (the i scale) on both of the dimensions. However, the D and i scales would be expected to have similar loading on one dimension but be opposite on the other dimension. This was observed, since both scales were positively loaded on the vertical dimension, but had opposite loadings on the horizontal dimension.

Table 4.9 shows the ideal and actual angular locations for the eight DiSC scales. The deviation column indicates that the actual angles are very similar to the ideal angles. The absolute average deviation is 3.8, which is lower than many of the interpersonal-based instruments currently available (Kiesler, Schmidt, & Wagner, 1997). Vector length, as shown in the last column of Table 4.9, reflects the extent to which the scale is represented

Table 4.8 Factor Loadings for the Eight DiSC Scales

Scale	Actual Loadings Vertical Dimension	Actual Loadings Horizontal Dimension	Ideal Loadings Vertical Dimension	Ideal Loadings Horizontal Dimension
D	.51	−.73	.707	−.707
Di	.83	.09	1.000	.000
i	.56	.67	.707	.707
iS	.06	.88	.000	1.000
S	−.76	.48	−.707	.707
SC	−.90	−.03	−1.000	.000
C	−.61	−.56	−.707	−.707
CD	−.09	−.85	.000	−1.000

Table 4.9 Angular Locations for the Eight DiSC Scales

Scale	Actual Angle	Ideal Angle	Deviation	Vector Length
D	325	315	10	.89
Di	6	0	6	.83
i	40	45	−5	.87
iS	86	90	−4	.88
S	122	135	−13	.90
SC	182	180	2	.90
C	223	225	−2	.82
CD	276	270	6	.85

by the two underlying dimensions (Gurtman & Balakrishnan, 1998). The mean vector length of .87 suggests that the scales have a strong relationship with the dimensions they are intended to measure.

The circumplex structure was also evaluated using the Fisher Test. According to the circumplex theory, variables, in this case scales, should be equidistant from the center of the circle (Acton & Revelle, 2002). The Fisher test provides a statistic that represents the variance of the vectors divided by the mean vector. The desired result is a value that is very small, as a circle would have no variance in radius. The results were based on the first pair of varimax rotated factors. The analysis indicated that the DiSC scales had a constant radius (Fisher = .031) with circumplex structure.

Scale Correlations with Other Measures of Personality

Another method used to provide evidence of construct validity involves correlating an assessment with other well-respected assessments of similar traits. For this purpose, a sample of respondents took the *Everything DiSC* assessment and two established measures of personality: the *NEO™ Personality Inventory*–3 (NEO-PI-3) (McCrae & Costa, 2010) and the *Sixteen Personality Factor Questionnaire®* (16PF®) (IPAT, 2009). This sample (*N* = 760) is described in Table B.1.

The NEO-PI-3 is a 240-item assessment designed to measure the Five-Factor Model of Personality: Extraversion, Agreeableness, Conscientiousness, Neuroticism, and Openness to Experience, and produces a scale score for each. In addition, the NEO-PI-3 produces six facet scales within each of the five domains. The 16PF is a 185-item assessment designed to measure 16 primary personality traits, as well as the Five-Factor Model of Personality. The assessment also provides scores on 19 additional scales in the following areas: self-esteem and adjustment, vocational interests, social skills, leadership, and creativity.

The correlations among the *Everything DiSC* scales and the NEO-PI-3 and the 16PF scales are shown in Appendix C. For the purposes of interpretation, a summary is provided here. For each *Everything DiSC* scale, the ten strongest correlations with either the NEO-PI-3 or 16PF are listed.

The Di Scale. The scales listed in Table 4.10 reflect the active, socially influential disposition that is measured by the Di scale. Although not listed, this scale also demonstrated high correlations with the Excitement Seeking ($r = .51$) and Achievement Striving ($r = .48$) scales of the NEO-PI-3. This reflects the adventurous, pioneering aspects of the Di scale. The high correlation with the Creative Potential scale of the 16PF was unexpected, but may reflect an openness to new activities that is tapped by the Di scale.

The i Scale. The scales listed in Table 4.11 reflect the extraverted, lively disposition that is measured by the i scale, as well as some elements of social poise or competence. Although not listed, this scale also demonstrated high correlations with Positive Emotions ($r = .50$) and Self-consciousness ($r = -.48$) scales of the NEO-PI-3. The i scale

Table 4.10 Strongest Correlations Between the Di Scale and the NEO-PI-3 and 16PF Scales

Scale	Instrument	r
Assertiveness	NEO-PI-3	.68
Creative Potential	16PF	.62
Independence	16PF	.60
Activity	NEO-PI-3	.57
Emotional Expressivity	16PF	.56
Social Expressivity	16PF	.55
Dominance	16PF	.54
Social Control	16PF	.53
Enterprising	16PF	.53
Social Boldness	16PF	.52

Table 4.11 Strongest Correlations Between the i Scale and the NEO-PI-3 and 16PF Scales

Scale	Instrument	r
Social Expressivity	16PF	.74
Extraversion	16PF	.70
Social Boldness	16PF	.70
Extraversion	NEO-PI-3	.69
Social Adjustment	16PF	.68
Gregariousness	NEO-PI-3	.65
Social Control	16PF	.62
Liveliness	16PF	.62
Warmth	NEO-PI-3	.60
Leadership Potential	16PF	.60

also had high correlations with Social ($r = .56$) and Enterprising ($r = .53$) vocational interest scales.

The iS Scale. The scales listed in Table 4.12 reflect the warm, accepting, and empathetic disposition measured by the iS scale. Although not listed, the iS scale also had significant correlations with the Emotional Sensitivity ($r = .42$) scale of the 16PF. Significant negative correlations with the Angry Hostility ($r = -.46$; NEO-PI-3), Tension ($r = -.43$; 16PF), and Anxiety ($r = -.41$; 16PF) scales reflect the more cheerful, easy-going disposition measured by the iS scale.

The S Scale. The scales listed in Table 4.13 reflect the agreeable, peaceful, and accommodating disposition measured by the S scale. The original conceptualization of the S scale also included a number of submissive tendencies, which is reflected by correlations with Compliance, Independence, and Dominance. It is worth noting the Straightforwardness scale is designed to measure sincerity or genuineness (rather than directness or bluntness), which is consistent with the S construct.

The SC Scale. The scales listed in Table 4.14 reflect the self-controlled, cautious, and passive disposition measured by the SC scale. Although not listed, the SC scale had significant positive correlations with a number of scales, particularly on the NEO-PI-3. These include Self-consciousness ($r = .44$), Compliance ($r = .41$), and Modesty ($r = .37$). The strong correlation with the Creative Potential scale of the 16PF was unexpected, but perhaps reflects a preference for stability over change, which is measured by the SC scale.

Table 4.12 Strongest Correlations Between the iS Scale and the NEO-PI-3 and 16PF Scales

Scale	Instrument	r
Warmth	NEO-PI-3	.61
Positive Emotions	NEO-PI-3	.57
Empathy	16PF	.56
Trust	NEO-PI-3	.55
Altruism	NEO-PI-3	.53
Agreeableness	NEO-PI-3	.52
Extraversion	NEO-PI-3	.52
Extraversion	16PF	.51
Warmth	16PF	.49
Compliance	NEO-PI-3	.47

Table 4.13 Strongest Correlations Between the S Scale and the NEO-PI-3 and 16PF Scales

Scale	Instrument	r
Agreeableness	NEO-PI-3	.67
Compliance	NEO-PI-3	.65
Altruism	NEO-PI-3	.47
Trust	NEO-PI-3	.39
Straightforwardness	NEO-PI-3	.39
Creative Potential	16PF	−.32
Independence	16PF	−.40
Dominance	16PF	−.45
Tension	16PF	−.45
Angry Hostility	NEO-PI-3	−.53

Table 4.14 Strongest Correlations Between the SC Scale and the NEO-PI-3 and 16PF Scales

Scale	Instrument	*r*
Dominance	16PF	−.63
Social Adjustment	16PF	−.64
Enterprising	16PF	−.65
Social Boldness	16PF	−.66
Social Expressivity	16PF	−.67
Social Control	16PF	−.67
Emotional Expressivity	16PF	−.69
Independence	16PF	−.71
Creative Potential	16PF	−.72
Assertiveness	NEO-PI-3	−.75

The C Scale. The scales listed in Table 4.15 reflect the introverted and emotionally reserved disposition measured by the C scale. Although not listed, the C scale had significant positive correlations with the Self-reliance ($r = .51$; 16PF), Self-consciousness ($r = .41$; NEO-PI-3), and Privateness ($r = .33$; 16PF) scales. Correlations with the Order ($r = .07$; NEO-PI-3), Perfectionism ($r = .15$; 16PF), and Conscientiousness ($r = .11$; NEO-PI-3) scales were significant, but smaller than expected. It is important to note that the C scale is designed to measure a reserved, methodical, analytical disposition rather than directly measuring a preference for order.

The CD Scale. The scales listed in Table 4.16 reflect the skeptical, challenging disposition measured by the CD scale. Although not listed, the CD scale had significant positive correlations with the Vigilance ($r = .31$; which measures an expectation of being misunderstood or taken advantage of) and Self-reliance ($r = .30$; which is opposed with group-orientation) scales of the 16PF.

The D Scale. The scales listed in Table 4.17 reflect the forceful, outspoken disposition that is measured by the D scale. Although not listed, the D scale also had significant positive correlations with the Social Boldness ($r = .32$; 16PF) and Activity ($r = .32$; NEO-PI-3) scales. As mentioned earlier, the Straightforwardness scale of the NEO-PI-3 is designed to measure sincerity rather than bluntness. Low scorers are described as more likely to manipulate others or to be cunning.

Table 4.15 Strongest Correlations Between the C Scale and the NEO-PI-3 and 16PF Scales

Scale	Instrument	r
Liveliness	16PF	−.55
Warmth	NEO-PI-3	−.55
Social	16PF	−.57
Empathy	16PF	−.57
Gregariousness	NEO-PI-3	−.59
Social Boldness	16PF	−.60
Social Adjustment	16PF	−.60
Extraversion	NEO-PI-3	−.63
Social Expressivity	16PF	−.66
Extraversion	16PF	−.67

Table 4.16 Strongest Correlations Between the CD Scale and the NEO-PI-3 and 16PF Scales

Scale	Instrument	r
Tension	16PF	.55
Angry Hostility	NEO-PI-3	.51
Anxiety	16PF	.45
Positive Emotions	NEO-PI-3	−.41
Altruism	NEO-PI-3	−.42
Warmth	NEO-PI-3	−.43
Empathy	16PF	−.44
Trust	NEO-PI-3	−.47
Agreeableness	NEO-PI-3	−.48
Compliance	NEO-PI-3	−.55

Table 4.17 Strongest Correlations Between the D Scale and the NEO-PI-3 and 16PF Scales

Scale	Instrument	r
Dominance	16PF	.63
Independence	16PF	.60
Assertiveness	NEO-PI-3	.55
Creative Potential	16PF	.51
Emotional Expressivity	16PF	.50
Enterprising	16PF	.44
Social Control	16PF	.35
Straightforwardness	NEO-PI-3	−.35
Agreeableness	NEO-PI-3	−.58
Compliance	NEO-PI-3	−.63

Scale Correlations with Self-Descriptions

Descriptive paragraphs were created to reflect the distinct characteristics of the different DiSC styles. As shown in Table 4.18, the paragraphs are rough approximations of the narrative feedback that respondents see in the DiSC profile, and are intended to capture a broad description of the different DiSC styles. Note that the two-letter styles (e.g., DC and CD) were collapsed into a single description that addresses the common characteristics of both styles. Participants taking the DiSC assessment were presented with descriptive paragraphs and asked to rate how well each described them on a 7-point scale from "Doesn't describe me at all" to "Describes me extremely well."

Data were collected in two batches, with two separate samples. Each batch included four descriptive paragraphs. The first sample included 7,200 participants and the second sample included 24,965 participants. The characteristics of these samples are included in Table B.4. A z-test for proportions (independent groups) was completed to test if the samples were significantly different from each other based on the twelve styles and eight DiSC scale scores. The results indicated that there is not a significant difference between the two observed proportions on any scale or style, using an alpha of .05. Table 4.19 shows the resulting correlations between the eight DiSC scales and the eight descriptive paragraphs. The results were as expected according to the theoretical model. For example, the D scale had its strongest positive correlation with the D descriptive paragraph and its strongest

Table 4.18 DiSC Descriptive Paragraphs

Style	Descriptive Paragraph Text
Di	I tend to be very active and assertive, and I am always pushing myself to try new things. When a good opportunity comes along, I'm usually the first one to jump on it. In fact, most people would describe me as very high energy with a bold, adventurous spirit. I'm a bit of a risk taker. Along those lines, I like things to move at a fast pace and change things up frequently. My personality is naturally very inspiring and dynamic, and I'm quick to take charge in a group situation.
i	I am a people person, tending to be a very outgoing and sociable. I love getting to know new people, hearing their stories and telling them mine. Even people who've just met me can sense that I'm very positive and optimistic. I usually come across as talkative and lively, and can help create an energetic, fun environment. I can be the life of the party, and have no problem helping everyone to feel included and have a good time.
iS	I am very cheerful by nature and can't help but see the best in everyone around me. In fact, I can be a little too optimistic about people, not recognizing when I need to be more skeptical. I go out of my way to make sure that everyone is comfortable and notice quickly if someone's feelings are hurt. If someone's got a problem, I really enjoy being there to listen and provide support. Most people would consider me to be highly empathetic and trusting. First and foremost, people see me as really caring, upbeat, and warm-hearted.
S	I tend to be very patient with other people and usually come across as warm and even-tempered. When people first meet me, they can usually sense that I'm gentle, welcoming, and sympathetic. I will go out of my way to make sure other people are happy. I prefer a harmonious environment where everyone gets along and, consequently, I'd rather keep my opinions to myself than hurt someone's feelings. I like relating to people in a calm and compassionate way, and I have no problem silently listening and empathizing with people when they talk about their feelings.
SC	I tend to be naturally cautious and prefer to move at a more steady, reflective pace. I frequently keep a low profile and don't mind working behind the scenes. Other people would probably describe me as very humble and soft-spoken. I often come across as quiet because I think things through for a long time before I speak. In general, I tend to be moderately paced and don't show a lot of assertiveness or boldness unless I really have to.
C	I tend to be reserved, analytical, and a bit skeptical. I put a strong emphasis on logic and accuracy. I choose my words carefully and can come across as a little impersonal if you don't know me well. When I'm working on a project, I'm extremely careful to ensure that I get things right. I'm often a little bit cynical toward people who are highly emotional or enthusiastic. Similarly, I prefer to have my privacy and don't show a lot of emotion with people that I don't know very well. As a consequence, some people may read me as detached or unexpressive. Ultimately, I like having a quiet, analytical environment where logic and critical thinking is highly valued.

(continued)

Table 4.18 continued.	
Style	**Descriptive Paragraph Text**
CD	I like to think of myself as a strong critical thinker and pride myself on being highly rational. Admittedly, I also have a bit of a cynical side. I have high standards for myself and others, and I don't have much tolerance for incompetent people. In fact, I can be a little dismissive if someone comes to me with work that is sloppy or flawed. I pride myself on my ability to make highly logical decisions and expect others to be able to do the same. At work, I prefer people to be fairly task-oriented and set strong emotions to the side. Along those lines, I know that my skeptical, matter-of-fact feedback can sometimes be a little tough for others to swallow.
D	My determination and insistence keep things moving and help me get real results. I'm fairly direct and candid and may even be seen as blunt by others. I don't usually sugarcoat my opinions, and I'm straightforward and frank with my feedback even if it's not what the other person wants to hear. I can also come across as dominant or forceful when I have a clear sense of how things should be. I may become a little aggressive, persistent, or even demanding if I know it will get the job done. I feel that it's more important to have things done right than make everyone happy. As a result, many people see me as tough-minded and focused on the bottom line.

Table 4.19 DiSC Scale Correlations with the Descriptive Paragraphs

Descriptive Paragraph	DiSC Scale							
	Di	i	iS	S	SC	C	CD	D
Di Paragraph	**.70**	.48	.16	−.26	−.58	−.45	−.17	.36
i Paragraph	.37	**.75**	.48	.03	−.43	−.57	−.34	.07
iS Paragraph	−.03	.35	**.62**	.43	.03	−.27	−.51	−.34
S Paragraph	−.36	.00	.38	**.60**	.40	.06	−.42	−.58
SC Paragraph	−.59	−.48	−.16	.29	**.70**	.48	−.02	−.45
C Paragraph	−.34	−.56	−.48	−.07	.37	**.57**	.31	−.10
CD Paragraph	.07	−.22	−.45	−.40	−.15	.18	**.49**	.32
D Paragraph	.38	.04	−.33	−.57	−.40	−.09	.30	**.63**

Note: The highest correlations for each DiSC scale are bolded.

negative correlation with the S paragraph. Similarly, the D scale demonstrated low correlations with theoretically independent descriptions (i.e., the C and i paragraphs).

Criterion Validity of the Scales

Criterion validity asks if an assessment's results relate to outside criteria (e.g., outcomes, behaviors, benchmarks) in a manner that is consistent with theoretical expectations.

Scale Correlations with Observer Ratings of Behavior

As part of a 360-degree feedback experience, respondents were asked to complete the DiSC assessment. At the same time, a group of observers were asked to rate the respondent on a series of 24 leadership practices scales, as measured in the *Everything DiSC 363® for Leaders* assessment. Each of these practices represents a desirable behavior associated with leadership (e.g., Being Fair-minded, Showing Confidence). Analyses were performed to investigate the correlations between the respondent's DiSC scale scores and the leadership practices scale scores. In all cases, the respondent sample ($N = 3,287$) was paired with at least three raters ($n = 19,881$). (See Table B.4 for demographics and Appendix D for leaders' style distributions.) The correlations between the DiSC scale scores and the practice ratings were largely as expected, with the highest correlations ranging between .3 and .5. These results are in line with other studies that have calculated correlations between adult subjects rating their own personality and raters who know the subject (Kendrick & Funder, 1988). The complete correlation matrices are shown in Appendix E. For the purposes of interpretation, a summary is provided here.

The analyses were performed first without controlling for the quality of the leaders and then controlling for the quality of the leaders. More specifically, preliminary analyses suggested that respondents with particular DiSC styles (e.g., iS, S) consistently received higher ratings across all practice scales than respondents with other styles (e.g., D, DC). As a result, a general factor (titled *leader quality*) appeared to boost correlations for some DiSC scales while muting correlations for others. To compensate for this effect, analyses were performed in which overall leadership quality was controlled for. In this sense, respondents are being rated on their relative performance of these 24 leadership practices.

Di Scale. The six most positive and six least positive correlations with the Di scale are listed in Tables 4.20 and 4.21.

The two tables demonstrate a large degree of similarity, and the scales listed reflect the socially influential and active disposition measured by the Di scale. Positive correlations were found with practice scales measuring bold, adventurous behavior (e.g., Promoting Bold Action, Finding Opportunities) and outward shows of confidence (e.g., Taking Charge, Showing Confidence). Negative correlations were with scales measuring humble behavior (e.g., Showing Modesty) and tactful behavior (e.g., Showing Diplomacy, Being Fair-minded). Across both tables, the only unexpected correlation was with the Creating a Positive Environment scale.

i Scale. The six most positive and six least positive correlations with the i scale are listed in Tables 4.22 and 4.23.

Table 4.20 Six Most Positive and Six Least Positive Correlations with the Di Scale

Practices	*r*
Showing Confidence	.30
Promoting Bold Action	.26
Taking Charge	.24
Focusing on Results	.21
Finding Opportunities	.21
Stretching the Boundaries	.20
Being Approachable	−.18
Staying Open to Input	−.19
Being Fair-minded	−.20
Maintaining Composure	−.23
Showing Diplomacy	−.24
Showing Modesty	−.29

N = 3,287

Table 4.21 Six Most Positive and Six Least Positive Correlations with the Di Scale Controlling for Leader Quality

Practices	*r*
Promoting Bold Action	.45
Stretching the Boundaries	.41
Finding Opportunities	.38
Focusing on Results	.38
Taking Charge	.37
Showing Confidence	.35

Table 4.21 continued.	
Practices	*r*
Creating a Positive Environment	−.31
Providing a Sense of Stability	−.32
Staying Open to Input	−.33
Being Fair-minded	−.37
Showing Diplomacy	−.41
Showing Modesty	−.47
N = 3,287	

Table 4.22 Six Most Positive and Six Least Positive Correlations with the i Scale	
Practices	*r*
Building Professional Networks	.32
Showing Enthusiasm	.26
Rallying People to Achieve Goals	.21
Promoting Bold Action	.20
Showing Confidence	.17
Stretching the Boundaries	.15
Providing a Sense of Stability	−.05
Communicating with Clarity	−.06
Being Fair-minded	−.08
Showing Modesty	−.09
Promoting Disciplined Analysis	−.11
Maintaining Composure	−.12
N = 3,287	

Table 4.23 Six Most Positive and Six Least Positive Correlations with the i Scale Controlling for Leader Quality

Practices	r
Showing Enthusiasm	.44
Building Professional Networks	.37
Rallying People to Achieve Goals	.35
Promoting Bold Action	.21
Stretching the Boundaries	.14
Acknowledging Contributions	.13
Communicating with Clarity	−.22
Providing a Sense of Stability	−.26
Maintaining Composure	−.27
Showing Modesty	−.29
Being Fair-minded	−.31
Promoting Disciplined Analysis	−.37

N = 3,287

Both Tables 4.22 and 4.23 exhibit strong similarities reflecting the lively and extraverted disposition measured by the i scale. Positive correlations were found with practice scales measuring sociable behaviors (e.g., Building Professional Networks) and liveliness and high-energy behaviors (e.g., Showing Enthusiasm, Rallying People to Achieve Goals). Negative correlations were with scales measuring precision (e.g., Communicating with Clarity) and reserved behaviors (e.g., Showing Modesty, Providing a Sense of Stability).

iS Scale. The six most positive and six least positive correlations with the iS scale are listed in Tables 4.24 and 4.25.

Tables 4.24 and 4.25 both reflect the empathetic, warm, and accepting disposition measured by the iS scale. Positive correlations are seen in the practice scales measuring cheerful behaviors (e.g., Being Approachable, Showing Enthusiasm) and empathetic behaviors (e.g., Acknowledging Contributions, Rallying People to Achieve Goals). Negative correlations were found in scales measuring analytic behaviors (e.g., Improving Methods, Promoting Disciplined Analysis) and in-charge behaviors (e.g., Taking Charge, Setting High Expectations).

S Scale. The six most positive and six least positive correlations with the S scale are listed in Tables 4.26 and 4.27.

Table 4.24 Six Most Positive and Six Least Positive Correlations with the iS Scale

Practices	r
Being Approachable	.31
Building Professional Networks	.30
Showing Enthusiasm	.27
Acknowledging Contributions	.26
Rallying People to Achieve Goals	.24
Showing Diplomacy	.23
Improving Methods	.03
Promoting Disciplined Analysis	.02
Taking Charge	.02
Setting High Expectations	−.01
Showing Confidence	−.04
Speaking Up About Problems	−.07

$N = 3,287$

Table 4.25 Six Most Positive and Six Least Positive Correlations with the iS Scale Controlling for Leader Quality

Practices	r
Being Approachable	.33
Showing Enthusiasm	.31
Acknowledging Contributions	.28
Rallying People to Achieve Goals	.26
Creating a Positive Environment	.23
Showing Diplomacy	.23

(continued)

Table 4.25 continued.

Practices	r
Taking Charge	−.17
Setting High Expectations	−.22
Showing Confidence	−.22
Improving Methods	−.27
Promoting Disciplined Analysis	−.30
Speaking Up About Problems	−.35

$N = 3,287$

Table 4.26 Six Most Positive and Six Least Positive Correlations with the S Scale

Practices	r
Maintaining Composure	.38
Showing Diplomacy	.37
Being Approachable	.34
Showing Modesty	.34
Creating a Positive Environment	.29
Staying Open to Input	.29
Promoting Bold Action	−.07
Focusing on Results	−.09
Speaking Up About Problems	−.12
Taking Charge	−.13
Setting High Expectations	−.14
Showing Confidence	−.27

$N = 3,287$

Table 4.27 Six Most Positive and Six Least Positive Correlations with the S Scale Controlling for Leader Quality

Practices	r
Showing Diplomacy	.50
Creating a Positive Environment	.39
Maintaining Composure	.39
Being Approachable	.36
Showing Modesty	.34
Staying Open to Input	.33
Stretching the Boundaries	−.34
Focusing on Results	−.35
Setting High Expectations	−.35
Taking Charge	−.37
Speaking Up About Problems	−.38
Showing Confidence	−.45

$N = 3,287$

Tables 4.26 and 4.27 demonstrate a large degree of similarity, and the scales listed reflect the accommodating, agreeable, and peaceful disposition measured by the S scale. Positive correlations were found with practice scales measuring accommodating and thoughtful behaviors (e.g., Showing Diplomacy, Staying Open to Input) and mild-mannered behaviors (e.g., Maintaining Composure, Being Approachable, Showing Modesty). Negative correlations were found with scales measuring results-oriented behaviors (e.g., Focusing on Results, Setting High Expectations) and commanding behaviors (e.g., Taking Charge, Showing Confidence).

SC Scale. The six most positive and six least positive correlations with the SC scale are listed in Tables 4.28 and 4.29.

Both Tables 4.28 and 4.29 exhibit strong similarities and reflect the passive, cautious, and self-controlled disposition measured by the SC scale. Positive correlations were found with practice scales measuring quiet, slow-paced behaviors (e.g., Showing Modesty, Maintaining Composure) and unassertive behaviors (e.g., Showing Diplomacy, Being Fair-minded). Negative correlations were with scales measuring commanding

Table 4.28 Six Most Positive and Six Least Positive Correlations with the SC Scale

Practices	r
Showing Modesty	.24
Maintaining Composure	.22
Showing Diplomacy	.19
Being Fair-minded	.16
Staying Open to Input	.14
Creating a Positive Environment	.12
Setting High Expectations	−.19
Stretching the Boundaries	−.19
Focusing on Results	−.21
Promoting Bold Action	−.24
Taking Charge	−.25
Showing Confidence	−.34

$N = 3,287$

Table 4.29 Six Most Positive and Six Least Positive Correlations with the SC Scale Controlling for Leader Quality

Practices	r
Showing Modesty	.46
Showing Diplomacy	.36
Being Fair-minded	.35
Maintaining Composure	.32
Staying Open to Input	.30
Creating a Positive Environment	.28
Showing Enthusiasm	−.28
Focusing on Results	−.32

Table 4.29 continued.	
Practices	*r*
Stretching the Boundaries	−.34
Taking Charge	−.35
Showing Confidence	−.36
Promoting Bold Action	−.36
N = 3,287	

behaviors (e.g., Focusing on Results, Taking Charge) and energetic behaviors (e.g., Showing Enthusiasm, Promoting Bold Action).

C Scale. The six most positive and six least positive correlations with the C scale are listed in Tables 4.30 and 4.31.

The two tables demonstrate a large degree of similarity, and the scales listed reflect the emotionally reserved and introverted disposition measured by the C scale. Positive

Table 4.30 Six Most Positive and Six Least Positive Correlations with the C Scale	
Practices	*r*
Promoting Disciplined Analysis	.10
Showing Modesty	.06
Being Fair-minded	.05
Communicating with Clarity	.05
Providing a Sense of Stability	.05
Maintaining Composure	.05
Finding Opportunities	−.15
Stretching the Boundaries	−.15
Promoting Bold Action	−.20
Rallying People to Achieve Goals	−.20
Showing Enthusiasm	−.23
Building Professional Networks	−.30
N = 3,287	

Table 4.31 Six Most Positive and Six Least Positive Correlations with the C Scale Controlling for Leader Quality

Practices	r
Promoting Disciplined Analysis	.37
Being Fair-minded	.28
Providing a Sense of Stability	.26
Showing Modesty	.25
Improving Methods	.23
Communicating with Clarity	.22
Stretching the Boundaries	−.14
Being Approachable	−.15
Promoting Bold Action	−.20
Rallying People to Achieve Goals	−.31
Building Professional Networks	−.33
Showing Enthusiasm	−.33

$N = 3,287$

correlations were found with practice scales measuring precision (e.g., Promoting Disciplined Analysis, Communicating with Clarity) and steady, level-headed behaviors (e.g., Showing Modesty, Providing a Sense of Stability, Being Fair-minded). Negative correlations were with scales measuring bold behaviors (e.g., Finding Opportunities, Stretching the Boundaries, Promoting Bold Action) and social behaviors (e.g., Showing Enthusiasm, Rallying People to Achieve Goals).

CD Scale. The six most positive and six least positive correlations with the CD scale are listed in Tables 4.32 and 4.33.

Both Tables 4.32 and 4.33 exhibit strong similarities reflecting the challenging and skeptical disposition measured by the CD scale. Positive correlations were found with practice scales measuring efficiency-improving behaviors (e.g., Speaking Up About Problems, Improving Methods) and commanding behaviors (e.g., Taking Charge, Showing Confidence). Negative correlations were with scales measuring accommodating behaviors (e.g., Showing Diplomacy, Being Approachable) and socially positive or encouraging behaviors (e.g., Showing Enthusiasm, Acknowledging Contributions).

D Scale. The six most positive and six least positive correlations with the D scale are listed in Tables 4.34 and 4.35.

Table 4.32 Six Most Positive and Six Least Positive Correlations with the CD Scale

Practices	r
Speaking Up About Problems	.07
Showing Confidence	.06
Taking Charge	−.01
Setting High Expectations	−.01
Improving Methods	−.04
Promoting Disciplined Analysis	−.05
Creating a Positive Environment	−.17
Maintaining Composure	−.17
Showing Enthusiasm	−.18
Acknowledging Contributions	−.18
Showing Diplomacy	−.20
Being Approachable	−.21

$N = 3,287$

Table 4.33 Six Most Positive and Six Least Positive Correlations with the CD Scale Controlling for Leader Quality

Practices	r
Speaking Up About Problems	.30
Showing Confidence	.22
Promoting Disciplined Analysis	.17
Improving Methods	.16
Setting High Expectations	.15
Taking Charge	.15

(continued)

Table 4.33 continued.

Practices	r
Rallying People to Achieve Goals	−.17
Showing Enthusiasm	−.17
Acknowledging Contributions	−.18
Creating a Positive Environment	−.18
Being Approachable	−.21
Showing Diplomacy	−.22

$N = 3{,}287$

Table 4.34 Six Most Positive and Six Least Positive Correlations with the D Scale

Practices	r
Showing Confidence	.35
Taking Charge	.20
Setting High Expectations	.20
Speaking Up About Problems	.14
Focusing on Results	.13
Promoting Bold Action	.13
Creating a Positive Environment	−.27
Staying Open to Input	−.27
Being Approachable	−.31
Maintaining Composure	−.34
Showing Modesty	−.34
Showing Diplomacy	−.34

$N = 3{,}287$

Table 4.35 Six Most Positive and Six Least Positive Correlations with the D Scale Controlling for Leader Quality

Practices	r
Showing Confidence	.51
Taking Charge	.44
Stretching the Boundaries	.38
Setting High Expectations	.38
Focusing on Results	.37
Promoting Bold Action	.36
Being Approachable	−.36
Maintaining Composure	−.37
Staying Open to Input	−.37
Creating a Positive Environment	−.41
Showing Modesty	−.42
Showing Diplomacy	−.50

$N = 3{,}287$

Tables 4.34 and 4.35 demonstrate a large degree of similarity, and the behavioral scales listed reflect the outspoken, forceful, and result-oriented disposition measured by the D scale. Positive correlations were found with practice scales measuring commanding behaviors (e.g., Showing Confidence, Taking Charge) and behaviors associated with goal striving (e.g., Setting High Expectations, Stretching the Boundaries, Focusing on Results). Negative correlations were with scales measuring empathetic behaviors (e.g., Showing Diplomacy, Creating a Positive Environment) and restraint behaviors (e.g., Maintaining Composure, Showing Modesty).

The DiSC Scales and Occupational Membership

An analysis was performed to examine the relationship between DiSC scale scores and occupational membership. Broadly speaking, DiSC is not expected to be a powerful predictor of occupational choice, satisfaction, or tenure. A sizable amount of research is available to support Prediger's (1982) proposal that vocational interests can most succinctly described by two attitudinal dimensions: (1) data versus ideas and (2) people versus things. One of these two dimensions (i.e., data versus ideas) is not measured by the DiSC model. This dimension involves a preference for abstract, conceptual tasks as opposed to a preference for more concrete tasks. The people versus things dimension, however, is addressed within the DiSC model, most distinctively by the i-C axis. Other dimensions within the DiSC model are also expected to show a relationship with specific occupations, but not necessarily with all occupations. It is more useful to consider the task preferences conceptually related to specific DiSC styles and then consider which occupations require those tasks. For instance, certain occupations, such as manager, require directing others, a task that is related to the D scale. Table 4.36 shows a sample of the task preferences that are expected to have a relationship with the eight DiSC scales. The theory, then, would suggest that members of certain occupations (i.e., occupations that require given tasks) would score higher than average on the corresponding DiSC scale.

A large sample of respondents was separated into their self-reported occupational groups from the larger sample of 57,648 (see Table B.1 for demographics). For each group, the means were calculated on all eight DiSC scales. The highest mean scale score and the second-highest scale score are shown in Table 4.37.

The results were generally as expected, with a few exceptions. Those in warehouse/general labor jobs were not expected to score as high on the D scale as they did. In this sample, the SC scale was noticeably higher than all other scales, with the D scale being a distant second. Finally, those in the skilled trades were not expected to score as high on the Di scale as they did. None of the occupations listed on Table 4.37 had the CD scale as one of their top two highest scales. Analyses did suggest that both police officers and military personal had the CD scale as their highest and second-highest DiSC scale, respectively.

Task Preference	Related DiSC Scale
Table 4.36 Relationship Between Task Preferences and the DiSC Scales	
Directing others	D
Promoting action	Di
Interpersonal enthusiasm	i
Nurturance	iS
Serving others	S
Tolerance of routine	SC
Analysis	C
Showing mental toughness	CD

Table 4.37 Occupations and Highest DiSC Scale Scores

Occupation	n	Highest Mean Scale	Second-Highest Mean Scale	Task Preferences as Measured by DiSC Scales
Assembly Worker	317	SC	C	Tolerance for routine, Analysis
Customer Service	2,611	S	iS	Serving others, Nurturance
Executive	3,760	Di	D	Promoting action, Directing others
Health Care Worker	1,761	iS	S	Nurturance, Serving others
IT	164	SC	C	Tolerance of routine, Analysis
Mechanical/ Technical	1,832	C	SC	Analysis, Tolerance of routine
Mid-level Management	10,240	Di	D	Promoting action, Directing others
Sales	5,197	i	Di	Interpersonal enthusiasm, Promoting action
Secretarial/ Clerical	1,988	SC	S	Tolerance of routine, Serving others
Skilled Trades	604	C	Di	Analysis, Promoting action
Supervisory	3,452	D	Di	Directing others, Promoting action
Teacher/ Educator	1,497	iS	i	Nurturance, Interpersonal enthusiasm
Warehouse/ General Labor	410	SC	D	Tolerance of routine, Directing others

These results are not presented on the table because the sample sizes were too small. For each occupational group, an effect size was calculated for the highest DiSC scale, comparing the occupational sample mean to the larger sample mean ($N = 57,648$). The effect sizes for the occupations listed in the table ranged from .08 to .54, with a median of .29. The smallest effect sizes were within the supervisory (.08) and management (.18) groups. The largest effect sizes were within the executive (.54), secretarial/clerical (.47), sales (.43), and mechanical/technical (.42) groups. Overall, these results suggest that DiSC does have a relationship to occupational membership for selected occupations, but, as expected, this relationship is modest.

Evidence for the Validity of the DiSC Styles

The eight DiSC scales are used to assign each participant a DiSC style, as described in Chapter 3. This section will explore the evidence for the validity of those styles.

Construct Validity of the Styles

Relationship Between the DiSC Styles and Other Measures of Personality

Respondents were asked to take the DiSC assessment, the NEO-PI-3 (McCrae & Costa, 2010) assessment, and the 16PF (IPAT, 2009) assessment, as described earlier in this chapter.

Based on the results of the assessment, respondents were separated into subsamples by style. Because some style groups were too small, some of these groups were combined with adjacent groups: Di and iD, iS and Si, SC and CS, CD and DC. An analysis of variance (ANOVA) was performed across the eight style groups on all 78 scales across the NEO-PI-3 and 16PF assessments. For each style group on every scale, an effect size was calculated. Here, the total sample scale mean was subtracted from the style group mean and then the difference was divided by the total sample standard deviation. These effect sizes provided a way to examine how much higher or lower a style group was on a given scale when compared to the total sample. Although no official guidelines are available for interpreting the magnitude of effect sizes, Cohen (1992) suggests the following rough guidelines: 0.3 = small, 0.5 = moderate, 0.8 = large. The full results of this analysis are shown in Appendix F.

The tables in the following section include the strongest (positive and negative) effect sizes for each style group across all NEO-PI-3/16PF scales. This information provides a snapshot of distinctive characteristics within each style group relative to the larger sample.

The Di/iD Style. The six strongest effect sizes for the Di/iD style group are shown in Table 4.38.

For each of the scales listed in Table 4.38, post hoc analyses indicated that the Di/iD group was significantly different than the S, SC/CS, and C style groups at a .01 level. Although not included here, the Di/iD group also had large negative effect sizes on the following scales: Social Sensitivity, Self-consciousness, and Apprehension. In total, these results suggest people with the Di/iD styles are likely to be assertive, energetic, self-assured, non-self-conscious, expressive, and socially bold.

The i Style. The six strongest effect sizes for the i style group are shown in Table 4.39.

For each of the scales listed in Table 4.39, post hoc analyses indicated that the i group was significantly different than the SC/CS, C, and CD/DC style groups at a .01 level. Although not included here, the i group also had large negative effect sizes on the following scales: Self-reliance, Self-consciousness, and Privateness. In total, these results suggest people with the i style are likely to be energetic, sociable, open, expressive, and positive.

The iS/Si Style. The six strongest effect sizes for the iS/Si style group are shown in Table 4.40.

Table 4.38 Six Strongest Effect Sizes for the Di/iD Style on the NEO-PI-3/16PF Scales

NEO-PI-3/16PF Scale	Effect Size	Instrument
Assertiveness	1.13	NEO-PI-3
Social Expressivity	1.08	16PF
Liveliness	1.01	16PF
Leadership Potential	.99	16PF
Independence	.98	16PF
Creative Potential	.95	16PF

Table 4.39 Six Strongest Effect Sizes for the i Style on the NEO-PI-3/16PF Scales

NEO-PI-3/16PF Scale	Effect Size	Instrument
Extraversion	1.08	NEO-PI-3
Gregariousness	1.07	NEO-PI-3
Social Expressivity	1.06	16PF
Liveliness	1.05	16PF
Extraversion	1.03	16PF
Warmth	.91	NEO-PI-3

Table 4.40 Six Strongest Effect Sizes for the Si/iS Style on the NEO-PI-3/16PF Scales

NEO-PI-3/16PF Scale	Effect Size	Instrument
Empathy	1.02	16PF
Extraversion	1.01	16PF
Warmth	.96	NEO-PI-3
Social	.96	16PF
Positive Emotions	.95	NEO-PI-3
Social Expressivity	.93	16PF

For each of the scales listed in Table 4.40, post hoc analyses indicated that the iS/Si group was significantly different than the C, CD/DC, and D style groups at a .01 level. Although not included here, the iS/Si group also had large negative effect sizes on the following scales: Tension and Angry Hostility. In total, these results suggest people with the iS/Si styles are likely to be empathetic, warm, positive, expressive, outgoing, and nurturing.

The S Style. The six strongest effect sizes for the S style group are shown in Table 4.41.

For each of the scales listed in Table 4.41, post hoc analyses indicated that the S group was significantly different than the CD/DC, D, and Di/iD style groups at a .01 level. Although not included here, the S group also had large negative effect sizes on the following scales: Tension and Anxiety. In total, these results suggest people with the S style are likely to be agreeable, accommodating, submissive, warm, positive, and calm.

The SC/CS Style. The six strongest effect sizes for the SC/CS style group are shown in Table 4.42.

Table 4.41 Six Strongest Effect Sizes for the S Style on the NEO-PI-3/16PF Scales

NEO-PI-3/16PF Scale	Effect Size	Instrument
Agreeableness	.59	NEO-PI-3
Angry Hostility	−.58	NEO-PI-3
Compliance	.58	NEO-PI-3
Warmth	.54	NEO-PI-3
Altruism	.52	NEO-PI-3
Positive Emotions	.51	NEO-PI-3

For each of the scales listed in Table 4.42, post hoc analyses indicated that the SC/CS group was significantly different than the D, Di/iD, and i style groups at a .01 level. Although not included here, the SC/CS group also had large positive effect sizes on the following scales: Compliance, Agreeableness, Self-consciousness, and Modesty. In total, these results suggest people with the SC/CS styles are likely to be deferential, modest, passive, quiet, and controlled.

The C Style. The six strongest effect sizes for the C style group are shown in Table 4.43.

For each of the scales listed in Table 4.43, post hoc analyses indicated that the C group was significantly different than the Di/iD, i, and iS/Si style groups at a .01 level. Although not included here, the C group also had large positive effect sizes on the following scales: Self-consciousness, Privateness, and Self-reliance. The mean score on the Reasoning scale of the 16PF for people with the C style was higher than any other style group. This difference was statistically significant at least at a .03 level when compared

Table 4.42 Six Strongest Effect Sizes for the SC/CS Style on the NEO-PI-3/16PF Scales

NEO-PI-3/16PF Scale	Effect Size	Instrument
Assertiveness	−.73	NEO-PI-3
Independence	−.62	16PF
Creative Potential	−.61	16PF
Emotional Expressivity	−.60	16PF
Dominance	−.58	16PF
Social Expressivity	−.55	16PF

Table 4.43 Six Strongest Effect Sizes for the C Style on the NEO-PI-3/16PF Scales

NEO-PI-3/16PF Scale	Effect Size	Instrument
Social Expressivity	−.88	16PF
Extraversion	−.83	16PF
Emotional Expressivity	−.80	16PF
Social Boldness	−.80	16PF
Social Adjustment	−.79	16PF
Extraversion	−.77	NEO-PI-3

to all other style groups except the CD/DC group. This scale is reported to measure problem solving through logical reasoning. Note that the C scale and style are not intended to measure/reflect a high level of structure or responsibility. In total, these results suggest people with the C style are likely to be socially reserved and private.

The CD/DC Style. The six strongest effect sizes for the CD/DC style group are shown in Table 4.44.

For each of the scales listed in Table 4.44, post hoc analyses indicated that the CD/DC group was significantly different than the i, iS/Si, and S style groups at a .01 level. In total, these results suggest people with the CD/DC styles are likely to be skeptical, defiant, and quick to frustrate.

The D Style. The six strongest effect sizes for the D style group are shown in Table 4.45.

For each of the scales listed in Table 4.45, post hoc analyses indicated that the D group was significantly different than the iS/Si, S, and SC/CS style groups at a .01 level. Although not included here, the D group also had large negative effect sizes on the following scales: Self-consciousness, Modesty, and Compliance. In total, these results suggest people with the D styles are likely to be assertive, driven, outspoken, strong-willed, and self-assured.

Style Agreement with Self-Descriptions

Descriptive paragraphs were created to reflect the distinct characteristics of each of the eight styles of DiSC. As previously shown in Table 4.18, the paragraphs are rough approximations of the narrative feedback that respondents would see in the DiSC profile, and are intended to capture a broad description of the different DiSC styles. Participants were asked to take the DiSC assessment and then indicate on a 7-point scale the degree to which they felt these paragraphs described them, with higher scores representing a greater identification with the paragraph.

Participants were subdivided into style groups (i.e., subsamples of participants all sharing the same DiSC style). The mean rating of each paragraph was calculated

Table 4.44 Six Strongest Effect Sizes for the CD/DC Style on the NEO-PI-3/16PF Scales

NEO-PI-3/16PF Scale	Effect Size	Instrument
Compliance	−.80	NEO-PI-3
Agreeableness	−.71	NEO-PI-3
Angry Hostility	.59	NEO-PI-3
Tension	.58	16PF
Trust	−.56	NEO-PI-3
Dominance	.55	16PF

according to the twelve styles. The results are consistent with the theoretical model. Participants assigned a Di style also highly endorsed the Di paragraph. Similarly, those with a CS style endorsed the Di paragraph the least. Table 4.46 shows the results of the calculations.

In addition to the previous analysis, ratings of the descriptive paragraphs were grouped into low (1–2), medium (3–4), and high (5–7) categories based on the scale

Table 4.45 Six Strongest Effect Sizes for the D Style on the NEO-PI-3/16PF Scales

NEO-PI-3/16PF Scale	Effect Size	Instrument
Assertiveness	1.09	NEO-PI-3
Creative Potential	.98	16PF
Independence	.95	16PF
Enterprising	.92	16PF
Emotional Expressivity	.89	16PF
Dominance	.85	16PF

Table 4.46 Style and Highest Mean Endorsement of Descriptive Paragraph

Descriptive Paragraph	Style											
	iD	i	iS	Si	S	SC	CS	C	CD	DC	D	Di
Di Paragraph	**6.9**	6.6	5.8	5.5	4.6	4.1	4.1	4.2	4.9	5.0	6.1	**6.7**
i Paragraph	6.8	**7.2**	7.0	6.5	5.5	4.8	4.4	4.0	4.3	5.2	5.5	6.1
iS Paragraph	5.7	6.5	**6.9**	6.8	6.5	5.9	5.6	4.7	4.3	4.4	4.6	5.3
S Paragraph	5.0	5.7	6.4	6.7	**6.9**	6.8	6.5	5.6	4.7	4.4	4.2	4.6
SC Paragraph	3.5	3.5	4.0	4.3	5.6	**6.3**	6.5	6.0	4.8	4.2	3.5	3.4
C Paragraph	4.0	3.7	3.6	3.9	4.4	5.4	6.0	**6.5**	6.1	5.3	4.7	4.1
CD Paragraph	5.6	5.0	4.7	4.5	4.6	4.9	5.3	6.2	**6.8**	6.5	6.5	5.9
D Paragraph	5.9	5.2	4.5	4.1	3.7	4.0	4.3	5.2	5.8	6.3	**6.7**	6.5

Note: Bolded numbers were expected to be highest in their column under the DiSC theory.

ratings of 1 (doesn't describe me at all) to 7 (describes me extremely well). For each style subsample, the percentage of participants to give the eight descriptive paragraphs a high rating was calculated, as shown in Table 4.47. In addition, the percentage of participants to give each paragraph a low rating was also calculated, as shown in Table 4.48.

For each style subsample, Table 4.49 shows the paragraph that was most often rated as high and the paragraph most often rated as low. For instance, among participants with the Di style, the most highly endorsed paragraph was the Di paragraph and the least endorsed paragraph was the SC paragraph.

The results of the analysis are largely consistent with the expectations. Of the twelve styles, there were three instances in which the style subsample did not most highly endorse the expected paragraph (i.e., the iS, SC, and CS styles). In all of these cases, the expected paragraph was the second-most highly endorsed paragraph.

Table 4.47 Percentage of Participants Rating a Paragraph as High, by Style Subgroup

Style Subgroup	Descriptive Paragraph							
	Di	i	iS	S	SC	C	CD	D
iD	**90.7**	88.0	59.3	43.7	11.1	19.0	60.4	69.5
i	85.0	**94.9**	80.1	60.8	11.1	14.2	43.4	50.0
iS	63.3	**92.3**	89.0	79.5	19.0	12.8	35.9	33.8
Si	55.5	81.8	**89.2**	87.6	25.5	16.1	33.3	25.5
S	30.3	12.9	81.9	**89.7**	58.4	30.2	33.8	16.1
SC	21.6	37.8	67.8	**89.3**	78.4	53.7	43.0	21.7
CS	20.6	42.7	57.7	**83.3**	81.9	69.1	49.9	29.6
C	22.1	20.0	34.0	60.3	68.8	**81.3**	78.0	50.4
CD	38.2	27.7	22.7	37.1	36.7	72.8	**90.3**	67.6
DC	42.2	46.9	26.4	29.0	22.9	53.1	**85.1**	80.3
D	74.8	56.1	28.5	23.7	11.6	34.7	84.9	**87.5**
Di	**87.7**	70.3	47.6	32.9	9.7	20.5	68.8	82.9

Note: The highest percentages for each row are shown in bold.

Table 4.48 Percentage of Participants Rating a Paragraph as Low, by Style Subgroup

Style Subgroup	Descriptive Paragraph							
	Di	i	iS	S	SC	C	CD	D
iD	1.0	1.7	9.0	22.1	**63.2**	46.2	14.2	9.6
i	2.4	0.3	2.8	11.6	**61.8**	56.5	26.0	20.8
iS	8.5	1.0	1.4	3.6	46.5	**59.9**	30.0	35.2
Si	12.2	3.6	1.6	2.3	39.0	**46.9**	34.5	45.9
S	30.1	56.4	2.4	1.5	11.8	34.5	33.9	**57.1**
SC	41.6	23.3	6.1	1.8	4.0	15.7	26.2	**48.2**
CS	**41.9**	35.6	9.5	3.2	3.2	7.6	17.3	27.7
C	40.7	**47.3**	25.3	12.2	8.5	3.7	5.2	21.9
CD	22.4	**42.0**	36.2	28.5	25.0	6.3	2.1	11.0
DC	16.7	17.0	32.3	34.8	**40.3**	16.4	3.6	5.4
D	3.9	15.3	27.0	40.7	**59.3**	27.3	4.0	2.4
Di	1.4	7.1	13.4	31.6	**63.4**	42.6	10.2	2.5

Note: The highest percentages for each row are shown in bold.

Table 4.49 Highest and Lowest Endorsed Paragraphs Among Each Style

Style	Paragraph Most Often Rated as High		Paragraph Most Often Rated as Low	
	Descriptive Paragraph	Percentage	Descriptive Paragraph	Percentage
iD	Di Paragraph	90.7	SC Paragraph	63.2
i	i Paragraph	94.9	SC Paragraph	61.8
iS	i Paragraph	92.3	C Paragraph	59.9
Si	iS Paragraph	89.2	C Paragraph	46.9

(continued)

Table 4.49 continued.

| Style | Paragraph Most Often Rated as High | | Paragraph Most Often Rated as Low | |
	Descriptive Paragraph	Percentage	Descriptive Paragraph	Percentage
S	S Paragraph	89.7	D Paragraph	57.1
SC	S Paragraph	89.3	D Paragraph	48.2
CS	S Paragraph	83.3	Di Paragraph	41.9
C	C Paragraph	81.3	i Paragraph	47.3
CD	DC Paragraph	90.3	i Paragraph	42.0
DC	DC Paragraph	85.1	SC Paragraph	40.3
D	D Paragraph	87.5	SC Paragraph	59.3
Di	Di Paragraph	87.7	SC Paragraph	63.4

Criterion Validity of the Styles

Agreement with DiSC Style

In three separate samples, respondents completed the DiSC assessment and were given their DiSC profile. After being debriefed on the model and allowed to review their profile results, participants were asked the degree to which they felt the results fit them. The results are shown in Table 4.50.

Table 4.50 Participants' Rating of the Overall Fit of Their DiSC Style

Quality of Fit	Sample 1		Sample 2		Sample 3	
Excellent Fit	63	56%	101	39%	286	48%
Good Fit	34	30%	133	51%	253	43%
OK Fit	13	12%	26	10%	54	9%
Poor Fit	2	2%	1	0%	2	0%
Very Poor Fit	0	0%	0	0%	0	0%
N	112		261		595	

Overall, participants report that the DiSC fit is good or excellent approximately 90% of the time. As documented under the Forer effect (1949), however, it is not unusual for participants to show a high level of agreement with psychological test results, especially when those results include broad interpretations that could accurately describe most individuals in the population. Consequently, analyses such as these should be supplemented with analyses that include evidence of both convergent and discriminant validity.

Relationship Between the DiSC Styles and Observer Ratings of Behavior

As described earlier in this chapter, a study was conducted to examine the relationship between DiSC assessment results and observer ratings of leadership behavior. Respondents were asked to complete the DiSC assessment, and observers were asked to rate them on 24 leadership practices, as measured by the *Everything DiSC 363 for Leaders* assessment.

Subsamples of respondents were created to represent each of the twelve styles. The largest subsamples were Di and D, $n = 541$ and $n = 448$, respectively. The smallest subsamples were CD and SC, $n = 165$ and $n = 157$. The mean sample size for each of the twelve styles was 274 with a standard deviation of 119. For each DiSC style subgroup, the means on each of the 24 practices were calculated and the three highest-rated leadership practices were identified, as shown in descending order in Table 4.51. Practices were standardized to have a mean of zero and standard deviation of one.

Table 4.51 Three Highest Practices for Each Style

Style	Highest Practices	*n*
iD	Promoting Bold Action Showing Enthusiasm Rallying People to Achieve Goals	220
i	Being Approachable Showing Enthusiasm Building Professional Networks	274
iS	Building Professional Networks Showing Enthusiasm Being Approachable	197
Si	Creating a Positive Environment Being Approachable Showing Diplomacy	237
S	Being Approachable Maintaining Composure Showing Diplomacy	229

(continued)

Table 4.51 continued.

Style	Highest Practices	n
SC	Showing Diplomacy Maintaining Composure Showing Modesty	157
CS	Showing Diplomacy Maintaining Composure Showing Modesty	228
C	Maintaining Composure Showing Modesty Promoting Disciplined Analysis	279
CD	Improving Methods Speaking Up About Problems Promoting Disciplined Analysis	165
DC	Setting High Expectations Speaking Up About Problems Showing Confidence	272
D	Promoting Bold Action Taking Charge Showing Confidence	488
Di	Taking Charge Showing Confidence Promoting Bold Action	541

$N = 3,287$

The results were largely as expected under the DiSC model. Behaviors that require assertiveness and exertion (e.g., Promoting Bold Action, Showing Confidence, Taking Charge) were high among styles in the upper-left region of the model (e.g., D, Di). Behaviors that require positivity and socializing (e.g., Showing Enthusiasm, Building Professional Networks) were high among styles in the upper-right region of the model (e.g., i, iS). Behaviors that promote stability and harmony (e.g., Maintaining Composure, Showing Diplomacy) were high among styles in the lower-right region of the model (e.g., S, SC). Behaviors that require analysis (i.e., Promoting Disciplined Analysis) and insistence on accuracy (i.e., Speaking Up About Problems) were high among styles in the lower-left region of the model (e.g., C, CD).

As shown in Table 4.52, another analysis was conducted to determine which style was most likely to demonstrate each of the 24 practices. For each practice, the style

Table 4.52 The Highest Style Means for Each of the Practices

Practice	Highest Mean	Second-Highest Mean	Third-Highest Mean
Finding Opportunities*	**Di**	**iD**	D
Stretching the Boundaries*	**Di**	D	**iD**
Promoting Bold Action*	**Di**	**iD**	D
Showing Enthusiasm	**i**	iS	iD
Building Professional Networks	iS	**i**	iD
Rallying People to Achieve Goals	**i**	iD	iS
Being Approachable*	**iS**	S	**Si**
Acknowledging Contributions*	**iS**	**Si**	S
Creating a Positive Environment*	S	SC	CS
Staying Open to Input	**S**	SC	CS
Showing Diplomacy	**S**	SC	Si
Facilitating Dialogue	**S**	SC	CS
Maintaining Composure*	S	**SC**	**CS**
Showing Modesty*	**SC**	**CS**	S
Being Fair-minded*	**SC**	**CS**	S
Communicating with Clarity	**C**	CD	CS
Promoting Disciplined Analysis	**C**	CD	CS
Providing a Sense of Stability	CS	SC	CD
Setting High Expectations*	D	Di	**DC**
Speaking Up About Problems*	D	**DC**	**CD**
Improving Methods*	**CD**	**DC**	C
Showing Confidence	**D**	Di	DC
Taking Charge	**D**	Di	DC
Focusing on Results	Di	**D**	iD

Note: For each practice, the style that was theoretically expected to have the highest mean score is bolded.

*Two styles were expected to have equally high means for these practices.

subsample with the highest, second-highest, and third-highest mean rating is listed. For example, the practice Finding Opportunities was most commonly observed among respondents with the Di, iD, and D styles. For each practice, one or two specific styles were expected to be the highest mean. For instance, for the Showing Enthusiasm practice, the style with the highest mean was expected to be i. For Promoting Bold Action, the styles expected to have the highest means were Di and iD. For each practice, the style that was theoretically expected to have the highest mean score is bolded. Note that each style was expected to be the highest on three and only three practices. The expected relationship between the DiSC model and the 24 practices is more thoroughly illustrated in Chapter 6.

The results of the analysis were largely as expected under the theoretical DiSC model. For 71% of the practices, the expected style had the highest mean. For 88% of the practices, the expected style was among the top two highest means. The iS and Si styles were expected to be among the styles with the highest mean on the Creating a Positive Environment practice, but were not. Likewise, the C style was expected to be among the styles with the highest mean on the Providing a Sense of Stability practice, but was not.

Relationship Between Styles and Occupations

Although DiSC is not expected to be a strong predictor of occupational choice, certain occupations are expected to have characteristics that would be more enticing to people with specific DiSC styles compared to other DiSC styles. For instance, some occupations, such as sales, typically require a higher level of activity and a higher level social interaction. Consequently, it is reasonable to expect that people with the i or iD style would be more attracted to these jobs. As discussed earlier in this chapter, DiSC is expected to have a moderate relationship with occupational membership in selected fields. In this study, analyses were conducted for occupational groups in which a large enough sample was available (i.e., $N > 150$).

Analyses were performed to determine the mean angle of members of certain occupations. First, respondents were divided into samples according to occupation. For each respondent, an x and y coordinate were calculated within the DiSC map. After calculating the mean x and y coordinates for each occupation, the mean x and y coordinates were used to calculate an angle. The occupation and corresponding angles are listed in Table 4.53. Further illustration of the relationship between the DiSC styles and the circular angles is included in the Test-Retest Reliability of the Styles section earlier in this chapter.

Eleven DiSC subject-matter experts (SME) were recruited. On average, the SMEs had been using DiSC products for 23 years and had been facilitating professional development sessions in the workplace for 30 years. They held a variety of education and

Table 4.53 Actual and SME Estimated Occupation Angle

Occupation	N	Actual Angle	Actual Style	SME Mean Estimated Angle	SME Style Estimate	Difference in Angle
Assembly Worker	317	173	SC	180	SC/CS	7
Customer Service	2,611	125	S	108	Si	17
Executive	3,760	341	Di	326	D	15
Health Care Worker	1,761	129	S	170	SC	41
IT	164	163	SC	219	C	56
Mechanical/ Technical	1,832	225	C	215	C	10
Mid-level Management	10,240	328	D	335	Di	7
Sales	5,197	26	iD	33	i	7
Secretarial/ Clerical	1,988	154	SC	147	S	7
Skilled Trades	604	253	CD	203	CS	50
Supervisory	3,452	289	DC	147	S	142
Teacher/ Educator	1,497	113	Si	113	Si	0
Warehouse/ General Labor	410	187	CS	164	SC	23

Note: Sample data were used to determine actual angle and actual style. Subject-matter experts' evaluations of the estimated angle were averaged to determine the mean estimated angle and the style.

facilitation certifications such as MBA, master's degree, and Ph.D. For each occupation, the SMEs were asked to indicate the angular location where they expected the group to plot on the DiSC map (see Table 4.53). Mean estimates were calculated by transforming angles into Cartesian coordinates, calculating means, and then transforming those means back into angular estimates.

The median angle difference between the sample data and the SME estimates was 15 degrees. The difference expected by chance is 90 degrees. The largest difference between the data and the SME estimates was in the supervisory occupation. This occupation showed a large variance in SME estimates, second only to the mid-level management estimates. The occupations with the most SME consensus were sales, IT, and mechanical/technical.

CHAPTER 5

Demographic Considerations

The *Everything DiSC®* assessment was developed and normed on a representative sample of U.S. adults. As such, some subgroups in the population make up a relatively small percentage of the sample. The analyses in this chapter are intended to explore the psychometric qualities of the DiSC® assessment within these subgroups. Likewise, additional analyses are included on demographic variables (e.g., gender, education) that have traditionally had large social, political, or economic implications. Analyses were conducted for subsamples within a larger sample of 26,703 respondents (see Table B.2 for demographics of this sample) who responded to the *Everything DiSC* assessment.

Internal Reliability by Gender, Heritage, and Education

For the eight DiSC scales, alpha reliabilities were calculated separately based on gender, heritage, and education, as shown in Tables 5.1 through 5.3. Across these demographic categories, there did not appear to be major differences in scale reliability. All scale reliabilities within all subgroups were well above .7, indicating good to quite good reliability.

Correlation Matrices by Gender, Heritage, and Education

Correlations among the eight DiSC scales were calculated for subsets of data based on gender, heritage, and education, as shown in Tables 5.4 through 5.13. The DiSC model proposes that adjacent scales (e.g., Di and i) should be most strongly correlated. Similarly, scales that are theoretically opposite (e.g., D and S) should have strong negative correlations. Scales that are positioned at 90 degree from each other (e.g., the D and i scales) should have low correlations. In the tables, Cronbach's alpha coefficients are shown in bold along the diagonal, and the correlation coefficients among scales are shown within the body of the table. The pattern of correlations did not vary substantially across subsamples, and within the subsamples, the pattern of intercorrelations was as expected by the model.

Table 5.1 Internal Reliability by Gender

Scale	Number of Items	Cronbach's Alpha	
		Males	Females
Di	9	.84	.85
i	7	.88	.88
iS	9	.81	.82
S	10	.81	.81
SC	12	.85	.86
C	11	.78	.79
CD	12	.81	.82
D	8	.82	.84

Table 5.2 Internal Reliability by Heritage

Scale	Number of Items	Cronbach's Alpha				
		Asian	African-American	Caucasian	Hispanic	Native American
Di	9	.85	.84	.85	.84	.81
i	7	.87	.87	.88	.87	.86
iS	9	.82	.80	.82	.79	.82
S	10	.80	.79	.82	.77	.79
SC	12	.86	.82	.86	.84	.85
C	11	.77	.76	.79	.77	.75
CD	12	.80	.80	.82	.80	.81
D	8	.82	.82	.85	.80	.83

Table 5.3 Internal Reliability by Education

Scale	Number of Items	Cronbach's Alpha		
		Some High School and High School Graduate	Technical School and Some College	College Degree and Graduate School
Di	9	.85	.84	.85
i	7	.87	.88	.88
iS	9	.81	.82	.82
S	10	.81	.81	.81
SC	12	.84	.85	.86
C	11	.75	.78	.80
CD	12	.81	.82	.81
D	8	.84	.84	.83

Correlation Matrices by Gender

Table 5.4 Correlations Among the DiSC Scales; Sample: Male

	D	Di	i	iS	S	SC	C	CD
D	.82							
Di	.49	.84						
i	.14	.46	.88					
iS	−.29	.11	.52	.81				
S	−.66	−.35	−.01	.47	.81			
SC	−.60	−.73	−.56	−.20	.31	.85		
C	−.25	−.46	−.67	−.51	−.06	.48	.78	
CD	.37	−.08	−.36	−.66	−.59	−.08	.19	.82

$N = 13{,}358$

Table 5.5 Correlations Among the DiSC Scales; Sample: Female

	D	Di	i	iS	S	SC	C	CD
D	.84							
Di	.52	.85						
i	.12	.48	.88					
iS	−.34	.08	.52	.82				
S	−.68	−.38	.00	.49	.81			
SC	−.62	−.75	−.55	−.16	.35	.86		
C	−.25	−.47	−.68	−.47	−.04	.48	.79	
CD	.38	−.09	−.38	−.66	−.59	−.10	.17	.82

N = 13,345

Correlation Matrices by Education

Table 5.6 Correlations Among the DiSC Scales; Sample: Some High School and High School Graduate

	D	Di	i	iS	S	SC	C	CD
D	.84							
Di	.52	.85						
i	.07	.41	.87					
iS	−.39	−.01	.49	.81				
S	−.68	−.39	.05	.53	.81			
SC	−.59	−.73	−.51	−.11	.31	.84		
C	−.20	−.40	−.63	−.44	−.08	.40	.75	
CD	.40	−.03	−.40	−.65	−.60	−.11	.19	.81

N = 3,962

Table 5.7 Correlations Among the DiSC Scales; Sample: Technical School and Some College

	D	Di	i	iS	S	SC	C	CD
D	**.84**							
Di	.51	**.84**						
i	.09	.44	**.88**					
iS	−.34	.06	.52	**.82**				
S	−.67	−.36	.03	.51	**.81**			
SC	−.61	−.74	−.54	−.17	.31	**.85**		
C	−.24	−.44	−.66	−.47	−.06	.47	**.78**	
CD	.39	−.08	−.39	−.68	−.61	−.08	.18	**.82**

$N = 9,057$

Table 5.8 Correlations Among the DiSC Scales; Sample: College Degree and Graduate School

	D	Di	i	iS	S	SC	C	CD
D	**.83**							
Di	.51	**.85**						
i	.13	.47	**.88**					
iS	−.31	.10	.54	**.82**				
S	−.68	−.38	−.02	.47	**.81**			
SC	−.61	−.74	−.57	−.20	.34	**.86**		
C	−.26	−.49	−.69	−.50	−.03	.51	**.80**	
CD	.38	−.08	−.36	−.66	−.59	−.10	.17	**.81**

$N = 13,684$

Correlation Matrices by Heritage

Table 5.9 Correlations Among the DiSC Scales; Sample: Asian

	D	Di	i	iS	S	SC	C	CD
D	**.82**							
Di	.50	**.85**						
i	.17	.47	**.87**					
iS	−.25	.16	.55	**.82**				
S	−.66	−.37	−.05	.42	**.80**			
SC	−.61	−.71	−.57	−.24	.33	**.86**		
C	−.29	−.50	−.66	−.49	.01	.49	**.77**	
CD	.36	−.08	−.33	−.62	−.56	−.13	.15	**.80**

N = 1,861

Table 5.10 Correlations Among the DiSC Scales; Sample: African-American

	D	Di	i	iS	S	SC	C	CD
D	**.82**							
Di	.43	**.84**						
i	.06	.43	**.87**					
iS	−.34	.09	.51	**.80**				
S	−.64	−.35	.02	.48	**.79**			
SC	−.56	−.71	−.52	−.17	.31	**.82**		
C	−.22	−.42	−.64	−.46	−.06	.43	**.76**	
CD	.37	−.11	−.37	−.65	−.58	−.07	.17	**.80**

N = 3,266

Table 5.11 Correlations Among the DiSC Scales; Sample: Caucasian

	D	Di	i	iS	S	SC	C	CD
D	**.85**							
Di	.53	**.85**						
i	.11	.45	**.88**					
iS	−.35	.06	.53	**.82**				
S	−.69	−.38	.01	.51	**.82**			
SC	−.61	−.76	−.56	−.17	.33	**.86**		
C	−.24	−.47	−.69	−.49	−.05	.49	**.79**	
CD	.39	−.06	−.38	−.68	−.61	−.08	.19	**.82**

$N = 18,458$

Table 5.12 Correlations Among the DiSC Scales; Sample: Hispanic

	D	Di	i	iS	S	SC	C	CD
D	**.80**							
Di	.48	**.84**						
i	.10	.42	**.87**					
iS	−.29	.10	.54	**.79**				
S	−.63	−.36	.01	.44	**.77**			
SC	−.60	−.72	−.52	−.18	.30	**.84**		
C	−.24	−.43	−.66	−.49	−.04	.45	**.77**	
CD	.37	−.07	−.35	−.64	−.57	−.11	.15	**.80**

$N = 2,711$

Table 5.13 Correlations Among the DiSC Scales; Sample: Native American

	D	Di	i	iS	S	SC	C	CD
D	**.83**							
Di	.53	**.81**						
i	.01	.38	**.86**					
iS	−.36	.01	.56	**.82**				
S	−.67	−.44	.06	.46	**.79**			
SC	−.55	−.72	−.54	−.16	.37	**.85**		
C	−.25	−.40	−.60	−.43	−.06	.43	**.75**	
CD	.42	−.01	−.38	−.63	−.59	−.17	.15	**.81**

$N = 407$

Variance Accounted for by Gender, Heritage, and Education

Variance Accounted for by Gender

An analysis of variance (ANOVA) was performed on the eight DiSC scales across gender groups to identify differences (see Table 5.14). These differences are generally small. The largest differences are seen on the iS scale, in which gender accounted for 3.7% of scale variance. Women tended to score higher on the i, iS, S, and SC scales, and men tended to score higher on the D, Di, C, and CD scales. Although statistically significant differences were found on all eight scales, in practical terms these differences were not large.

Variance Accounted for by Heritage

An analysis of variance (ANOVA) was performed on the eight DiSC scales across heritage groups to identify differences (see Table 5.15). These differences are generally small. The largest differences are seen on the CD scale, in which heritage accounted for 2.5% of scale variance. Although statistically significant differences were found on all eight scales, in practical terms these differences are not large.

Variance Accounted for by Education

An analysis of variance (ANOVA) was performed on the eight DiSC scales across education groups—Some High School and High School Graduate, Technical School and

Table 5.14 Percentage of Variance Accounted for by Gender

Scale	Percentage
D	1.8
Di	1.1
i	1.6
iS	3.7
S	1.7
SC	< .1
C	.1
CD	1.7

$N = 26{,}703$

Table 5.15 Percentage of Variance Accounted for by Heritage

Scale	Percentage
D	.4
Di	.4
i	.9
iS	.2
S	.2
SC	.7
C	.2
CD	2.5

$N = 26{,}703$

Some College, College Degree and Graduate School—to determine any differences (see Table 5.16). These differences are generally very small. The largest differences are seen on the Di scale, in which education accounted for .7% of scale variance. The Some High School and High School Graduate group scored highest on the S and SC scales. The Technical School and Some College group scored highest on the D, i, and iS scales. The College Degree and Graduate School group scored highest on the Di, C, and CD scales. Although statistically significant differences were found on all of the eight scales, in practical terms these differences are not large.

Table 5.16 Percentage of Variance Accounted for by Education

Scale	Percentage
D	< .1
Di	.7
i	.3
iS	.2
S	.3
SC	.6
C	.1
CD	.4
$N = 26{,}703$	

Distribution of Style by Gender, Heritage, and Education

Analyses were conducted to see if the distribution of styles differed across various demographic categories. Based on the norming of the DiSC assessment, the expected theoretical distribution is 8.3% for each of the twelve styles. For each of the demographic subsamples, the style distributions are presented in Tables 5.17 through 5.19. The first column in all the tables shows the overall distribution of the larger sample, $N = 26{,}703$. As previously determined by other analyses, certain subsamples tend to score higher in some DiSC scales than other subsamples and this is reflected in the distributions. Female participants are more represented in the i, iS, Si, S, SC, and CS styles, while male participants are more heavily represented in the C, CD, DC, D, Di, and iD styles. As noted earlier,

Table 5.17 Style Distribution by Gender

	All	Male	Female
iD	7.1%	7.8%	6.5%
i	10.4%	9.0%	11.8%
iS	7.6%	5.2%	10.0%
Si	8.4%	6.7%	10.2%
S	9.2%	7.8%	10.6%
SC	8.1%	7.8%	8.4%
CS	9.9%	10.0%	9.8%
C	9.2%	10.3%	8.0%
CD	5.3%	5.9%	4.6%
DC	7.5%	8.3%	6.6%
D	8.8%	10.9%	6.8%
Di	8.5%	10.4%	6.6%

Table 5.18 Style Distribution by Education

	All	Some High School and High School Graduate	Technical School and Some College	College Degree and Graduate School
iD	7.1%	4.9%	7.2%	7.7%
i	10.4%	9.1%	10.3%	10.9%
iS	7.6%	8.5%	8.2%	6.9%
Si	8.4%	8.6%	8.7%	8.2%
S	9.2%	11.0%	9.4%	8.5%
SC	8.1%	11.0%	8.2%	7.1%
CS	9.9%	10.6%	9.6%	9.9%
C	9.2%	7.6%	8.9%	9.8%

(continued)

Table 5.18 continued.

	All	Some High School and High School Graduate	Technical School and Some College	College Degree and Graduate School
CD	5.3%	4.0%	5.0%	5.8%
DC	7.5%	7.1%	7.6%	7.5%
D	8.8%	9.8%	8.6%	8.7%
Di	8.5%	7.8%	8.3%	8.8%

Table 5.19 Style Distribution by Heritage

	All	Asian	African-American	Caucasian	Hispanic	Native American
iD	7.1%	7.7%	8.5%	6.4%	10.2%	7.6%
i	10.4%	8.0%	12.6%	9.8%	13.3%	13.3%
iS	7.6%	5.3%	8.1%	7.5%	8.6%	7.9%
Si	8.4%	6.4%	8.4%	8.8%	7.7%	6.6%
S	9.2%	9.9%	10.0%	9.1%	7.8%	12.0%
SC	8.1%	11.8%	9.2%	7.5%	7.8%	9.1%
CS	9.9%	16.4%	11.9%	8.8%	10.4%	10.8%
C	9.2%	10.2%	7.9%	9.6%	7.6%	7.1%
CD	5.3%	4.6%	3.1%	6.0%	3.5%	3.9%
DC	7.5%	5.9%	4.5%	8.6%	5.1%	5.2%
D	8.8%	5.9%	7.7%	9.6%	7.3%	9.8%
Di	8.5%	8.0%	8.1%	8.3%	10.7%	6.6%

however, these differences do not account for a large percentage of the measured variance. Participants in the Some High School and High School Graduate category were less likely to be assigned the iD style and more likely to be assigned the SC style. The other two education groups did not demonstrate marked differences from the total sample.

Compared to other groups, participants with Asian heritage were particularly less likely to be assigned the i, Si, iS, and DC styles and more likely to be assigned the SC and

CS styles. African-Americans tended to have lower representation particularly in the DC and CD styles, while they were more represented in the i and CS styles. Caucasian participants tended to have especially lower representation in the iD and CS styles while having noticeably higher representation in the DC and CD styles. Relative to other groups, participants with Hispanic heritage had particularly high representation in the iD and i styles and lower representation in the C, CD, and DC styles. Participants with Native American heritage had high relative representation in the i and S styles and low representation in the Si, DC, and Di styles. As mentioned earlier, however, mean differences based on ethnicity were, overall, very small. Practically speaking, knowing someone's ethnic background will tell a practitioner almost nothing about that person's DiSC style.

Distribution of Inclination by Gender and Heritage

The distance that a respondent's dot is located from the center of the circle is known as inclination. People with stronger inclinations are expected to have more pronounced DiSC styles, as discussed in Chapter 8. A sample of 26,703 respondents was evaluated to estimate the distribution of DiSC inclinations in the population. As shown in Figure 5.1, most respondents' dots (81.8%) were located in the outer half of the circle. Inclination is

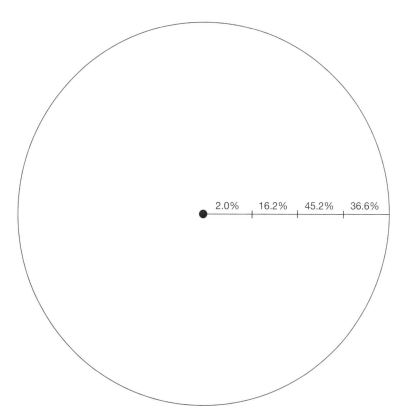

Figure 5.1 Distribution of DiSC Inclination

measured on a scale from 0 to 2. Scores of 0 are plotted at the center of the circle, scores of 1 are plotted in the center of the radius, and scores of 2 are plotted on the edge of the circle.

As shown in Table 5.20, analyses were also conducted to estimate the distribution of inclination across two demographic variables: heritage and gender. For this analysis, the radius of the circle was divided into four equal segments, with the first quarter being the segment closest to the center of the circle. For each quarter, the percentage of respondents in that segment is listed. The distributions suggest that Caucasians were significantly more likely to have inclinations in the fourth quarter compared to other groups. An ANOVA confirmed that significant differences ($p < .01$) did exist among heritage groups. For each group, effect sizes were calculated by subtracting the mean across all five groups from the specific group mean, and dividing the difference by the sample standard deviation. The resulting effect sizes suggest that the relationship between heritage and inclination is of little practical importance. An ANOVA comparing men and women on inclination also produced statistically significant results at $p < .01$. Gender differences, however, accounted for less than 1% of the variance.

Table 5.20 Distribution of DiSC Inclination by Heritage and Gender

Demographic Group	N	% in 1st Quarter	% in 2nd Quarter	% in 3rd Quarter	% in 4th Quarter	Effect Size
All	26,703	2.0	16.2	45.2	36.6	
Heritage						
Asian	1,861	2.6	19.7	45.1	32.6	.00
African-American	3,266	2.6	19.3	49.3	28.8	−.08
Caucasian	18,458	1.7	14.9	43.8	39.6	.18
Hispanic	2,711	2.8	18.4	49.1	29.7	−.05
Native American	407	3.7	17.7	50.1	28.5	−.05
Gender						
Male	13,358	2.2	17.6	46.3	33.9	−.06
Female	13,345	1.9	14.8	44.1	39.2	.06

CHAPTER 6

The Everything DiSC Applications

Everything DiSC® reports are available in six different application-specific profiles. Table 6.1 lists these different profiles and their intended uses. The measurement of a participant's DiSC® style is the same across all profiles, but the information presented to the participant in his or her report will be specific to that application. For instance, DiSC information is presented in a management context within the *Management Profile* and presented in a sales context within the *Sales Profile.*

One important way in which the profiles differ is in the presentation of the DiSC map. All DiSC maps include eight priorities wrapped around the circumference. An example of the priorities in the *Workplace Profile* is shown in Figure 6.1. These priorities are used to help participants understand the DiSC model in practical terms. In particular, the eight priorities help participants to understand the relationship between their location on the

Table 6.1 Descriptions of the Everything DiSC Applications

Application	Intended Audience	Intended Use
Workplace	All Adults	• help people understand their personality • help people better understand their colleagues • provide tips and guidance for improving their relationships
Sales	Sales Professionals	• help sales professionals understand their sales style • help sales professionals better understand their customers • provide tips and guidance for improving sales effectiveness

(continued)

Table 6.1 continued.		
Application	**Intended Audience**	**Intended Use**
Management	Managers	• help managers understand their management style • help managers better understand their direct reports • provide tips and guidance for improving management effectiveness
Productive Conflict	All Adults	• help people understand their style in conflict • help people understand their destructive responses and the automatic thoughts that drive them • help people understand how to "catch themselves" and make more productive choices
Work of Leaders	Leaders	• help leaders understand their style of leadership • give leaders a framework for understanding leadership best practices • provide tips and guidance for improving leadership effectiveness
363 for Leaders	Leaders	• give leaders feedback from their colleagues • give leaders a framework for understanding leadership best practices • provide tips and guidance for improving leadership effectiveness

DiSC map (i.e., dot location) and other locations. In the example in Figure 6.1, the priority of Accuracy suggests that people whose dots fall close to the lower, left-hand corner of the map place a particularly strong priority on precision within their work. A summary list of all the priorities across all of the different profiles is included in Table 3.3. For a discussion of the interpretation of the priorities, see Chapter 8 .

The following sections describe the development of the priorities in each of the different DiSC profiles.

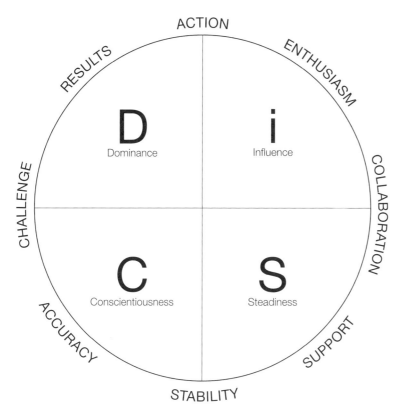

Figure 6.1 Everything DiSC Workplace Model

Everything DiSC Workplace

The application-specific model used in the *Everything DiSC Workplace® Profile*, as shown in Figure 6.1, helps participants better understand their own work style as well as the perspective of their colleagues.

Development of the Workplace Priorities

The first step in developing the *Workplace* priorities was to generate a list of possible priorities that would be relevant at each of the eight points around the DiSC map. Because *Workplace* is intended for a broad audience of working adults, only priorities that were applicable to a broad range of employees were considered. In addition, only priorities that had a strong conceptual link to the DiSC model were considered. So, for instance, the priorities considered for the S location on the DiSC map included words like *sincerity*, *support*, *harmony*, and *listening*. After considering a variety of options, the profile designers settled on a list of eight final candidates. Data were then collected from working adults to ensure that these candidates showed a strong empirical link to the model.

As part of a beta test, participants ($N = 2,270$; see Table B.4 for demographics) were presented with a series of statements describing work tasks and asked to rate the importance of each task to job effectiveness. For instance, participants were asked to rate the importance of "speaking up about problems" on a 5-point scale, ranging from "Not Important" (1) to "Crucially Important" (5). Statements were grouped into eight categories that represent the eight priorities on the circle in Figure 6.1. Each category contained three statements that were used to form a scale. The 24 individual statements are shown in Table 6.2.

After participants rated each statement, the average response for statements within a priority category was then calculated. Consequently, all participants had a category score for all eight priorities.

A statistical technique called multidimensional scaling analysis (MDS) is a highly useful assessment for examining the fit of the data to the conceptual model. First, this technique allows for a visual inspection of the relationships among the eight approach scales or the 24 practice scales. Second, this technique makes it possible to look at all of the scales simultaneously. The category scores were analyzed using MDS. The results of the analysis are presented in Figure 6.2. Categories that are closer together share more in common and categories that are farther apart are more dissimilar.

As expected, the eight priority categories are arranged in a circular shape, in the manner predicted by the *Everything DiSC Workplace* model. That is, the sequence around the circle proceeds as follows: Action, Enthusiasm, Collaboration, Support, Stability, Accuracy, Challenge, and Results. Although the eight priority scales do not form a perfectly equidistant circle, this theoretical ideal is nearly impossible to obtain with actual data.

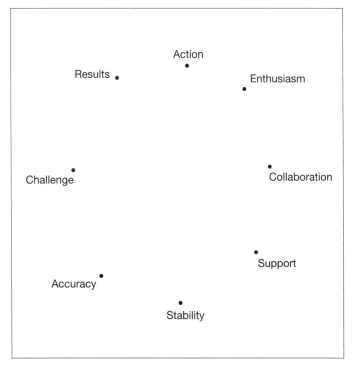

Figure 6.2 MDS Map of Workplace Priorities During Development
Note: Stress = .08137; RSQ = .93595; *N* = 2,270.

Table 6.2 Statements Used to Measure Each of the Eight Workplace Priorities

Priority	Statement
Action	Remaining active
	Being on the lookout for new opportunities
	Being open to taking risks
Enthusiasm	Showing enthusiasm for the projects you are working on
	Being optimistic about the work you are doing
	Encouraging people to have fun at work
Collaboration	Communicating frequently with the people you work with
	Taking opportunities to collaborate with other people
	Encouraging teamwork
Support	Letting people know that you are there to help out if they need it
	Being patient with other people's mistakes
	Delivering feedback in a tactful manner
Stability	Working at a consistent, steady pace
	Creating schedules for projects
	Following established rules or procedures
Accuracy	Taking extra time to ensure quality
	Making decisions that are based on logic, not emotion
	Taking time to analyze choices in-depth before making a decision
Challenge	Speaking up about problems
	Questioning ideas that don't seem logical
	Questioning procedures or practices that aren't efficient
Results	Being direct with your opinions and ideas
	Constantly pushing yourself toward new goals
	Setting high expectations for yourself and others

Validation of the Workplace Priorities

After the beta test, items were collected to measure each of the eight priorities. Most of these items were taken from 78 items that were already included in the basic *Everything DiSC* assessment. Analyses suggested, however, that additional items were needed for three of the priority scales: Collaboration, Accuracy, and Results. These extra items were developed and data were collected on all of the priority scale items. These data were analyzed (e.g., internal reliability, MDS) and refinements were made to the scales. The rest of this section describes the evidence for reliability and validity on these priority scales. As mentioned in Chapter 3, the priority scales should be regarded as supplemental and have no role in determining DiSC style. They play a subtle role in shaping the output of a respondent's *Workplace Profile*, but are not nearly as important as the DiSC scales.

The internal reliabilities of the *Workplace* priority scales were calculated on a sample of 2,270 adults. The median alpha was .80 and the values ranged from .76 to .82, as shown in Table 6.3.

The two-week test-retest reliabilities of the *Workplace* priority scales were calculated using a sample of 599 adults (see Table B.4 for characteristics of this sample). The median test-retest reliability was .86 and the values ranged from .81 to .88, as shown in Table 6.4.

The validation sample was composed of participants ($N = 39,607$; see Table B.5 for demographics) taking the *Everything DiSC Workplace* assessment. Multidimensional scaling analysis showed that the priorities are arranged in a manner predicted by the model. It is important to note that the original MDS rotation is arbitrary and the axes are meaningless. Distortions of distance are smaller when the stress is closer to zero and when the distances are relatively large (Kruskal & Wish, 1978). In Figure 6.3, the

Table 6.3 Internal Reliability of the Workplace Priority Scales

Priority	Alpha
Action	.78
Enthusiasm	.82
Collaboration	.77
Support	.81
Stability	.81
Accuracy	.80
Challenge	.76
Results	.81
$N = 2,270$	

Table 6.4 Test-Retest Reliability of the Workplace Priority Scales

Priority	Test-Retest Reliability
Action	.86
Enthusiasm	.88
Collaboration	.86
Support	.88
Stability	.88
Accuracy	.81
Challenge	.83
Results	.83

N = 599

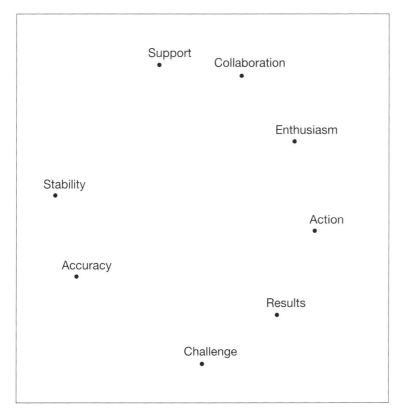

Figure 6.3 MDS Map of the Workplace Priorities
Note: Stress = .01240; RSQ = .99858; *N* = 39,607.

data are circularly represented and the order of the scale is as predicted by the model: Action, Enthusiasm, Collaboration, Support, Stability, Accuracy, Challenge, and Results. Additionally, the stress value of .01240 and the RSQ value of .99858 suggest that the two-dimensional model fits the validation sample very well. Lower stress values approaching zero are preferred while RSQ values closer to one are considered ideal.

Overall, the analysis suggests a good fit between the data and the model. Stress values suggest that the eight scales are well represented by two dimensions and that additional dimensions are not needed. The MDS results do show relatively larger gaps between Support and Stability ($r = .26$) and between Accuracy and Challenge ($r = .11$). The correlations between these variables were statistically significant, but were much lower than the median correlation between adjacent pairs, which was .46.

Everything DiSC Sales

The application-specific model used in the *Everything DiSC® Sales Profile*, shown in Figure 6.4, helps salespeople better understand themselves and their customers. In this model, the eight words around the map indicate the priorities of both customers and

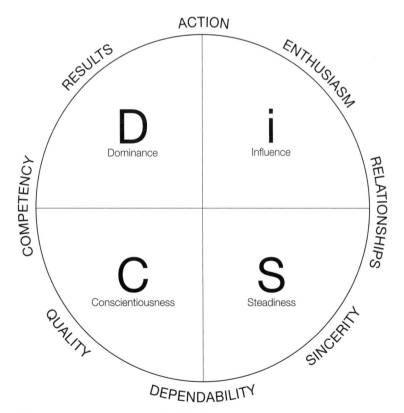

Figure 6.4 Everything DiSC Sales Model

salespeople of different DiSC styles during sales interactions. For example, the priorities of "i" salespeople and customers are Enthusiasm, Action, and Relationships. The development of this model was based on empirical data gathered from both customers and salespeople.

Development of the Sales Priorities

First, participants ($N = 1,047$; see Table B.5 for demographics) were presented with a series of statements and asked the importance of each when working with a salesperson. For instance, participants were asked to rate the importance of "working with a salesperson who is friendly and personable" on a 5-point scale, ranging from "Not Important" (1) to "Vitally Important" (5). Statements were grouped into eight categories that represent the eight priorities on the circle shown in Figure 6.4. Each category contained two to four statements. The individual statements for each category are shown in Table 6.5.

After participants rated each statement, the average response for statements within a priority category was calculated. Consequently, all participants had a category score for all eight priorities. The category scores were analyzed using MDS. The results of the analysis are presented in Figure 6.5. Categories that are closer together share more in common, and categories that are farther apart are more dissimilar.

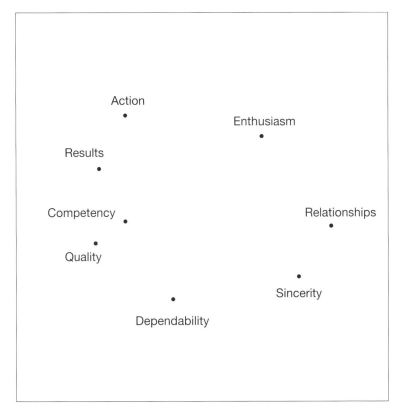

Figure 6.5 MDS Map for Customers
Note: Stress = .06642; RSQ = .96801; $N = 1,047$.

Table 6.5 Statements Used to Measure the Sales Priorities from the Customer's Perspective

Priority	Statement
Action	Being assured that things will happen quickly and easily once I make a decision
	Getting things moving as soon as possible after the sale
Enthusiasm	Seeing a product/service that I'm excited about
	Working with salespeople who are enthusiastic and passionate about the product/service
Relationships	Working with salespeople who are friendly and personable
	Working with salespeople that I connect with
	Knowing that the salesperson doesn't see me as just another sales opportunity
	Working with a salesperson I enjoy talking to
Sincerity	Working with salespeople who are sincere
	Working with salespeople who I sense are genuinely looking out for my best interest
	Working with a salesperson who genuinely seems to care about my needs and concerns
	Working with a salesperson who is a good listener
Dependability	Being sure that the salesperson is dependable
	Working with salespeople who are thorough, careful, and responsible
Quality	Being sure that I'm getting the highest quality
	Seeing demonstrations of the quality of the product/service
Competency	Being sure that the salesperson is competent to handle my business
	Working with salespeople who are experts in their field
Results	Having salespeople show me how I can get immediate, practical results
	Seeing how the product/service can have a big impact on my success
	Seeing the immediate benefits of the product/service

As expected, the eight priorities are arranged in a circular shape, with the priorities arranged in the manner predicted by the sales model. That is, the sequence around the circle proceeds as follows: Action, Enthusiasm, Relationships, Sincerity, Dependability, Quality, Competency, and Results. Although the eight scales do not form a perfectly equidistant circle (as predicted by the model), this theoretical ideal is nearly impossible to obtain with actual data.

Because the *Everything DiSC Sales* model speaks to the priorities of salespeople as well as customers, a second sample of data was collected on salespeople ($N = 1,800$; see Table B.5 for demographics). In this study, salespeople were presented with sales behaviors, such as "showing the customer that you're an expert in your field," and asked to rate the importance of each statement on a 5-point scale, ranging from "Not Important" (1) to "Vitally Important" (5). Each category contained three to five statements. Sample statements for each category are shown in Table 6.6.

As described in the previous study, statement ratings within a priority category were averaged. The category scores were then submitted to a MDS analysis. The results of this analysis are shown in Figure 6.6.

As with the customer data, the priority categories are arranged in a circle. Further, the categories are plotted in the expected order: Action, Enthusiasm, Relationships, Sincerity, Dependability, Quality, Competency, and Results. The categories are not spaced in a perfectly even manner, but again, this standard is almost impossible to meet with real data.

Table 6.6 Statements Used to Measure the Sales Priorities from the Salesperson's Perspective

Priority	Statement
Action	Showing the customer that you can make things happen quickly and easily
	Helping customers see how they can use your product/service immediately
	Inspiring customers that your product/service can help them right away
Enthusiasm	Getting the customer excited about your product/service
	Creating enthusiasm in the customer
	Having fun with the customer

(*continued*)

Table 6.6 continued.

Priority	Statement
Relationships	Developing a comfortable, friendly relationship with the customer
	Building a personal connection with the customer
	Being friendly, warm, and personable
	Showing that you care about the customer as a person, not just as a customer
	Showing the customer that you empathize with his/her needs and concerns
Sincerity	Showing that you're sincere
	Showing that you're genuinely looking out for the customer's best interest
	Showing that you truly care about the customer's problems
Dependability	Showing that you and your product/service are a dependable choice
	Showing that you'll be available to provide support after the sale
	Showing that you're thorough and careful
Quality	Explaining the quality of your product/service
	Showing that you can back up your claims with evidence
	Making sure customers get all of the information they need to make an informed decision
Competency	Demonstrating your expertise on the product/service you're selling
	Showing the customer that you're an expert in your field
	Showing customers that you can get things done without wasting a lot of their time
	Backing up claims with specific information
Results	Showing customers how you can get them immediate, practical results
	Showing customers that you can have an impact on their success
	Getting the customer to see the benefits of your product/service

Figure 6.6 MDS Map for Salespeople
Note: Stress = .08733; RSQ = .94534; *N* = 1,800.

Validation of the Sales Priorities

The validation sample for the *Sales* priority scales included 3,487 participants. The characteristics of this sample are included in Table B.5. The internal reliabilities of the *Sales* priority scales were calculated; the median alpha was .74 and the values ranged from .68 to .86 (see Table 6.7).

Multidimensional scaling analysis suggests that the priorities are arranged in a way that is expected by the model. It is important to note that the original MDS rotation is arbitrary and the axes are meaningless. In Figure 6.7, the data are circularly represented and the order of the data is as expected by the model: Action, Enthusiasm, Relationships, Sincerity, Dependability, Quality, Competency, and Results. The distances from the ordered data points are roughly equal. Additionally, the stress value of .01217 and the RSQ value of .99853 suggest that the two-dimensional model fits the validation sample very well. Lower stress values approaching zero are preferred while RSQ values closer to one are considered ideal.

Table 6.7 Internal Reliability of the Sales Priority Scales

Priority	Alpha
Action	.79
Enthusiasm	.86
Relationships	.68
Sincerity	.81
Dependability	.70
Quality	.76
Competency	.72
Results	.71

N = 3,487

Figure 6.7 MDS Map of the Sales Priorities
Note: Stress = .01217; RSQ = .99853; *N* = 3,487.

Everything DiSC Management

The management model in the *Everything DiSC® Management Profile*, shown in Figure 6.8, helps managers understand how they approach their work. The eight words around the map indicate the top priorities of managers with different DiSC styles. For example, the priorities assigned to managers with the S style are Support, Reliability, and Collaboration. The development of this model was based on empirical data gathered from both managers and employees.

Development of the Management Priorities

First, participants with management experience ($N = 427$; see Table B.5 for demographics) were presented with a series of statements describing management tasks and asked the importance of each when working as a manager. For instance, participants were asked to rate the importance of "setting high expectations" on a 5-point scale, ranging from "Not Important" (1) to "Crucially Important" (5). Statements were grouped into eight categories that represent the eight priorities in Figure 6.8. Each category contained four to five statements. The 36 individual statements are shown in Table 6.8.

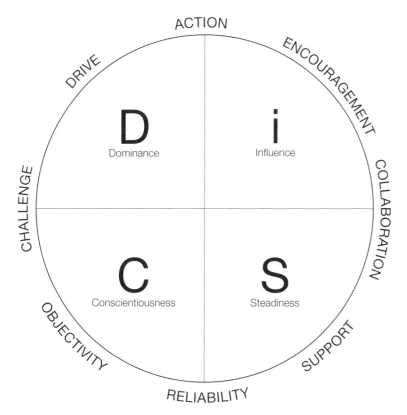

Figure 6.8 Everything DiSC Management Model

Table 6.8 Statements Used to Measure the Management Priorities from the Manager's Perspective

Priority	Statement
Action	Maintaining forward momentum on your team
	Creating goals for the team that are inspiring
	Getting new projects moving quickly
	Encouraging the team to maintain an energetic pace
	Encouraging people to take risks
Encouragement	Celebrating group victories
	Praising people for good work
	Letting people know that you're optimistic about their progress
	Creating enthusiasm in the team
Collaboration	Building a sense of collaboration
	Encouraging teamwork
	Providing feedback in a way that's warm and understanding
	Making sure that everyone's getting along
Support	Letting people know that you are there to help them out whenever they need it
	Checking in with people to make sure they are doing okay
	Taking time to listen to people's concerns and fears
	Letting people know that you're patient with their mistakes
Reliability	Creating a stable work environment
	Being consistent in your management
	Checking to make sure people have the resources they need
	Giving people time to adjust to changes
	Providing people with clear guidelines for doing their work

Priority	Statement
Objectivity	Maintaining objectivity in your management decisions
	Ensuring that decisions are based on logical analysis
	Emphasizing the need for quality work
	Making accuracy a top priority
	Separating out emotions from facts when making decisions
Challenge	Challenging ideas that don't make sense to you
	Questioning employee's actions when they don't seem logical to you
	Letting people know when they aren't performing up to your standards
	Questioning procedures or practices that aren't efficient
	Providing people with new challenges
Drive	Constantly pushing yourself and others toward results
	Creating a sense of urgency in the team
	Getting results that are practical and concrete
	Setting high expectations

Table 6.8 continued.

After participants rated each statement, the average response for statements within a priority category was calculated. Consequently, all participants had a category score for all eight priorities. The category scores were analyzed using MDS. The results of the analysis are presented in Figure 6.9. Categories that are closer together share more in common, and categories that are further apart are more dissimilar.

As expected, the eight priorities form a circular shape, with the priorities arranged as predicted by the management model. That is, the sequence around the circle proceeds as follows: Action, Encouragement, Collaboration, Support, Reliability, Objectivity, Challenge, and Drive. Although the eight scales do not form a perfectly equidistant circle (as predicted by the model), this theoretical ideal is nearly impossible to obtain with actual data.

To capture management priorities from the perspective of employees, a second study was performed. In this study, 699 participants (see Table B.5 for demographics) were asked to think of their previous experiences reporting to a manager. They were then presented with a series of management tasks and asked to rate how important each was for a manager to perform. For instance, participants rated how important "taking time to listen to my concerns and fears" was on a 5-point scale ranging from "Not Important" (1) to "Crucially Important" (5).

Figure 6.9 MDS Map for Managers
Note: Stress = .05577; RSQ = .97257; *N* = 427.

Again, statements were grouped into eight categories that represent the eight priorities in Figure 6.8. Each category contained three to five statements. As described in the previous study, statement ratings within a priority category were averaged to arrive at a category score. The individual statements used in this study are shown in Table 6.9.

The priority category scores were analyzed using MDS. The results of this analysis are shown in Figure 6.10.

As with the manager data, the priority categories are arranged in a circle. Further, the categories are plotted in the expected order: Action, Encouragement, Collaboration, Support, Reliability, Objectivity, Challenge, and Drive. The categories are not spaced in a perfectly even manner, but, again, this standard is almost impossible to meet with real data.

Validation of the Management Priorities

The validation sample for the *Management* priority scales included 10,237 participants (see Table B.6 for the characteristics of this sample). The internal reliabilities of the *Management* priority scales were calculated. The median alpha was .77 and the values ranged from .65 to .83, as shown in Table 6.10.

Multidimensional scaling analysis was conducted and the results suggested that the priorities are arranged in a manner that is expected by the model. It is important to note that the original MDS rotation is arbitrary and the axes are meaningless. As shown in

Table 6.9 Statements Used to Measure the Management Priorities from an Employee's Perspective

Priority	Statement
Drive	Setting high expectations
	Creating a sense of urgency in the team
	Getting quick results
	Constantly pushing himself/herself and others toward results
Action	Maintaining forward momentum on our team
	Creating goals for the team that are inspiring
	Encouraging the team to maintain an energetic pace
	Encouraging me to take risks
Encouragement	Celebrating group victories
	Letting me know that he/she is optimistic about my progress
	Creating enthusiasm in the team
Collaboration	Providing feedback in a way that's warm and understanding
	Building a sense of collaboration
	Encouraging teamwork
	Making sure that everyone's getting along
Support	Letting me know that he/she is there to help me out whenever I need it
	Checking in with me to make sure I'm doing okay
	Taking time to listen to my concerns and fears
	Letting me know that he/she is patient with my mistakes
Reliability	Creating a stable work environment
	Being consistent in his/her management
	Checking to make sure I have the resources I need
	Giving me time to adjust to changes
	Providing me with clear guidelines for doing my work

(continued)

Priority	Statement
Objectivity	Emphasizing the need for quality work
	Ensuring that decisions are based on logical analysis
	Maintaining objectivity in his/her management decisions
	Making accuracy a top priority
	Separating out emotions from facts when making decisions
Challenge	Challenging ideas that don't make sense to him/her
	Questioning employee's actions when they don't seem logical
	Questioning procedures or practices that aren't efficient
	Providing me with new challenges

Table 6.9 continued.

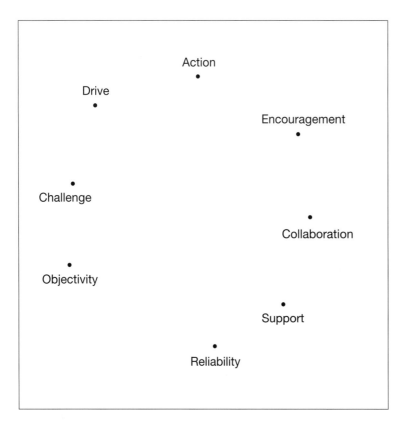

Figure 6.10 MDS Map for Employees
Note: Stress = .04956; RSQ = .97730; *N* = 699.

Table 6.10 Internal Reliability of the Management Priority Scales

Priority	Alpha
Drive	.83
Action	.77
Encouragement	.83
Collaboration	.65
Support	.77
Reliability	.77
Objectivity	.76
Challenge	.75
$N = 10,237$	

Figure 6.11, the scales were circularly represented and the order of the data was as expected by the model: Action, Encouragement, Collaboration, Support, Reliability, Objectivity, Challenge, and Drive. The stress value of .01112 and the RSQ value of .99890 suggest that a two-dimensional model fits the validation sample very well. Lower stress values approaching zero are preferred while RSQ values closer to one are considered ideal.

The distances between the *Management* priority scales were roughly similar, although not perfectly equidistant. Most notably, the Collaboration and Encouragement scales were much closer than other adjacent scales. The correlation between these two scales was .78, compared to a median of .46 for all adjacent scales.

Figure 6.11 MDS Map of the Management Priorities
Note: Stress = .01112; RSQ = .99890; *N* = 10,237.

Everything DiSC Productive Conflict

The application-specific model used in the *Everything DiSC® Productive Conflict Profile*, shown in Figure 6.12, helps learners understand how they approach conflict situations. The eight words around the map indicate the top priorities of learners with different DiSC styles. For example, the priorities of "S" individuals are Harmony, Stability, and Reassurance. The development of this model was based on empirical data.

Development of the Productive Conflict Priorities

Twenty-five new items were created to supplement the measurement of the eight *Productive Conflict* priorities. These items were intended to be combined with specific Everything DiSC base items in order to measure the eight priorities. Responses were collected from a total of 3,509 participants in preparation for an upcoming classroom training session. These data were analyzed using multidimensional scaling, intercorrelation matrixes, and internal reliability analyses. As a result, a total of six items were eliminated and replacement items were written for the final version of the priorities assessment.

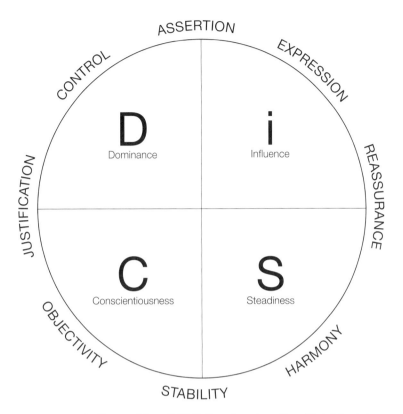

Figure 6.12 Everything DiSC Productive Conflict Model

Validation of the Productive Conflict Priorities

A total of 8,332 participants were asked to take the *Everything DiSC Productive Conflict* assessment in preparation for an upcoming classroom training session. The demographics for this sample are shown in Table B.6. This assessment measured the eight DiSC scales as well as eight *Productive Conflict* priority scales. These scales are shown in Table 6.11, along with sample items included within each scale. Items were rated on a five-point Likert scale ranging from Strongly Disagree to Strongly Agree. The *Productive Conflict* priority scales are standardized to have a mean of zero and standard deviation of one.

The priority scales were first submitted to a multidimensional scaling analysis, which allows researchers to look at the relationship among the eight scales and compare this against the expected relationships, as predicted by the model. The results of this analysis are presented in Figure 6.13. Scales that are closer together share more in common and scales that are farther apart are more dissimilar.

Table 6.11 Sample Items for the Productive Conflict Priority Scales

Priority	Sample Items
Assertion	When I'm in a conflict, I confront the topic without waiting
	When I'm in a conflict, I tackle the issue head on
Expression	When I'm in a conflict, I tend to verbalize my emotions
	When I'm in a conflict, I have a strong need to express my feelings
Reassurance	When I'm in a conflict, I'm still very empathetic with the other person
	When I'm in a conflict, I'm eager to forgive the other person (even if I probably shouldn't)
Harmony	When I'm in a conflict, the lack of harmony in the relationship really bothers me
	When I'm in a conflict, I do whatever it takes to calm the situation down
Stability	When I'm in a conflict, the lack of stability in my world is very unnerving for me
	When I'm in a conflict, I sometimes cave in just to make things stable again
Objectivity	When I'm in a conflict, I'm very disciplined at stepping outside myself and analyzing the situation objectively
	When I'm in a conflict, I prefer that we leave emotion out of the discussion
Justification	When I'm in a conflict, I'm great at quickly coming up with an airtight justification for my position
	When I'm in a conflict, I'm very good at logically dissecting and dismantling the other person's argument
Control	When I'm in a conflict, I make sure I'm in control
	When I'm in a conflict, I often take charge of the conversation

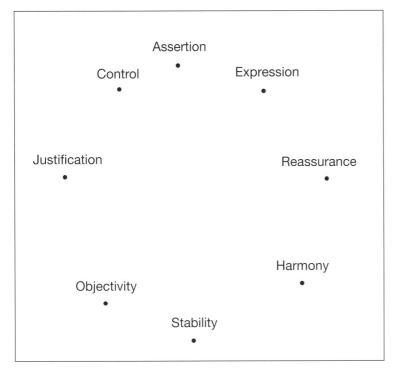

Figure 6.13 MDS Map of the Productive Conflict Priorities
Note: Stress = .0130; RSQ = .9980.

The results suggest that the scales are related in a manner consistent with the conceptual model. That is, the priority scales are arranged in a roughly equally spaced circle in the predicted order. For instance, Harmony is equally distant from both Reassurance and Stability, and is between the two of them. Table 6.12 shows the intercorrelations among the priority scales.

The intercorrelation matrix further suggests that the relationships among the priority scales are as predicted by the theoretical model. That is, each scale has its strongest positive correlation with the two scales adjacent to it. The degree of correlation among adjacent scales, however, does vary more than expected. As well, all scales demonstrate their strongest negative correlation with scales that are theoretically opposite, as shown in the grey shaded boxes.

Figure 6.14 shows the relationship among the priority scales (plotted as unfilled circles) and the DiSC scales (plotted as filled circles). The results suggest that each priority scale tends to be most strongly correlated with the DiSC scale specified in the theoretical model. For instance, the Control scale is most strongly correlated with the D scale.

Finally, Table 6.13 shows the internal reliability (i.e., Cronbach's Alpha) coefficients for the eight priority scales. The median alpha was .76 and the values ranged from .60 to .79.

Table 6.12 Intercorrelations Among Productive Conflict Priority Scales

	Control	Assertion	Expression	Reassurance	Harmony	Stability	Objectivity	Justification
Control		.67	.23	-.34	-.72	-.59	-.19	.47
Assertion	.67		.55	.02	-.50	-.81	-.43	.10
Expression	.23	.55		.49	-.07	-.528	-.70	-.23
Reassurance	-.34	.02	.49		.53	-.13	-.50	-.63
Harmony	-.72	-.50	-.07	.53		.38	-.06	-.58
Stability	-.59	-.81	-.58	-.13	.38		.42	-.11
Objectivity	-.19	-.43	-.70	-.50	-.06	.42		22
Justification	.47	.10	-.23	-.63	-.58	-.11	22	

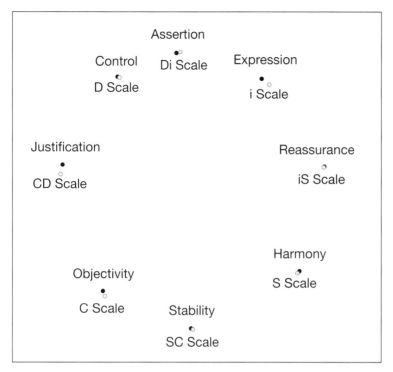

Figure 6.14 MDS Map for Productive Conflict Priority
Scales and DiSC Scales
Note: Stress = .0200; RSQ = .9970.

Table 6.13 Internal Reliability of the Productive Conflict
Priority Scales

Priority	Alpha
Control	.79
Assertion	.77
Expression	.76
Reassurance	.76
Harmony	.79
Stability	.75
Objectivity	.60
Justification	.71

In summary, these results provide support for the *Everything DiSC Productive Conflict* model and the measurement of that model. The priority scales are correlated in a manner predicted under the theoretical model and the priority scales are correlated with the DiSC scales as expected. Finally, the scales demonstrate an acceptable level of internal reliability. This type of empirical support should give managers confidence that the *Productive Conflict* model accurately reflects real-life conflict approaches and is useful for understanding various approaches to conflict.

Everything DiSC Work of Leaders

In addition to the DiSC model, the *Everything DiSC Work of Leaders® Profile* includes a second model: the *Work of Leaders* model. Consequently, this section will explain the development of this additional model.

The *Everything DiSC Work of Leaders* assessment includes the eight DiSC scales and the eight priority scales, but also includes 18 additional bipolar scales that address important leadership dispositions. The 18 *Work of Leaders* scales are listed in Table 6.14. Note that these scales are arranged by drivers, which is an organizing principle used in the *Work of Leaders* model. The "Right Label" and "Left Label" columns indicate the labels on either end of a given driver continuum.

To measure these 18 scales, the *Everything DiSC Work of Leaders* assessment includes 75 items in addition to the basic *Everything DiSC* assessment. Each of these items is composed of two statements placed at opposite ends of a 4-point continuum. The respondent is asked to choose the point on the continuum that best describes him or her. For instance, one continuum has the statement "I am an optimist" on one end and the statement "I am a realist" on the other. Some items are reverse scored. Items are standardized to have a mean of zero and a standard deviation of one. Each scale is calculated by averaging its assigned items. The criteria for selecting the scale items closely mirrors the selection criteria outlined in Chapter 2.

Validation of the Work of Leaders Scales

The analyses presented below are based on a sample of 349 participants. The sample is 52% female and 48% male. Within the sample, 90% of participants were between the ages of 25 and 60. The majority of participants (52%) have at least some college. Ethnic backgrounds are as follows: African-American (6%), Asian (5%), Caucasian (79%), Hispanic (6%), Native American (1%), and other (3%).

Internal Reliability
The median internal reliability alpha coefficient for the eighteen scales was .81, as shown in Table 6.15. The alphas range from .69 to .89. These findings suggest that each of the scales measures a unified construct.

Table 6.14 The Work of Leaders Scales

Driver	Left Label	Right Label	Measures a tendency to . . .
Exploration	Seeking closure	Remaining open	seek new information and explore new options rather than make conclusive decisions
	Prioritizing details	Prioritizing the big picture	focus on broad, abstract relationships and structures rather than on concrete details
Boldness	Being cautious	Being adventurous	take chances in the face of uncertain circumstances rather than choose predict-able options
	Holding back	Speaking out	vocalize bold or uncon-ventional ideas rather than keep them to oneself
Testing Assumptions	Deciding independently	Seeking counsel	ask others for input about one's options rather than make decisions without assistance
	Pushing forward	Exploring implications	investigate the conse-quences of a proposal rather than take immediate action
Clarity	Offering intuition	Explaining rationale	explain proposals in logical, objective terms rather than in subjective, idiosyncratic terms
	Impromptu messaging	Structured messages	take time organizing the presentation of a mes-sage rather than speaking spontaneously
Dialogue	Presenting information	Exchanging perspectives	give information in the con-text of a two-way dialogue rather than in a top-down, authoritative manner
	Being challenging	Being receptive	assume an accepting posture when listening to others' opinions rather than a skeptical posture

(continued)

Table 6.14 continued.

Driver	Left Label	Right Label	Measures a tendency to . . .
Inspiration	Being reserved	Being expressive	articulate feelings or ideas rather than inhibit expression
	Being matter-of-fact	Being encouraging	communicate empathetic or reassuring sentiments rather than simply sticking with facts
Momentum	Being low-key	Being driven	pressure others to push themselves and try harder rather than remaining laissez-faire
	Being reactive	Initiating action	originate new projects and enterprises rather than accepting the current state of affairs
Structure	Improvising	Providing a plan	create structured, detailed plans before starting projects rather than making it up along the way
	Following first impressions	Analyzing in-depth	spend time thinking deeply about complex issues rather than accepting a situation at face value
Feedback	Maintaining harmony	Addressing problems	speak up about problems or unhealthy behavior rather than avoiding interpersonally difficult issues
	Offering less praise	Offering more praise	praise or recognize people for good work rather than remaining silent on such topics

Table 6.15 Internal Reliability Coefficients for Work of Leaders Scales

Work of Leaders Scale	Alpha	Number of Items
Remaining Open	.71	8
Prioritizing the Big Picture	.69	8
Being Adventurous	.75	7
Speaking Out	.85	13
Seeking Counsel	.74	4
Exploring Implications	.86	9
Explaining Rationale	.72	5
Structuring Messages	.80	5
Exchanging Perspectives	.72	14
Being Receptive	.89	30
Being Expressive	.88	14
Being Encouraging	.86	12
Being Driven	.86	19
Initiating Action	.87	13
Providing a Plan	.74	9
Analyzing In-depth	.75	9
Addressing Problems	.85	22
Offering Praise	.82	11
Median	**.81**	**10**

Intercorrelations Among the Work of Leaders Scales

The analyses presented below are based on a sample of 777 participants in leadership classroom training sessions. The sample was 54% female and 46% male. Within the sample, 77% of participants were between the ages of 26 and 55, and 21% were 56 or older. Most participants (79%) had at least a college degree. Ethnic backgrounds were as follows: African-American (5%), Asian (3%), Caucasian (85%), Hispanic (2%), Native American (1%), and other (3%).

Intercorrelations among the 18 *Work of Leaders* scales are shown in Table 6.16. Coefficients ranged from −.94 to .77, with a median of −.01. Many of the stronger correlations are the result of overlapping items among the scales. For instance, the Praise scale, which measures a tendency to give praise to others at work, has many items in common with the Receptive scale, which measures a tendency to come across as warm and welcoming.

Overall, correlations were as expected. For instance, we would expect a high positive correlation between the Adventurous scale and the Speaking Out scale, whereas we would expect a high negative correlation between the Adventurous scale and the Planning scale. Further, scales that are conceptually independent generally showed small correlations, such as the Being Adventurous scale and the Offering Praise scale.

Correlations Among Work of Leaders Scales and DiSC Scales

Correlations among the *Work of Leaders* scales and the DiSC scales are shown in Table 6.17. These correlations are largely as expected. The largest positive correlation for each of the DiSC scales is as follows: Di-Adventurous, i-Expressive, iS-Encouraging, S-Receptive, SC-Exchanging Perspectives, C-Providing a Plan, CD-Addressing Problems, D-Addressing Problems. Most *Work of Leaders* scales show a significant correlation with several of the DiSC scales. Further, the pattern of these correlations is consistent with the DiSC circumplex model. That is, if a given *Work of Leaders* scale has a high positive correlation with a particular DiSC scale, then the *Work of Leaders* scale has a high negative correlation with the DiSC scale on the opposite side of the DiSC circumplex. The correlations range from −.85 to .87, with a median of .81.

Correlations Among the Work of Leaders Scales and the NEO-PI-3 and the 16PF Scales

Correlation coefficients were calculated among the 18 *Work of Leaders* scales and 35 scales on the NEO™-PI-3 inventory (McCrae & Costa, 2010), as shown in Tables G.1 through G.5. Correlations were also calculated among the *Work of Leaders* scales and 43 scales on the 16PF® (IPAT, 2009), as shown in Table G.6.

The strongest correlations among the *Work of Leaders* scales and the scales of these instruments are summarized below. Note that the *Work of Leaders* scales are paired according to the driver under which they are assigned in the *Work of Leaders* model. For instance, Exchanging Perspectives and Being Receptive are both included under the Dialogue driver. In this case, both of these scales measure behaviors that facilitate having an open, two-way conversation with the people a leader leads.

The Exploration Scales. The Exploration driver includes the Prioritizing the Big Picture and Remaining Open scales. Table 6.18 shows the six strongest correlations between these two scales and the combined 78 scales of the NEO-PI-3 and the 16PF.

As reported in Table 6.16, these two scales have a correlation of .73, which reflects the sizable conceptual overlap between them. As can be seen in Table 6.18, they both show a similar pattern of correlations with specific scales on the 16PF. The 16PF correlations suggest that the Exploration scales measure open-mindedness, comfort with ambiguity, and a freedom from conventional thought. The Tough-mindedness scale of the 16PF shows strong negative correlations with both of the Exploration scales, which is not surprising given that this scale is a negatively weighted composite of the Warmth, Sensitivity, Abstractedness, and Openness to Change scales of the 16PF. People scoring high in the Tough-mindedness scale are regarded as highly pragmatic but low in flexibility.

Compared to the Big Picture scale, the Remaining Open scale showed stronger positive correlations with Creative Potential (16PF) and Openness to Actions (NEO-PI-3). It showed stronger negative correlations with Conscientiousness (NEO-PI-3), Order (NEO-PI-3), Self-discipline (NEO-PI-3), Rule-consciousness (16PF), and Perfectionism (16PF). In this regard, the Remaining Open scale is more a measure of a low need for structure or order (i.e., closure) and a desire to keep oneself open to new options.

Compared to the Remaining Open scale, the Big Picture scale had stronger positive correlations with the Openness to Fantasy (NEO-PI-3), Openness to Ideas (NEO-PI-3), and Abstractedness (16PF) scales. In this regard, the Big Picture scale is more a measure of tendencies toward abstract or conceptual thinking.

The Boldness Scales. The Boldness driver includes the Adventurousness and Speaking Out scales. Table 6.19 shows the six strongest correlations between these two scales and the combined 78 scales of the NEO-PI-3 and the 16PF.

As expected, both of the Boldness scales show a strong correlation with Independence and Assertiveness. Although the high correlations with the Creative Potential scale of the 16PF were not expected, they were understandable given that this scale (Creative Potential) also correlates highly with the Social Boldness, Dominance, and Openness to Change scales of the 16PF. These results suggest that the Boldness scales both measure a daring, assertive, self-reliant disposition.

Compared to the Speaking Out scale, the Adventurousness scale demonstrated stronger positive correlations with Excitement Seeking (NEO-PI-3) and Openness to Actions (NEO-PI-3) and stronger negative correlations with Anxiety (NEO-PI-3), Rule-consciousness (16PF), and Self-control (16PF). In this regard, the Adventurousness scale is more a measure of risk-taking and freedom from fear.

Compared to the Adventurousness scale, the Speaking Out scale demonstrated stronger positive correlations with Emotional Expressivity (16PF), Social Expressivity (16PF), Dominance (16PF), Social Boldness (16PF), Independence (16PF), Assertiveness (NEO-PI-3), Enterprising (16PF), Social Control (16PF), and Leadership Potential (16PF).

Table 6.16 Intercorrelations Among Work of Leaders Scales

	Remaining Open	Prioritizing the Big Picture	Being Adventurous	Speaking Out	Seeking Counsel	Exploring Implications	Explaining Rationale	Structuring Messages	Exchanging Perspectives
Remaining Open		.77	.51	.53	.00	−.63	−.46	−.49	−.04
Prioritizing the Big Picture	.77		.48	.53	.06	−.54	−.38	−.36	−.04
Being Adventurous	.51	.48		.75	−.03	−.44	−.32	−.33	−.27
Speaking Out	.53	.53	.75		.01	−.46	−.32	−.39	−.29
Seeking Counsel	.00	.06	−.03	.01		.03	−.06	.04	.71
Exploring Implications	−.63	−.54	−.44	−.46	.03		.60	.55	.12
Explaining Rationale	−.46	−.38	−.32	−.32	−.06	.60		.43	−.08
Structuring Messages	−.49	−.36	−.33	−.39	.04	.55	.43		.14

Exchanging Perspectives	−.04	−.04	−.27	−.29	.71	.12	−.08	.14	
Being Receptive	.02	.01	−.23	−.26	.33	.04	−.17	.11	.72
Being Expressive	.29	.28	.45	.67	.23	−.34	−.39	−.35	−.03
Being Encouraging	.27	.28	.23	.21	.31	−.20	−.35	−.10	.42
Being Driven	.13	.15	.46	.57	−.12	−.25	−.05	−.22	−.59
Initiating Action	.55	.52	.52	.60	−.01	−.43	−.23	−.30	−.20
Providing a Plan	−.94	−.77	−.49	−.51	.00	.76	.52	.53	.04
Analyzing In-depth	−.30	−.11	−.18	−.16	−.04	.63	.70	.38	−.07
Addressing Problems	.09	.11	.42	.50	−.18	−.14	.06	−.18	−.61
Offering Praise	.17	.16	.07	.11	.34	−.12	−.34	−.03	.53

(continued)

Table 6.16 continued.

	Being Receptive	Being Expressive	Being Encouraging	Being Driven	Initiating Action	Providing a Plan	Analyzing In-depth	Addressing Problems	Offering Praise
Remaining Open	.02	.29	.27	.13	.55	-.94	-.30	.09	.17
Prioritizing Big Picture	.01	.28	.28	.15	.52	-.77	-.11	.11	.16
Being Adventurous	-.23	.45	.23	.46	.52	-.49	-.18	.42	.07
Speaking Out	-.26	.67	.21	.57	.60	-.51	-.16	.50	.11
Seeking Counsel	.33	.23	.31	-.12	-.01	.00	-.04	-.18	.34
Exploring Implications	.04	-.34	-.20	-.25	-.43	.76	.63	-.14	-.12
Explaining Rationale	-.17	-.39	-.35	-.05	-.23	.52	.70	.06	-.34
Structuring Messages	.11	-.35	-.10	-.22	-.30	.53	.38	-.18	-.03

	1	2	3	4	5	6	7	8	9	10
Exchanging Perspectives		.72	−.03	.42	−.59	−.20	.04	−.07	−.61	.53
Being Receptive	.72		−.05	.57	−.68	−.14	−.02	−.14	−.79	.69
Being Expressive	−.03	−.05		.40	.46	.37	−.29	−.28	.34	.35
Being Encouraging	.42	.57	.40		−.19	.23	−.24	−.21	−.24	.71
Being Driven	−.59	−.68	.46	−.19		.36	−.14	−.04	.77	−.30
Initiating Action	−.20	−.14	.37	.23	.36		−.52	−.09	.29	.10
Providing a Plan	.04	−.02	−.29	−.24	−.14	−.52		.41	−.08	−.16
Analyzing In-depth	−.07	−.14	−.28	−.21	−.04	−.09	.41		.07	−.21
Addressing Problems	−.61	−.79	.34	−.24	.77	.29	−.08	.07		−.40
Offering Praise	.53	.69	.35	.71	−.30	.10	−.16	−.21	−.40	

Table 6.17 Correlations Among Work of Leaders Scales and DiSC Scales

Work of Leaders Scales	DiSC Scales							
	Di	i	iS	S	SC	C	CD	D
Remaining Open	.22	.11	.02	−.14	−.16	−.24	.08	.15
Prioritizing the Big Picture	.23	.19	.09	−.12	−.22	−.34	.08	.17
Being Adventurous	.83	.44	.04	−.27	−.73	−.44	−.03	.46
Speaking Out	.71	.51	.05	−.46	−.85	−.44	.16	.70
Seeking Counsel	.09	.38	.43	.22	−.10	−.46	−.32	−.12
Exploring Implications	−.13	−.14	−.07	.12	.14	.24	−.10	−.15
Explaining Rationale	.05	−.17	−.28	−.11	−.02	.26	.09	.08
Structuring Messages	−.11	−.17	−.05	.13	.16	.23	−.10	−.17
Exchanging Perspectives	−.26	.18	.57	.67	.31	−.28	−.54	−.65
Being Receptive	−.21	.25	.75	.78	.23	−.27	−.74	−.65
Being Expressive	.61	.74	.28	−.29	−.79	−.59	−.02	.52
Being Encouraging	.14	.53	.87	.39	−.25	−.52	−.60	−.23
Being Driven	.64	.27	−.29	−.72	−.71	−.16	.44	.74
Initiating Action	.83	.50	.09	−.29	−.75	−.44	−.04	.47
Providing a Plan	−.20	−.18	−.07	.14	.17	.34	−.10	−.16
Analyzing In-depth	.13	−.14	−.23	−.17	−.12	.23	.11	.12
Addressing Problems	.36	.01	−.53	−.76	−.46	.01	.61	.75
Offering Praise	.04	.47	.79	.54	−.11	−.43	−.68	−.33

Table 6.18 Strongest Correlations Between the Exploration Scales and the NEO-PI-3 and 16PF Scales

	Scale	Instrument	r
Big Picture Scale	Self-control	16PF	−.54
	Conventional	16PF	−.52
	Artistic	16PF	.51
	Abstractedness	16PF	.48
	Tough-mindedness	16PF	−.47
	Openness to Change	16PF	.44
Remaining Open Scale	Self-control	16PF	−.59
	Artistic	16PF	.53
	Conventional	16PF	−.51
	Tough-mindedness	16PF	−.48
	Perfectionism	16PF	−.47
	Openness to Change	16PF	.46

In this regard, the Speaking Out scale is more a measure of being outspoken and socially dominant.

The Testing Assumptions Scales. The Testing Assumptions driver includes the Seeking Counsel and Exploring Implications scales. Table 6.20 shows the six strongest correlations between these two scales and the combined 78 scales of the NEO-PI-3 and the 16PF.

The Seeking Counsel scale demonstrated its strongest correlation with the Self-reliance scale of the 16PF. The intended purpose of the Seeking Counsel scale is to measure a tendency to seek input before making decisions (rather than making decisions independently), and of the 78 NEO-PI-3/16PF scales measured, Self-reliance comes the closest to measuring this construct. The Seeking Counsel scale also had strong correlations with scales that measure extraversion and interpersonal intimacy.

Conceptually, the Exploring Implications scale is designed to measure a tendency to investigate and research implications of an action before undertaking that action. As expected, the scale showed strong correlations with scales measuring a deliberate, measured approach to life. Although not shown here, the Exploring Implications scale also had significant correlations with the Order, Dutifulness, and Impulsiveness (negative) scales of the NEO-PI-3.

Table 6.19 Strongest Correlations Between the Boldness Scales and the NEO PI-3 and 16PF Scales

	Scale	Instrument	*r*
Adventurousness	Independence	16PF	.57
	Assertiveness	NEO-PI-3	.56
	Creative Potential	16PF	.56
	Emotional Expressivity	16PF	.55
	Social Expressivity	16PF	.52
	Excitement Seeking	NEO-PI-3	.51
Speaking Out	Independence	16PF	.76
	Creative Potential	16PF	.74
	Emotional Expressivity	16PF	.73
	Assertiveness	NEO	.70
	Dominance	16PF	.68
	Enterprising	16PF	.65

Table 6.20 Strongest Correlations Between the Testing Assumptions Scales and the NEO-PI-3 and 16PF Scales

	Scale	Instrument	*r*
Seeking Counsel	Self-reliance	16PF	−.65
	Gregariousness	NEO-PI-3	.55
	Extraversion	16PF	.55
	Warmth	NEO-PI-3	.46
	Warmth	16PF	.45
	Empathy	16PF	.45
Exploring Implications	Deliberation	NEO	.43
	Self-control	16PF	.42
	Perfectionism	16PF	.36
	Rule-consciousness	16PF	.33
	Conscientiousness	NEO	.31
	Conventional	16PF	.29

Work of Leaders Priorities

The validation sample for the *Work of Leaders* priority scales included 3,504 participants (see Table B.6 for the characteristics of this sample). The internal reliabilities of the leadership priority scales were calculated and are presented in Table 6.21. The median alpha was .85 and the values ranged from .80 to .89. A more in-depth discussion of these priorities is included in the *Everything DiSC 363® for Leaders* section of this chapter.

Table 6.21 Internal Reliability of the Work of Leaders Priority Scales

Priority	Alpha
Pioneering	.88
Energizing	.89
Affirming	.80
Inclusive	.82
Humble	.85
Deliberate	.85
Resolute	.84
Commanding	.87
$N = 3,504$	

Multidimensional scaling analysis showed that the priorities are arranged in a manner expected by the model. It is important to note that the original MDS rotation is arbitrary. As shown in Figure 6.15, the scales were circularly represented and the order of the scales was as predicted by the model: Pioneering, Energizing, Affirming, Inclusive, Humble, Deliberate, Resolute, and Commanding. The distances between scales was roughly, but not perfectly, equal. Additionally, the stress value of .00710 and the RSQ value of .99955 suggest that a two-dimensional model fits the validation sample very well. Lower stress values approaching zero are preferred while RSQ values closer to one are considered ideal. The median correlation between adjacent scales was .59. Among these eight correlations, the only unexpected correlation was between the Resolute scale and the Deliberate scale. At $r = .06$, this correlation was statistically significant, but was expected to be much higher.

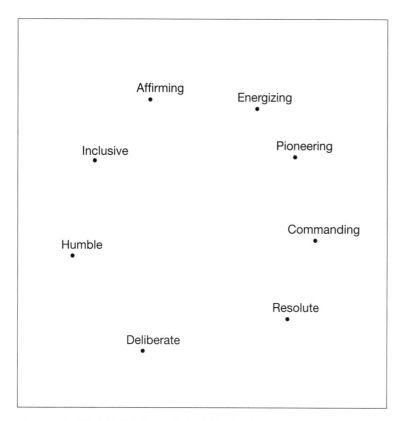

Figure 6.15 MDS Map of the Work of Leaders Priorities
Note: Stress = .00710; RSQ = .99955; *N* = 3,504.

Everything DiSC 363 for Leaders

Everything DiSC 363 for Leaders is a multi-rater assessment and profile that is designed to give participants feedback on their leadership performance. Figure 6.16 shows the *Everything DiSC 363 for Leaders* model that is the foundation for *Everything DiSC 363 for Leaders*.

The words around the circle represent eight leadership approaches, and are the same as the priorities discussed in the *Everything DiSC Work of Leaders* section of this chapter. In the theoretical model, each approach is most correlated with adjacent approaches and least correlated with opposite approaches. Three leadership practices are assigned to each approach for a total of 24 practices, and these can be seen inside the circle. Again, these practices are theoretically most correlated with practices within the same approach, and then most highly correlated with adjacent practices. Practices that sit opposite each other on the model are least correlated.

Development of the Practice Scales for 363 for Leaders

Alpha Phase. In the first development phase, a content analysis of contemporary leadership literature was conducted to identify leadership constructs that are relevant to the

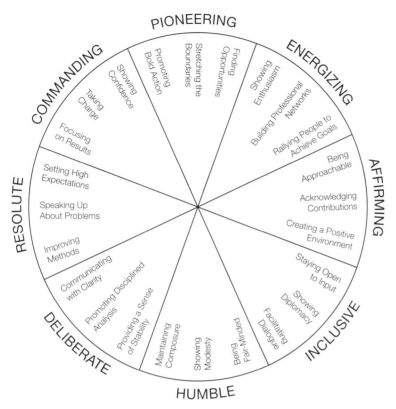

Figure 6.16 Everything DiSC 363 for Leaders Model

DiSC model. Data on these concepts were then gathered by asking participants who had just completed an online personality assessment to volunteer for research on a leadership project. Participants were asked questions about their own leadership performance, as well as the performance of leaders in their previous or current organizations. These data were used to identify and build initial approach and practice scales, as well as to understand the psychometric relationships among these leadership constructs. More than 26,000 participants were included in this stage of the research.

Beta Phase 1 (Exploratory). In the first beta phase, an initial *363 for Leaders* assessment was constructed for both leaders and raters. Leaders from a wide range of industries completed their portion of the assessment. Raters for each leader were selected by either the leader's manager or an HR professional within the organization. After these data were collected, they were analyzed. Based on this analysis, the *Everything DiSC* leadership model and scales were refined.

Beta Phase 2 (Confirmatory). In the second beta phase, the refined assessment was again completed by leaders and raters from a wide range of industries. The leader, the leader's manager, or an HR professional within the organization selected raters for each leader. Data from these participants were analyzed to evaluate the refined assessment for reliability and validity.

Validation of the 363 for Leaders Scales

The results are from a sample of 483 leaders (see Table B.6 for demographics). In all cases, leaders were rated by two or more raters, with a median of six raters per leader. The total number of raters was 3,043.

Scores were calculated by averaging the total responses for all items on each scale. Since the responses range from 1 to 7, so do the resulting scale scores. Each of the 24 practices contains three items, and each approach contains three of those 24 practices. Therefore, each approach scale contains nine items. Means and standard deviations for all scales are shown in Table 6.22.

Table 6.22 Scale Means and Standard Deviations

	Other-Rated		Self-Rated	
	Mean	*SD*	**Mean**	*SD*
Approaches				
Pioneering	5.49	.73	5.35	.94
Energizing	5.53	.80	5.65	.94
Affirming	5.79	.77	5.80	.76
Inclusive	5.72	.78	5.50	.75
Humble	5.53	.74	5.46	.77
Deliberate	5.64	.69	5.56	.82
Resolute	5.65	.64	5.72	.84
Commanding	5.83	.68	5.64	.87

Table 6.22 continued.

	Other-Rated		Self-Rated	
	Mean	*SD*	**Mean**	*SD*
Practices				
Finding Opportunities	5.56	.75	5.63	.96
Stretching the Boundaries	5.56	.76	5.17	1.26
Promoting Bold Action	5.35	.80	5.29	1.07
Showing Enthusiasm	5.62	.84	5.78	1.05
Building Professional Networks	5.59	.79	5.82	1.00
Rallying People to Achieve Goals	5.45	.86	5.57	.99
Being Approachable	6.00	.78	5.97	.84
Acknowledging Contributions	5.70	.85	5.69	.94
Creating a Positive Environment	5.66	.81	5.73	.86
Staying Open to Input	5.74	.81	5.45	1.05
Showing Diplomacy	5.83	.84	5.60	.84
Facilitating Dialogue	5.59	.77	5.46	.84
Maintaining Composure	5.63	.87	5.36	.99
Showing Modesty	5.43	.84	5.36	.99
Being Fair-minded	5.53	.75	5.67	.83
Communicating with Clarity	5.68	.75	5.38	1.02
Promoting Disciplined Analysis	5.60	.68	5.66	.93
Providing a Sense of Stability	5.64	.79	5.62	.92
Setting High Expectations	5.57	.74	5.67	.93
Speaking Up About Problems	5.78	.63	5.96	.93
Improving Methods	5.65	.76	5.66	1.05
Showing Confidence	5.93	.69	5.63	.98
Taking Charge	5.75	.77	5.56	.99
Focusing on Results	5.81	.74	5.74	.97

Internal Reliability

Cronbach's alpha is calculated separately for each of the assessment's scales. The following guidelines are frequently used to evaluate the quality of a scale's internal reliability: alpha values above .70 are generally considered acceptable and satisfactory, alpha values above .80 are usually considered quite good, and values above .90 are considered to reflect exceptional internal consistency.

The scales used in the *363 for Leaders* model demonstrate good-to-excellent internal consistency, as shown by the alpha values listed in Tables 6.23 and 6.24. For raters, all scales had an alpha well above .80. These high alpha coefficients probably also reflect, to at least some degree, a strong general factor among all of the items (e.g., overall leadership ability). For leaders, four of the 32 scale alphas fell below the preferred cutoff of .70. Given that the focus of the *363 for Leaders Profile* is on rater feedback and that these scales are reflecting self-assessment, these less-than-desirable alphas are within the tolerable range.

The median alpha on the approach scales was .95 for individual raters and .90 for leaders. The median alpha on the practice scales was .89 for individual raters and .80 for leaders. These results suggest that the rater-generated scales on the *363 for Leaders* assessment demonstrate excellent reliability. As well, the leader-generated scales demonstrate satisfactory to excellent reliability, with a few exceptions.

Table 6.23 Approach Scales Internal Reliabilities

Approaches	Alpha	
	Raters	Leaders
Pioneering	.95	.90
Energizing	.94	.91
Affirming	.96	.89
Inclusive	.96	.83
Humble	.94	.88
Deliberate	.95	.89
Resolute	.93	.90
Commanding	.94	.93

Table 6.24 Practice Scales Internal Reliabilities

Practices	Alpha	
	Raters	Leaders
Finding Opportunities	.87	.79
Stretching the Boundaries	.87	.80
Promoting Bold Action	.89	.83
Showing Enthusiasm	.89	.74
Building Professional Networks	.83	.88
Rallying People to Achieve Goals	.92	.84
Being Approachable	.89	.76
Acknowledging Contributions	.94	.69
Creating a Positive Environment	.91	.76
Staying Open to Input	.91	.83
Showing Diplomacy	.91	.59
Facilitating Dialogue	.90	.67
Maintaining Composure	.93	.86
Showing Modesty	.83	.64
Being Fair-minded	.86	.82
Communicating with Clarity	.90	.81
Promoting Disciplined Analysis	.85	.75
Providing a Sense of Stability	.90	.78
Setting High Expectations	.85	.77
Speaking Up About Problems	.84	.84
Improving Methods	.87	.82
Showing Confidence	.83	.83
Taking Charge	.91	.79
Focusing on Results	.88	.81

Inter-Rater Reliability

Inter-rater reliability evaluates the degree of agreement among raters. Interclass correlations were used to assess inter-rater reliability as described by Ebel (1951). Coefficients above .40 are considered to reflect moderate agreement. Those above .60 are considered to reflect substantial agreement. Those above .80 are considered to reflect outstanding agreement.

Raters were all direct reports of the person being rated. Reliability coefficients for the approach and practice scales can be seen in Tables 6.25 and 6.26, respectively. These coefficients suggest that the *363 for Leaders* scales have substantial to outstanding inter-rater reliability. The median reliabilities for the approach and practice scales were .78 and .76, respectively.

Table 6.25 Approach Scales Inter-Rater Reliabilities

Approaches	Alpha
Pioneering	.77
Energizing	.78
Affirming	.78
Inclusive	.76
Humble	.77
Deliberate	.79
Resolute	.81
Commanding	.76

Table 6.26 Practice Scales Inter-Rater Reliabilities

Practices	Alpha
Finding Opportunities	.76
Stretching the Boundaries	.77
Promoting Bold Action	.73
Showing Enthusiasm	.77
Building Professional Networks	.74
Rallying People to Achieve Goals	.74

Table 6.26 continued.

Practices	Alpha
Being Approachable	.81
Acknowledging Contributions	.73
Creating a Positive Environment	.75
Staying Open to Input	.75
Showing Diplomacy	.76
Facilitating Dialogue	.74
Maintaining Composure	.77
Showing Modesty	.73
Being Fair-minded	.74
Communicating with Clarity	.78
Promoting Disciplined Analysis	.77
Providing a Sense of Stability	.75
Setting High Expectations	.79
Speaking Up About Problems	.76
Improving Methods	.76
Showing Confidence	.86
Taking Charge	.79
Focusing on Results	.80

Multidimensional Scaling Analyses

The *363 for Leaders* model specifies a very specific set of relationships among its scales: it predicts that the eight approach scales and 24 practice scales will form a circumplex. That is, they will be arranged in a circular format at equal intervals. In Figures 6.17 and 6.18, scales that are plotted closer together have a stronger positive relationship. Scales that are farther apart are more dissimilar.

As can be seen in Figure 6.17, the approach scales are arranged in the order that is expected by the *363 for Leaders* model. Note that the original MDS rotation is presented, and this rotation is arbitrary. Although the eight scales do not form a perfectly equidistant circle (as predicted by the model), this theoretical ideal is nearly impossible to obtain

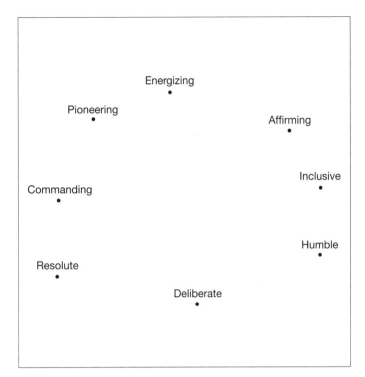

Figure 6.17 MDS Map of the Approach Scales
Note: Stress = .01302; RSQ = .99861; *N* = 483.

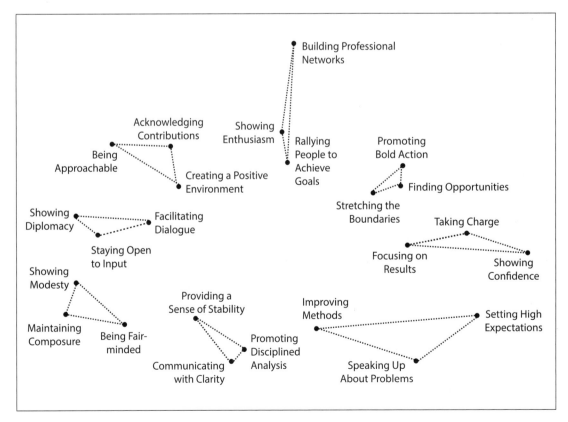

Figure 6.18 MDS Map of the Practice Scales
Note: Stress = .08097; RSQ = .96423; *N* = 483.

with actual data. The actual distance between the scales, however, is roughly equal, providing strong support for the model and its assessment.

The MDS results for the practice scales are shown in Figure 6.18. Again, the original MDS rotation is presented, and this rotation is arbitrary. Dashed lines have been added to help illustrate groups of scales that should theoretically cluster. This figure offers support for the *Everything DiSC 363 for Leaders* model in several ways. First, the scales are arranged in a circular fashion, and clusters of scales are ordered in the manner predicted by the model (although the rotation is presented in a counterclockwise fashion in this representation). Second, scales that should theoretically cluster together in the model do cluster together. For example, the practice of Taking Charge is located close to the practice of Showing Confidence, as predicted by the model. Third, clusters are spaced at roughly equal distances around the circle, although not perfectly equidistant.

Additionally, the stress values for the approach data and the practice data were .01302 and .08097, respectively. The RSQ values were .99861 and .96423, respectively. These values reflect the ability of a two-dimensional model to fit the data. Lower stress values are preferred (with a minimum of zero), whereas higher RSQ values are preferred (with a maximum of one). Stress values below .1 suggest an excellent fit of the data to a two-dimensional configuration. All of the stress and RSQ values reported here suggest that a third dimension is not needed to explain the relationship among these scales.

Intercorrelations

By examining the intercorrelations among scales, we can measure with more precision how well the data fits the *363 for Leaders* model. The model proposes that adjacent scales (e.g., Commanding and Pioneering) will have stronger positive correlations than opposite scales (e.g., Commanding and Inclusive). Further, if the data are controlled for overall leadership ability, opposite scales are expected to have negative correlations. For example, among leaders at the same skill level, leaders who are more Commanding than others are expected to be less Inclusive. To control for overall leadership ability, scale scores were ipsatized for each leader. That is, each leader's total average rating was calculated along with his or her total standard deviation across all items. The total mean was subtracted from individual item means, and then this number was divided by the total standard deviation. Ipsatized scale means were then calculated by summing ipsatized item scores for each scale. As a result, each leader's mean ipsatized scale score across all scales was zero. Ipsatized scale scores, then, represent relative strengths for the individual. Table 6.27 shows the ipsatized and non-ipsatized correlations among the approach scales. In this regard, the ipsatized means remove the variance due to a general factor (presumably overall leadership ability).

Because the *363 for Leaders* model proposes that the eight approach scales are arranged as a circumplex, an even more strict set of statistical assumptions are required of the data. The patterns of correlations for a given scale are expected to be arranged in a particular order. As seen in Table 6.28, the strongest theoretical correlation for two given

Table 6.27 Approach Scales Intercorrelations

	Pioneering	Energizing	Affirming	Inclusive	Humble	Deliberate	Resolute	Commanding
Pioneering		.85	.69	.62	.56	.65	.76	.81
Energizing	.26		.85	.74	.63	.65	.65	.70
Affirming	−.37	.34		.91	.81	.69	.52	.47
Inclusive	−.53	−.13	.56		.89	.76	.52	.40
Humble	−.57	−.52	.14	.52		.80	.55	.39
Deliberate	−.43	−.57	−.34	.01	.29		.78	.63
Resolute	.17	−.34	−.68	−.59	−.23	.26		.83
Commanding	.42	.03	−.65	−.79	−.59	−.06	.56	

Note: Ipsatized scales are shown below the diagonal and non-ipsatized scales are shown above the diagonal.

Table 6.28 Expected Scale Intercorrelations

	Pioneering	Energizing	Affirming	Inclusive	Humble	Deliberate	Resolute	Commanding
Pioneering	1							
Energizing	r_1	1						
Affirming	r_2	r_1	1					
Inclusive	r_3	r_2	r_1	1				
Humble	r_4	r_3	r_2	r_1	1			
Deliberate	r_3	r_4	r_3	r_2	r_1	1		
Resolute	r_2	r_3	r_4	r_3	r_2	r_1	1	
Commanding	r_1	r_2	r_3	r_4	r_3	r_2	r_1	1

scales is labeled r_1. The second strongest is labeled r_2, and so on. In this case, r_4 represents the correlation between two theoretically opposite scales. Consequently, r_4 should be a reasonably strong negative correlation. For each scale, we should observe the following relationship if the scales do, in fact, support a circumplex structure: $r_1 > r_2 > r_3 > r_4$.

Looking at Table 6.29, we do, in fact, observe a $r_1 > r_2 > r_3 > r_4$ pattern for each scale. In addition, we can examine the magnitude of these correlations in comparison to the theoretically expected magnitudes. The predicted magnitudes of r_1, r_2, r_3, and r_4 under a circumplex structure are listed in Table 6.29, as described by Wiggins (1995). The "actual" r_x values are the median correlations for a given r_x. Although the actual and predicted values are not exactly the same (a near impossible standard for practical purposes), the magnitude of the (ipsatized) actual and predicted correlation values is quite similar, thus providing additional support for the *363 for Leaders* model and the *363 for Leaders* assessment.

Additionally, intercorrelations for the practice scales are shown in Table 6.30 (shading indicates clusters of practices grouped under the same approach). Of the 24 practices, 21 demonstrated their highest correlation with one of the other two practices assigned to the same approach.

With both ipsatized and non-ipsatized scales, the average correlations among scales in the same approach was higher than the average correlation of individual scales with scales in adjacent approaches. As with the approach scales, we do observe a $r_1 > r_2 > r_3 > r_4$ pattern for each cluster of practice scales.

Table 6.29 Actual and Predicted Scale Relationships

r_1	>	r_2	>	r_3	>	r_4	
.84	>	.71	>	.58	>	.53	Actual (non-ipsatized average)
.40	>	−.05	>	−.50	>	−.65	Actual (ipsatized average)
.42	>	.03	>	−.36	>	−.73	Predicted

Comparing Self and Other Ratings

The correlations among the self-rated scale scores and the other-rated scale scores are shown in Table 6.31.

These correlations show greater consensus on some scales than on others. Scales that measure outwardly assertive behavior (e.g., Energizing and Commanding) demonstrate the highest correlations. Scales measuring more subtle, perhaps inward behaviors, (e.g., Humble, Deliberate) have smaller correlations.

Analyses were also performed to examine the relationship between overall leadership ability and self and other agreement. For each leader, an overall average rating was computed by averaging all scale scores. Leaders were then divided into three categories: the bottom 25%, the middle 50%, and the top 25%. Table 6.32 shows the correlations between self and other ratings for each of the approach scales by overall leadership ability.

Interestingly, those leaders who received the lowest ratings show the highest correlations between self and other ratings. Conversely, those with the highest ratings show the lowest correlations. It is possible that poorly rated leaders have more pronounced strengths and challenges and thus show more agreement (between self and other ratings) in the relative magnitude of their leadership abilities.

As shown in Table 6.33, further analyses suggest that lower-rated leaders overestimate their scores and higher-rated leaders underestimate their scores, even though higher-rated leaders still rated themselves higher (self-rating $M = 5.77$) than lower-rated leaders (self-rating $M = 5.41$). This difference of .36 in self-ratings, however, is dwarfed by the difference between these same two groups in their ratings by others (1.49). These findings suggest that leaders' self-ratings improve slightly as their ability level increases, but not nearly at the same rate as their ratings by others.

Correlations with Ratings of Leadership Effectiveness

Raters were asked to rate leaders on three global leadership effectiveness variables. The raters were asked to rate the degree to which they agreed or disagreed with each of these three statements: "[This person] is a good leader," "[This person] is respected in the organization as a good leader," and "I enjoy working with [this person]." Each leader's ratings on these questions were then correlated with his or her scores on the approach scales and are included in Table 6.34.

All of the approach scales show sizable correlations with the first two effectiveness variables (i.e., "Good Leader" and "Respected as a Good Leader") and at least moderate correlations with the third variable (i.e., "Enjoy Working With"). These findings suggest that the approaches do, in fact, have a strong relationship with perceived leadership ability. It is not surprising that some approaches, like Commanding and Resolute, are less correlated with relationship enjoyment, as these approaches are often correlated with personal attributes such as aggressiveness and stubbornness.

Table 6.30 Practice Scales Intercorrelations

Practices	Finding Opportunities	Stretching the Boundaries	Promoting Bold Action	Showing Enthusiasm	Building Professional Networks	Rallying People to Achieve Goals	Being Approachable	Acknowledging Contributions	Creating a Positive Environment	Staying Open to Input	Showing Diplomacy	Facilitating Dialogue
Finding Opportunities		.87	.85	.75	.68	.85	.56	.64	.69	.58	.51	.67
Stretching the Boundaries	.51		.86	.77	.72	.85	.57	.65	.73	.59	.54	.67
Promoting Bold Action	.50	.55		.75	.71	.83	.53	.58	.66	.54	.44	.61
Showing Enthusiasm	.07	.12	.17		.78	.90	.72	.80	.84	.67	.66	.74
Building Professional Networks	.06	.06	.16	.28		.78	.69	.75	.73	.56	.58	.62
Rallying People to Achieve Goals	.28	.31	.36	.62	.22		.70	.79	.85	.69	.67	.77
Being Approachable	−.29	−.32	−.20	.22	.28	.01		.80	.84	.79	.86	.79
Acknowledging Contributions	−.23	−.23	−.22	.33	.18	.23	.37		.89	.79	.83	.82
Creating a Positive Environment	−.28	−.21	−.19	.37	.08	.33	.43	.53		.83	.87	.87

Staying Open to Input	−.35	−.40	−.30	−.09	−.12	−.19	.36	.28	.27	.87	.92
Showing Diplomacy	−.43	−.48	−.48	−.03	−.06	−.10	.57	.45	.50	.53	.86
Facilitating Dialogue	−.25	−.32	−.27	−.03	−.12	−.05	.27	.28	.32	.68	.48
Maintaining Composure	−.24	−.32	−.33	−.32	−.23	−.36	.22	−.03	.13	.21	.14
Showing Modesty	−.34	−.38	−.38	−.30	−.16	−.34	.12	.12	.08	.43	.29
Being Fair-minded	−.39	−.43	−.47	−.40	−.34	−.48	.07	−.03	.04	.38	.30
Communicating with Clarity	−.19	−.21	−.22	−.28	−.31	−.28	−.20	−.14	−.23	.05	−.02
Promoting Disciplined Analysis	−.11	−.16	−.29	−.58	−.39	−.49	−.36	−.33	−.36	−.12	−.02
Providing a Sense of Stability	−.44	−.36	−.49	−.23	−.37	−.31	−.16	−.04	.01	.12	.06
Setting High Expectations	.19	.27	.08	−.21	−.10	−.14	−.48	−.34	−.50	−.54	−.46
Speaking Up About Problems	.09	.17	.14	−.38	−.16	−.43	−.45	−.50	−.60	−.56	−.36
Improving Methods	.04	.02	−.07	−.25	−.43	−.29	−.35	−.30	−.33	−.27	−.21
Showing Confidence	.26	.38	.37	−.05	.06	−.06	−.41	−.46	−.53	−.70	−.52
Taking Charge	.18	.30	.33	.02	.04	.06	−.42	−.41	−.40	−.65	−.50
Focusing on Results	.30	.28	.18	.05	−.09	.14	−.44	−.37	−.41	−.56	−.45

(continued)

Table 6.30 continued.

Practices	Maintaining Composure	Showing Modesty	Being Fair-minded	Communicating with Clarity	Promoting Disciplined Analysis	Providing a Sense of Stability	Setting High Expectations	Speaking Up About Problems	Improving Methods	Showing Confidence	Taking Charge	Focusing on Results
Finding Opportunities	.48	.46	.55	.58	.61	.59	.65	.71	.68	.62	.70	.79
Stretching the Boundaries	.48	.51	.58	.60	.64	.64	.67	.75	.70	.65	.74	.80
Promoting Bold Action	.42	.41	.48	.53	.51	.52	.55	.70	.61	.65	.74	.72
Showing Enthusiasm	.50	.55	.59	.57	.50	.66	.48	.55	.61	.49	.62	.69
Building Professional Networks	.45	.51	.50	.51	.50	.54	.52	.50	.55	.52	.62	.65
Rallying People to Achieve Goals	.53	.57	.62	.61	.59	.68	.57	.60	.64	.53	.67	.77
Being Approachable	.68	.65	.72	.52	.49	.62	.23	.42	.49	.21	.34	.45
Acknowledging Contributions	.60	.68	.71	.58	.56	.68	.38	.49	.55	.27	.42	.53
Creating a Positive Environment	.72	.72	.79	.65	.64	.76	.39	.52	.63	.32	.49	.60

Staying Open to Input	.69	.77	.84	.64	.63	.73	.30	.49	.58	.22	.35	.48
Showing Diplomacy	.78	.78	.82	.63	.61	.72	.24	.38	.53	.11	.28	.43
Facilitating Dialogue	.70	.76	.83	.69	.69	.76	.37	.55	.63	.29	.44	.56
Maintaining Composure		.65	.78	.56	.59	.66	.24	.39	.53	.14	.28	.40
Showing Modesty	.29		.75	.64	.66	.72	.28	.48	.58	.13	.31	.43
Being Fair-minded	.42	.35		.68	.76	.82	.40	.57	.67	.27	.42	.55
Communicating with Clarity	.04	.13	.11		.81	.82	.49	.68	.72	.44	.54	.59
Promoting Disciplined Analysis	.09	.21	.32	.40		.81	.58	.77	.76	.48	.58	.65
Providing a Sense of Stability	.13	.25	.34	.41	.30		.53	.65	.78	.41	.54	.66
Setting High Expectations	−.26	−.20	−.16	−.03	.22	−.04		.77	.60	.66	.67	.79
Speaking Up About Problems	−.28	−.20	−.08	.10	.42	−.03	.47		.81	.79	.79	.78
Improving Methods	−.06	.03	.08	.20	.29	.28	.20	.48		.54	.66	.72
Showing Confidence	−.38	−.44	−.34	−.03	.09	−.19	.47	.58	.13		.81	.70
Taking Charge	−.42	−.38	−.35	−.06	.04	−.12	.36	.49	.20	.67		.80
Focusing on Results	−.36	−.35	−.29	−.07	.02	−.04	.53	.29	.24	.43	.51	

Note: Ipsatized scales are shown below the diagonal and non-ipsatized scales are shown above the diagonal.

Table 6.31 Correlation Between Self and Other Ratings

	Self-Other Correlations
Approach Scales	
Pioneering	.36
Energizing	.50
Affirming	.41
Inclusive	.30
Humble	.16
Deliberate	.26
Resolute	.34
Commanding	.46
Practice Scales	
Finding Opportunities	.31
Stretching the Boundaries	.21
Promoting Bold Action	.40
Showing Enthusiasm	.48
Building Professional Networks	.46
Rallying People to Achieve Goals	.41
Being Approachable	.35
Acknowledging Contributions	.35
Creating a Positive Environment	.35
Staying Open to Input	.25
Showing Diplomacy	.27
Facilitating Dialogue	.19
Maintaining Composure	.20
Showing Modesty	.11
Being Fair-minded	.16
Communicating with Clarity	.21

Table 6.31 continued.	
	Self-Other Correlations
Promoting Disciplined Analysis	.22
Providing a Sense of Stability	.26
Setting High Expectations	.34
Speaking Up About Problems	.33
Improving Methods	.21
Showing Confidence	.50
Taking Charge	.38
Focusing on Results	.37

Table 6.32 Correlation Between Self and Other Ratings by Overall Leadership Ability

	Self-Other Correlation		
Scale	**Bottom 25%**	**Middle 50%**	**Top 25%**
Pioneering	.52	.33	.09
Energizing	.55	.44	.11
Affirming	.53	.35	.03
Inclusive	.45	.17	.14
Humble	.37	.07	.15
Deliberate	.46	.21	.20
Resolute	.52	.37	.19
Commanding	.64	.35	.33
Median	**.52**	**.28**	**.15**

Table 6.33 Overall Mean Ratings by Leadership Ability

	Mean Rating		
Overall Rating Category	**Other Rating**	**Self-Rating**	**Difference**
Bottom 25%	4.85	5.41	−.56
Middle 50%	5.71	5.59	.12
Top 25%	6.34	5.77	.57

Table 6.34 Correlation Between Approach Scales and Overall Effectiveness

	Outcome Variables		
Approach	**Good Leader**	**Respected as Good Leader**	**Enjoy Working With**
Pioneering	.70	.66	.51
Energizing	.72	.69	.57
Affirming	.66	.65	.63
Inclusive	.63	.64	.65
Humble	.57	.61	.56
Deliberate	.66	.69	.58
Resolute	.60	.58	.42
Commanding	.61	.58	.35

Correlations with the DiSC Scales

The *Everything DiSC* assessment includes eight scales that each measure a personal disposition, as shown in Table 6.35. In the *363 for Leaders* model, each of the eight approaches corresponds to one of the eight DiSC scales.

Analyses were performed to determine if the approach scales demonstrate the predicted relationships with the *Everything DiSC* scales. The eight ipsatized other-rated approach scales and the eight DiSC scales were submitted to an MDS analysis. The results, as shown in Figure 6.19, suggest that the approach scales do, in fact, conform to the theoretical model. All approach scales are located closest to their corresponding DiSC scale. Further, all scales are in the order predicted by the model, and the spacing between each approach/DiSC scale pair is roughly equidistant. The stress value and RSQ value for this solution were .08346 and .95566, respectively. This suggests that two dimensions are sufficient to account for the relationships among these scales. Correlations among the *Everything DiSC* scales and the approach scales are also shown in Table 6.36.

Table 6.35 The Eight DiSC Scales

Scale	Description	Corresponding Leadership Approach
Di	active, fast-paced disposition	Pioneering
i	interactive, lively disposition	Energizing
iS	agreeable, warm disposition	Affirming
S	accommodating, patient disposition	Inclusive
SC	moderate-paced, cautious disposition	Humble
C	private, analytical disposition	Deliberate
CD	questioning, skeptical disposition	Resolute
D	direct, dominant disposition	Commanding

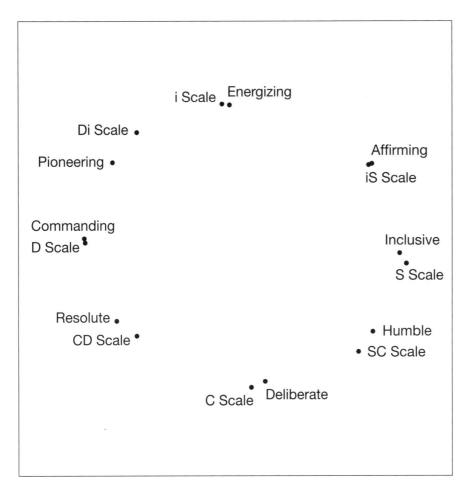

Figure 6.19 MDS Map of the Approach Scales and Everything DiSC Scales
Note: Stress = .08346; RSQ = .95566; *N* = 483.

Table 6.36 Correlations Among Everything DiSC Scales and Approach Scales

	Di	i	iS	S	SC	C	CD	D
Pioneering	.41	.18	−.13	−.25	−.40	−.18	.05	.27
Energizing	.44	.58	.30	−.11	−.41	−.52	−.31	.00
Affirming	−.03	.31	.52	.34	.06	−.32	−.40	−.42
Inclusive	−.29	−.10	.40	.49	.35	.01	−.23	−.52
Humble	−.44	−.37	.11	.42	.49	.27	−.05	−.35
Deliberate	−.41	−.50	−.24	.11	.37	.50	.22	−.04
Resolute	−.01	−.21	−.49	−.41	−.06	.29	.38	.43
Commanding	.29	.10	−.44	−.56	−.39	−.03	.33	.59

Note: Approach scales are ipsatized.

Differences Based on Demographic Categories

A series of ANOVAs were conducted to examine the degree to which approach scale scores were related to ethnic heritage and gender. A sample of 3,081 adult leaders who had been rated by at least three raters was divided into four subsamples based on heritage: African-American ($n = 123$), Asian ($n = 158$), Caucasian ($n = 2,707$), and Hispanic ($n = 93$) (see Table B.6 for demographics). Note that a Native American sample was not included in the analysis due to its small sample size. ANOVAs were conducted for each approach scale, as presented on Table 6.37. Statistically significant differences at the $p < .01$ level were found on all scales. In each case, however, the variance accounted for (i.e., eta-squared) by heritage was 1% or lower, suggesting that this variable did not play a large role in determining ratings.

ANOVAs on the 24 practice scales, as shown in Table 6.38, indicated that the most variance between heritage groups was accounted for by the Promoting Disciplined Analysis scale (2%). For all other scales, the percentage was 1% or less. Statistically significant differences, however, were found on 20 of the 24 scales ($p < .01$). The three scales with non-significant results were Promoting Bold Action, Speaking Up About Problems, and Taking Charge.

With regard to gender, analyses on 1,235 female and 1,846 male leaders showed that women received higher scores on all of the approach scales except Pioneering. In only three cases, however, were these differences statistically significant, as shown on Table 6.39. Variance accounted for by gender on the Affirming scale was 3%, suggesting that this was the most meaningful difference between men and women.

ANOVAs on the 24 practice scales, as shown in Table 6.40, indicated that the most variance between women and men was accounted for by the Acknowledging Contributions scale (3%), followed by the Being Approachable and Showing Diplomacy scales, both at 2%. In all three cases, women demonstrated a higher mean score. Statistically significant differences were found on 18 of the 24 scales ($p < .05$). All participants in the sample were at or above the age of 18 and had been rated by at least three raters.

Table 6.37 Differences Across the Heritage Subsamples on the Eight Approach Scales

Approach Scale	*F*-Value*	Variance Accounted for	Heritage	Mean	*SD*
Pioneering	5.82	.01	Asian	5.55	.79
			African-American	5.73	.80
			Caucasian	5.48	.84
			Hispanic	5.67	.80
Energizing	9.83	.01	Asian	5.38	.86
			African-American	5.67	.86
			Caucasian	5.33	.88
			Hispanic	5.58	.80
Affirming	9.49	.01	Asian	5.85	.77
			African-American	6.09	.64
			Caucasian	5.81	.71
			Hispanic	5.97	.70
Inclusive	10.67	.01	Asian	5.80	.73
			African-American	6.04	.65
			Caucasian	5.77	.67
			Hispanic	6.00	.68
Humble	10.87	.01	Asian	5.46	.80
			African-American	5.57	.73
			Caucasian	5.30	.75
			Hispanic	5.55	.75
Deliberate	14.17	.01	Asian	5.62	.71
			African-American	5.78	.66
			Caucasian	5.52	.67
			Hispanic	5.86	.64

Table 6.37 continued.

Approach Scale	*F*-Value*	Variance Accounted for	Heritage	Mean	*SD*
Resolute	5.02	< .01	Asian	5.69	.72
			African-American	5.86	.67
			Caucasian	5.70	.65
			Hispanic	5.88	.64
Commanding	2.49	< .01	Asian	5.67	.73
			African-American	5.84	.71
			Caucasian	5.73	.73
			Hispanic	5.87	.71

*All *F*-values were statistically significant at $p < .05$.

Table 6.38 Differences Across the Heritage Subsamples on the 24 Practice Scales

Practice Scale	*F*-Value	Variance Accounted for	Heritage	Mean	*SD*
Finding Opportunities	5.48*	.01	Asian	5.63	.88
			African-American	5.76	.94
			Caucasian	5.50	.94
			Hispanic	5.71	.93
Stretching the Boundaries	6.90*	.01	Asian	5.56	.87
			African-American	5.86	.80
			Caucasian	5.58	.85
			Hispanic	5.78	.86

(continued)

Table 6.38 continued.

Practice Scale	*F*-Value	Variance Accounted for	Heritage	Mean	*SD*
Promoting Bold Action	3.24	< .01	Asian	5.45	.87
			African-American	5.58	.95
			Caucasian	5.37	.97
			Hispanic	5.51	.89
Showing Enthusiasm	4.68*	< .01	Asian	5.79	.87
			African-American	5.89	.84
			Caucasian	5.68	.83
			Hispanic	5.85	.83
Building Professional Networks	5.80*	.01	Asian	4.94	1.16
			African-American	5.36	1.22
			Caucasian	4.96	1.27
			Hispanic	5.21	1.13
Rallying People to Achieve Goals	12.94*	.01	Asian	5.42	.95
			African-American	5.75	.93
			Caucasian	5.33	.98
			Hispanic	5.70	.90
Being Approachable	5.26*	.01	Asian	5.84	.92
			African-American	6.06	.81
			Caucasian	5.78	.92
			Hispanic	5.91	.85
Acknowledging Contributions	6.38*	.01	Asian	5.79	.93
			African-American	6.06	.86
			Caucasian	5.76	.89
			Hispanic	5.89	.87

Table 6.38 continued.

Practice Scale	*F*-Value	Variance Accounted for	Heritage	Mean	*SD*
Creating a Positive Environment	11.01*	.01	Asian	5.93	.75
			African-American	6.15	.64
			Caucasian	5.88	.69
			Hispanic	6.11	.74
Staying Open to Input	5.11*	< .01	Asian	6.01	.72
			African-American	6.16	.71
			Caucasian	5.98	.70
			Hispanic	6.16	.70
Showing Diplomacy	10.80*	.01	Asian	5.62	.93
			African-American	6.02	.79
			Caucasian	5.67	.85
			Hispanic	5.91	.86
Facilitating Dialogue	9.96*	.01	Asian	5.77	.80
			African-American	5.93	.74
			Caucasian	5.67	.76
			Hispanic	5.94	.70
Maintaining Composure	8.13*	.01	Asian	5.39	1.05
			African-American	5.59	1.01
			Caucasian	5.19	1.10
			Hispanic	5.39	1.10
Showing Modesty	5.83*	.01	Asian	5.51	.90
			African-American	5.46	.97
			Caucasian	5.32	.86
			Hispanic	5.60	.86

(continued)

Table 6.38 continued.

Practice Scale	*F*-Value	Variance Accounted for	Heritage	Mean	*SD*
Being Fair-minded	9.94*	.01	Asian	5.47	.92
			African-American	5.66	.73
			Caucasian	5.38	.79
			Hispanic	5.67	.78
Communicating with Clarity	6.31*	.01	Asian	5.53	.92
			African-American	5.67	.80
			Caucasian	5.44	.86
			Hispanic	5.70	.88
Promoting Disciplined Analysis	17.18*	.02	Asian	5.61	.82
			African-American	5.78	.81
			Caucasian	5.46	.79
			Hispanic	5.90	.69
Providing a Sense of Stability	8.56*	.01	Asian	5.73	.80
			African-American	5.88	.76
			Caucasian	5.67	.75
			Hispanic	5.99	.66
Setting High Expectations	6.98*	.01	Asian	5.51	.81
			African-American	5.76	.91
			Caucasian	5.52	.88
			Hispanic	5.82	.88
Speaking Up About Problems	1.74	< .01	Asian	5.75	.81
			African-American	5.91	.77
			Caucasian	5.87	.72
			Hispanic	5.95	.83

Table 6.38 continued.

Practice Scale	*F*-Value	Variance Accounted for	Heritage	Mean	*SD*
Improving Methods	5.32*	.01	Asian	5.82	.79
			African-American	5.91	.74
			Caucasian	5.72	.72
			Hispanic	5.86	.65
Showing Confidence	4.80*	< .01	Asian	5.58	.79
			African-American	5.87	.77
			Caucasian	5.70	.81
			Hispanic	5.89	.82
Taking Charge	.87	< .01	Asian	5.63	.87
			African-American	5.73	.98
			Caucasian	5.76	.87
			Hispanic	5.73	.86
Focusing on Results	5.40*	.01	Asian	5.81	.84
			African-American	5.93	.76
			Caucasian	5.74	.82
			Hispanic	5.98	.82

*F-value is statistically significant at a $p < .01$ level.

Table 6.39 Differences Between Gender Subsamples on the Eight Approach Scales

Approach Scale	F-Value	Variance Accounted for	Gender	Mean	SD
Pioneering	1.13	< .01	M	5.52	.82
			F	5.49	.86
Energizing	37.81*	.01	M	5.27	.88
			F	5.47	.86
Affirming	88.06*	.03	M	5.73	.72
			F	5.97	.67
Inclusive	55.50*	.02	M	5.72	.69
			F	5.91	.65
Humble	.18	< .01	M	5.32	.75
			F	5.33	.76
Deliberate	.32	< .01	M	5.55	.66
			F	5.56	.70
Resolute	.27	< .01	M	5.71	.64
			F	5.72	.68
Commanding	.14	< .01	M	5.74	.72
			F	5.75	.74

*F-value is statistically significant at a $p < .01$ level.

Table 6.40 Differences Across the Gender Subsamples on the 24 Practice Scales

Practice Scale	F-Value	Variance Accounted for	Gender	Mean	SD
Finding Opportunities	.31	< .01	M	5.53	.92
			F	5.51	.97
Stretching the Boundaries	.02	< .01	M	5.60	.83
			F	5.60	.89

Table 6.40 continued.

Practice Scale	*F*-Value	Variance Accounted for	Gender	Mean	*SD*
Promoting Bold Action	4.35	< .01	M	5.41	.94
			F	5.34	.99
Showing Enthusiasm	29.37*	< .01	M	5.63	.85
			F	5.80	.80
Building Professional Networks	41.09*	.01	M	4.87	1.27
			F	5.17	1.24
Rallying People to Achieve Goals	12.94*	< .01	M	5.32	.98
			F	5.45	.98
Being Approachable	56.89*	.02	M	5.70	.93
			F	5.95	.87
Acknowledging Contributions	91.07*	.03	M	5.65	.92
			F	5.96	.81
Creating a Positive Environment	44.54*	.01	M	5.83	.69
			F	6.00	.68
Staying Open to Input	33.48*	.01	M	5.94	.70
			F	6.09	.69
Showing Diplomacy	65.28*	.02	M	5.59	.86
			F	5.84	.82
Facilitating Dialogue	30.83*	.01	M	5.63	.77
			F	5.78	.74
Maintaining Composure	6.88*	< .01	M	5.27	1.10
			F	5.17	1.10
Showing Modesty	14.90*	< .01	M	5.29	.85
			F	5.42	.88

(continued)

Table 6.40 continued.

Practice Scale	*F*-Value	Variance Accounted for	Gender	Mean	*SD*
Being Fair-minded	.40	< .01	M	5.40	.80
			F	5.42	.79
Communicating with Clarity	.10	< .01	M	5.46	.86
			F	5.45	.88
Promoting Disciplined Analysis	2.36	< .01	M	5.52	.77
			F	5.47	.82
Providing a Sense of Stability	12.38*	< .01	M	5.66	.74
			F	5.75	.77
Setting High Expectations	1.21	< .01	M	5.52	.87
			F	5.56	.90
Speaking Up About Problems	5.70*	< .01	M	5.89	.71
			F	5.83	.76
Improving Methods	6.17	< .01	M	5.71	.71
			F	5.77	.74
Showing Confidence	1.45	< .01	M	5.72	.79
			F	5.69	.84
Taking Charge	.52	< .01	M	5.76	.86
			F	5.74	.89
Focusing on Results	8.77*	< .01	M	5.72	.81
			F	5.81	.83

*F-value is statistically significant at a $p < .01$ level.

CHAPTER 7

The Everything DiSC Comparison Report

The *Everything DiSC® Comparison Report* allows any two *Everything DiSC* participants to see their similarities and differences on a series of different continua. The report includes a narrative that explains these similarities and differences and guides participants in a discussion around them. Overall, the purpose of this report is to improve communication and efficiency, while reducing tension and misunderstandings.

The *Everything DiSC Comparison Report* begins with a brief comparison of the two participants' DiSC® styles. Each participant's style is calculated from the participant's responses to the basic *Everything DiSC* assessment. The focus of this chapter is on the continua contained in the second section of the *Everything DiSC Comparison Report*. Figure 7.1 shows an example of one such continuum.

Selection of the Continua Within Each Report

For each report, nine *Comparison Report* scales are calculated, which are presented in the form of continua. The names and definitions of these continua are shown in Table 7.1.

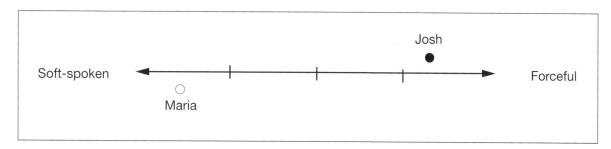

Figure 7.1 Continuum Example

Table 7.1 Definitions of the Nine Comparison Report Scales

Scale	Label	Definition
Soft-spoken— Forceful	Soft-spoken	People who are **soft-spoken** tend to shy away from leading discussions and withhold their opinion unless directly asked for it.
	Forceful	People who are **forceful** tend to be comfortable taking the lead in group settings and push strongly for their opinions.
Daring—Careful	Daring	People who are **daring** tend to see change as invigorating and pitch fresh ideas and new approaches.
	Careful	People who are **careful** tend to see major changes as risky or stressful, and they often rely on well-tested methods and solutions.
Patient—Driven	Patient	People who are **patient** tend to put up with annoyances or setbacks without complaint. They are often uncomfortable pressuring others and calmly accept delays.
	Driven	People who are **driven** tend to urge others to move quickly and get annoyed by others who seem to lack urgency.
Skeptical— Accepting	Skeptical	People who are **skeptical** tend to question and test other people's ideas and consider the things that could go wrong.
	Accepting	People who are **accepting** tend to validate other people's ideas and expect things to go relatively well.
Outgoing— Private	Outgoing	People who are **outgoing** tend to seek out social situations that allow them to meet new people, and they get restless if they have to work alone for too long.
	Private	People who are **private** tend to avoid social situations that require meeting a lot of new people and they are more comfortable working independently.
Tactful—Frank	Tactful	People who are **tactful** tend to find the most diplomatic way to convey information and hold back certain thoughts and feelings.
	Frank	People who are **frank** tend to get to the point fairly quickly and say what's on their mind, without holding back their thoughts and feelings.

Table 7.1 continued.

Scale	Label	Definition
Accommodating— Strong-willed	Accommo- dating	People who are **accommodating** tend to welcome input and advice from others and are willing to set their own ideas aside to maintain harmony.
	Strong- willed	People who are **strong-willed** tend to hold tightly to their opinions and may sometimes overlook advice and input from others.
Lively—Reserved	Lively	People who are **lively** tend to be upbeat and com- municate in an open and vivid manner.
	Reserved	People who are **reserved** tend to be unexpressive even when they are excited about something, and they're uncomfortable with excessive enthusiasm.
Calm—Energetic	Calm	People who are **calm** prefer to work at a measured pace and dislike last-minute deadlines or sudden changes.
	Energetic	People who are **energetic** prefer to work at a rapid pace and are energized by lots of activity and quick turn-around times.

Only the six continua that are expected to generate the most meaningful discussion for the participants are presented in the *Comparison Report*. This ensures that participants are not overwhelmed by the information and are better able to focus their discussions on meaningful topics. A panel of DiSC subject-matter experts reviewed each possible pairing on all nine continua and developed an algorithm to determine which six continua would be presented within a given *Everything DiSC Comparison Report*. The decision rules used in creating this algorithm include the following:

- If possible, at least two continua showing similarities should be presented.

- If possible, at least two continua showing differences should be presented.

- Continua on which there are larger differences are more likely to be presented than continua on which there are smaller differences.

- Among continua that have very high statistical correlations or conceptual overlap, only the continuum judged most meaningful should be presented.

Although other decision rules were used to create this algorithm, those presented above represent the major criteria. Within the report, the largest differences are presented first and the smallest differences (or greatest similarities) are shown last.

Scoring of the Comparison Report Scales

Each of the nine *Comparison Report* scales is calculated using the same item responses that are used to calculate the DiSC scale scores. Although there is substantial overlap in the items used to calculate DiSC scale scores and *Comparison Report* scores, an individual's *Comparison Report* scores are calculated separately from his or her DiSC style. Therefore, it is possible to have a person who tends toward the S style, for example, who is more Daring than Careful on that particular *Comparison Report* continuum, even though this is quite atypical for people with the S style. The number of items on each *Comparison Report* scale range from 7 to 13, with a median of 8. Scale scores are generated by reverse scoring the appropriate items and finding an average score. This score is then standardized, such that the population mean is zero and the standard deviation is one.

Reliability of the Comparison Report Scales

Internal Reliability

Alpha internal reliability coefficients were calculated for each of the nine continua, as shown in Table 7.2, using a sample of 752 participants. These coefficients range from .74 to .88, with a median reliability of .78. These findings suggest that each of the *Comparison Report* scales is measuring unified constructs.

Table 7.2 Alpha Coefficients of the Continua Scales

Scale	Number of Items	Alpha
Soft-spoken—Forceful	13	.85
Daring—Careful	7	.75
Patient—Driven	10	.74
Skeptical—Accepting	12	.82
Outgoing—Private	8	.88
Tactful—Frank	8	.75
Accommodating—Strong-willed	11	.75
Lively—Reserved	12	.85
Calm—Energetic	11	.78

N = 752

Test-Retest Reliability

The stability of the *Comparison Report* scales (i.e., test-retest reliability) was measured by asking a group of respondents to take a DiSC instrument and then asking those same respondents to take the same instrument again two weeks later.

The resulting data suggest that the *Comparison Report* scales are stable over different administrations (see Table 7.3). Consequently, test takers and test administrators should, on average, expect no more than small changes when the instrument is taken at different times. As the period between administrations increases, however, the divergent results of these administrations will become more and more noticeable.

Table 7.3 Comparison Report Scale Test-Retest Reliabilities

Scale	Reliability Coefficient
Soft-spoken—Forceful	.89
Daring—Careful	.84
Patient—Driven	.82
Skeptical—Accepting	.82
Outgoing—Private	.90
Tactful—Frank	.83
Accommodating—Strong-willed	.83
Lively—Reserved	.89
Calm—Energetic	.84
N = 599	

Validity of the Comparison Report Scales

Intercorrelations Among the Continua Scales

Intercorrelations among the continua scales were calculated using a sample of 752 participants. As shown in Table 7.4, many of the scale correlations are quite high, likely because these scales contain overlapping items. Although these scales may appear repetitive, they are included because each is used to help facilitate a different discussion between participants. For instance, the Calm—Energetic scale correlates at −.63 with the Outgoing—Private scale. The Calm—Energetic scale, however, is used to facilitate a discussion

Table 7.4 Continua Scale Intercorrelations

Continua Scales	Soft-spoken—Forceful	Daring—Careful	Patient—Driven	Skeptical—Accepting	Outgoing—Private	Tactful—Frank	Accommodating—Strong-willed	Lively—Reserved	Calm—Energetic
Soft-spoken—Forceful		-.59	.62	-.21	-.62	.66	.50	-.75	.64
Daring—Careful	-.59		-.74	.01	.50	-.33	-.24	.59	-.69
Patient—Driven	.62	-.74		-.07	-.48	.35	.26	-.63	.82
Skeptical—Accepting	-.21	.01	-.07		-.31	-.58	-.66	-.15	.06
Outgoing—Private	-.62	.50	-.48	-.31		-.13	.01	.89	-.63
Tactful—Frank	.66	-.33	.35	-.58	-.13		.78	-.29	.31
Accommodating—Strong-willed	.50	-.24	.26	-.66	.01	.78		-.14	.19
Lively—Reserved	-.75	.59	-.63	-.15	.89	-.29	-.14		-.83
Calm—Energetic	.64	-.69	.82	.06	-.63	.31	.19	-.83	

about the pace at which participants choose to complete tasks. On the other hand, the Outgoing—Private scale is used to facilitate a discussion about topics such as the need for personal space versus the need for interaction.

Correlations with the Other Measures of Personality

A sample of participants ($N = 752$) was asked to take the *Everything DiSC* assessment, the NEO™-PI-3 assessment, and the 16PF® assessment (for a description of the latter two assessments, see Chapter 4). The demographics for this sample are included in Table B.1. From this sample, intercorrelations among the scales on the instruments were calculated, as shown in Appendix C. Table 7.5 includes the six strongest correlations between the *Comparison Report* scales and the scales on the NEO-PI-3 and 16PF. Overall, these correlations suggest that the *Comparison Report* scales are measuring their intended constructs.

Table 7.5 Strongest Correlations Between the Comparison Report Scales and the NEO-PI-3 and 16PF Scales

Comparison Report Scale	NEO-PI-3/16PF Scale	Instrument	*r*
Soft-spoken—Forceful	Assertiveness	NEO-PI-3	.74
	Independence	16PF	.71
	Creative Potential	16PF	.68
	Dominance	16PF	.67
	Emotional Expressivity	16PF	.67
	Enterprising	16PF	.62
Daring—Careful	Independence	16PF	−.57
	Assertiveness	NEO-PI-3	−.56
	Creative Potential	16PF	−.56
	Emotional Expressivity	16PF	−.54
	Social Expressivity	16PF	−.52
	Excitement Seeking	NEO-PI-3	−.51

(continued)

Table 7.5 continued.

Comparison Report Scale	NEO-PI-3/16PF Scale	Instrument	r
Patient—Driven	Assertiveness	NEO-PI-3	.57
	Independence	16PF	.54
	Emotional Expressivity	16PF	.54
	Creative Potential	16PF	.54
	Activity	NEO-PI-3	.52
	Social Expressivity	16PF	.50
Skeptical—Accepting	Agreeableness	NEO-PI-3	.57
	Trust	NEO-PI-3	.56
	Compliance	NEO-PI-3	.53
	Warmth	NEO-PI-3	.51
	Altruism	NEO-PI-3	.51
	Empathy	16PF	.46
Outgoing—Private	Social Expressivity	16PF	−.79
	Social Boldness	16PF	−.77
	Social Adjustment	16PF	−.75
	Extraversion	16PF	−.74
	Extraversion	NEO-PI-3	−.72
	Social Control	16PF	−.72
Tactful—Frank	Compliance	NEO-PI-3	−.63
	Agreeableness	NEO-PI-3	−.61
	Dominance	16PF	.52
	Independence	16PF	.48
	Altruism	NEO-PI-3	−.40
	Assertiveness	NEO-PI-3	.39

Table 7.5 continued.

Comparison Report Scale	NEO-PI-3/16PF Scale	Instrument	*r*
Accommodating— Strong-willed	Compliance	NEO-PI-3	−.68
	Agreeableness	NEO-PI-3	−.63
	Tension	16PF	.47
	Dominance	16PF	.46
	Angry Hostility	NEO-PI-3	.42
	Altruism	NEO-PI-3	−.41
Lively—Reserved	Social Expressivity	16PF	−.74
	Social Boldness	16PF	−.71
	Social Adjustment	16PF	−.69
	Social Control	16PF	−.68
	Emotional Expressivity	16PF	−.67
	Extraversion	NEO-PI-3	−.67
Calm—Energetic	Social Expressivity	16PF	.63
	Activity	NEO-PI-3	.62
	Emotional Expressivity	16PF	.62
	Creative Potential	16PF	.60
	Assertiveness	NEO-PI-3	.60
	Social Boldness	16PF	.58

CHAPTER 8

Interpretation of Results

At its core, the DiSC® model is designed to be simple to understand and easy to remember. The respondent needs to be able to leave a DiSC experience with clear, simple principles that can be understood and applied in the real world. For this reason, the DiSC map is divided into four basic quadrants, even though there is a diversity of behavior represented in any single quadrant. For instance, the upper portion of the D quadrant captures bold, enterprising behavior, and the lower portion of the D quadrant captures direct, challenging behavior. The use of quadrants is an organizing principle that is designed to make abstract psychological constructs more memorable and applicable for a general audience.

Likewise, the *Everything DiSC®* assessment describes respondents as having a particular style, rather than placing a participant on a continuum, which is more customary in psychological measurement. The use of styles to present information (rather than continua) is an attempt at simplification that does (like all simplifications) result in the loss of some information. In a similar manner, the representation of an individual on a unidimensional continuum (which is common in academic and clinical assessment) is a simplification that inherently suggests that the individual's pattern of behavior, emotions, and thoughts exists at one and only one place on the continuum. A more accurate alternative might be to represent the individual's tendencies as a range rather than as an average. Nonetheless, the single point on a continuum is the most common method of representing an individual's standing on a trait because this simplification makes assessment results more interpretable and applicable, even for audiences that might have a strong background in measurement theory. Within the *Everything DiSC* model, the use of styles creates results that are more memorable for respondents and a simple language that helps people have meaningful conversations about interpersonal differences. As discussed in Chapter 4, however, the validity of these style assignments is crucial to the successful implementation of any tool such as this. Also, note that facilitators are encouraged to treat the two-dimensional DiSC circle as a continuous space (much like a one-dimensional continuum) where one style gradually transitions into neighboring styles.

Interpretations that describe the styles as fixed or rigid should be avoided. The shading on each respondent's *Everything DiSC* map is designed to reinforce the continuous nature of the model and of human nature.

Interpretation of Style

Dot placement conveys two pieces of information: (1) DiSC style and (2) style inclination. To start, the angle of the dot within the circle determines the assignment of style. As can be seen in Figure 8.1, the *Everything DiSC* map can be broken into 12 equally spaced segments, each corresponding to a set of angles. The iD style, for example, is represented by 0 to 30 degrees on the DiSC map. A person whose dot is located at the 45-degree angle would be assigned an i style. A person whose dot is located at the 338-degree angle would be assigned a Di style.

Each person who takes the *Everything DiSC* assessment is plotted on the *Everything DiSC* map with a dot. The example in Figure 8.2 shows a person (represented by the dot) who tends toward the D region, but also somewhat toward the i region. This represents a Di style. This person, therefore, is probably particularly active, bold, outspoken, and persuasive, as these qualities generally describe people who share both the D and i styles.

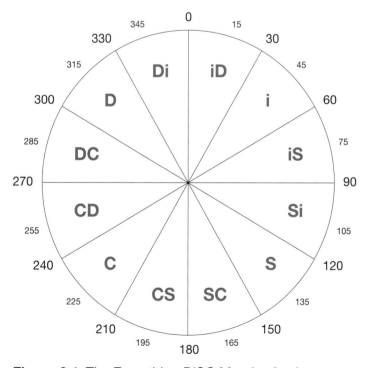

Figure 8.1 The Everything DiSC Map by Angle

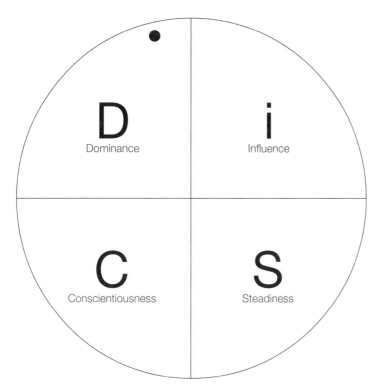

Figure 8.2 Everything DiSC Map with Plotted Dot

Interpretation of Inclination

The distance of the dot from the center of the circle is also meaningful. People whose dots fall toward the edge of the circle are said to be much more "inclined" toward their DiSC styles. On average, the characteristics (e.g., active, bold, outspoken, persuasive) associated with their style (e.g., Di) will be much more pronounced for them than they are for someone whose dot is closer to the center of the circle. By way of comparison, imagine a continuum that ranges from extrovert (on the left) to introvert (on the right). We can have two introverted people that are located on the right side of the continuum, but one (who is more introverted) will be placed further to the right than the other person (who is less introverted). One person will be expected to show more pronounced introverted traits than the other. In the context of DiSC, then, using our Di example, the person whose dot is close to the edge of the circle has a more pronounced Di style than someone whose dot is close to the center of the circle. The person whose dot is close to the center of the circle will be more likely to demonstrate characteristics (e.g., being cautious, deferring) of the style that is on the opposite side of the circle from his or her dot (SC in this example), although these opposite-side characteristics are not expected to be pronounced in either individual.

Interpretation of Shading

Each *Everything DiSC* map includes shading that surrounds the respondent's dot. This shading provides a rough approximation of the individual's comfort zone—behaviors and attitudes that will come naturally to the person and require little conscious effort. Figure 8.3 shows a person with a CD style. As with all maps, the shading includes the three priorities closest to his dot: accuracy, challenge, and results. These three priorities quickly explain some core behaviors associated with the CD style (e.g., speaking up about problems even when they are sensitive, insisting on efficiency even when it will upset the status quo).

The shading also communicates which regions of the map might require extra effort for the person. For instance, this person's shading does not come very close to the support priority, suggesting that listening empathetically may not be a natural strength for him or might make him uncomfortable. Likewise, the shading does not come very close to the enthusiasm priority, suggesting that outward displays of joy or excitement are probably infrequent. Not all people with the CD style, of course, are the same. For that reason, the *Everything DiSC* assessment measures every priority and will include extra shading for an individual if his or her score on the priority is over a pre-set threshold. This threshold was designed such that approximately one-third

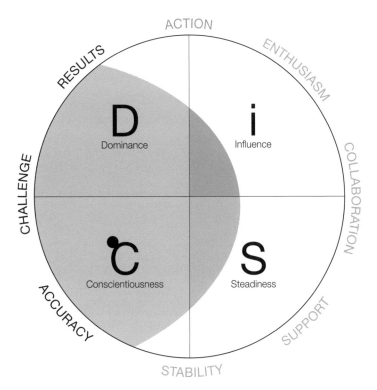

Figure 8.3 Example of Shading on an Everything DiSC Map

of respondents would receive an extra priority in their report. An example of extra shading is included in Figure 8.4 in the following section. As well, shading does reflect the respondent's inclination. Respondents with dots closer to the center will find that their shading is larger and more oblong than the shading illustrated in Figure 8.3. In such a case, the individual's dot is closer to priorities on the opposite side of the map, and, consequently, the individual would likely be more comfortable adopting those behaviors when they are needed. As mentioned earlier, however, the *Everything DiSC* shading is only designed to be a rough approximation of an individual's comfort level with different regions of the map.

Case Studies

The hypothetical case studies presented in this section are designed to (1) illustrate the relationship between profile results and real-life behavior and (2) model the appropriate interpretation of profile results. Note that these cases include specific characteristics that should not necessarily be generalized to every person sharing a particular style. In one of the cases, for instance, Andrea, who has a D style, is defensive and arrogant about receiving feedback. This should not be taken to mean that every person with a D style is defensive and arrogant in response to receiving feedback. This is simply one possible manifestation of that DiSC style.

The case studies presented here include the individual's *Everything DiSC* map, but also an umbrella graph. The umbrella graph shows the person's scores on the eight DiSC scales and can give a practitioner additional insight into the respondent's DiSC style. On this graph, scale scores are plotted such that higher scale scores are closer to the edge of the circle. Scale scores that are average are plotted at the halfway mark on each radius. These umbrella graphs are not included in the respondent's *Everything DiSC Profile*, but are available in the *Everything DiSC Supplement for Facilitators*.

Andrea: D Style

Andrea is a 31-year-old medical device salesperson. Over the past eight quarters, she has consistently been among the top five salespeople in her division. She is seemingly fearless when it comes to initiating contact with potential clients and pushing for their business, even in the face of repeated rejection. She particularly enjoys the part of her job that involves charming and persuading others. Some clients, however, have reported that her approach feels manipulative and insincere, and have asked to switch to other representatives from her company. The leadership at her organization has shown concern that her aggressive tactics may be hurting the company's brand in its tight-knit industry. Her response to this feedback has been perceived as defensive and, to some degree, cocky.

Ultimately, however, her history of results has allowed her to get away with some behaviors that might not be tolerated in others.

The assessment suggests that Andrea has a D style with an extra priority in Enthusiasm and a strong inclination toward her style (see Figure 8.4). Further, the umbrella graph indicates that her pattern of scores on the DiSC scales is as expected for someone with her dot placement and shading (see Figure 8.5). That is, she scored high on the D, CD, Di, and i scales and low on the S, CS, and C scales. This profile is associated with people who are bold, forceful, and enterprising. Her level of drive is typical for people with this style and, given her current level of immaturity, much of her self-worth may be wrapped up in her ability to achieve results. At her current stage of development, she has an exaggerated sense of her own rights, particularly relative to the rights of others. Likewise, she often only shows interest in the emotional experience of other people to the degree that it will help her achieve her goals.

The aspects of her behavior and personality that are entrepreneurial and charismatic are reflected in the extra priority of Enthusiasm. The D style is typically associated with more forceful persuasion tactics, whereas Andrea's atypical results suggest that she is also accustomed to smooth talking and charming others. Her approach is still heavy-handed, though, and consequently she can come across as manipulative in her relationships.

It is important to note that Andrea represents an immature example of the D style. Her arrogance and insensitivity is characteristic of people with the D style who also have a low level of ego integration and self-realization. The *Everything DiSC* assessment, however, does not measure psychological maturity or emotional intelligence. This is to say, by simply looking at her dot placement and shading, we would not know how healthy or adaptive Andrea's unique manifestation of the D style is. We would, however, expect

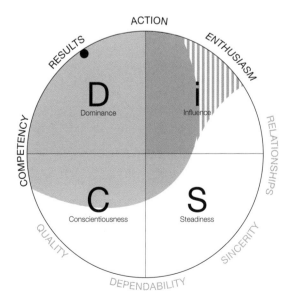

Figure 8.4 Andrea's DiSC Map

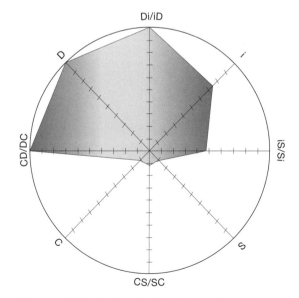

Figure 8.5 Andrea's Umbrella Graph

to see a predictable pattern of priorities, tendencies, and preferences (e.g., forcefulness, directness).

Rafael: CS Style

Rafael is a 54-year-old claims adjuster. He has worked at the same company for the past 9 years and in the same position for the last 6 years. He consistently receives positive reviews on his performance evaluations, and he is regarded as professional and competent by both clients and colleagues. His coworkers see him as the "go-to guy" for answers when they get stuck, and his manager enjoys the fact that she has to spend very little time supervising him. Despite his clear expertise and follow-through, however, Rafael has been passed up for promotion three times; twice these promotions went to colleagues with less seniority and skill than him. In addition, some coworkers feel that he can be unrealistically rigid about procedures. Although he doesn't force these views on others, they can slow down his team's progress.

The assessment indicates that Rafael has a CS style, with a strong inclination (see Figure 8.6). Further, his umbrella graph indicates that his pattern of DiSC scale scores is consistent with a strong CS style (see Figure 8.7). That is, he received very high scores on the C, CS, and S scales, moderate scores on the iS and CD scales, and very low scores on the D, Di, and i scales. This profile is associated with someone who is modest, self-controlled, and systematic. Like others with this style, Rafael places a particularly strong priority on stability and accuracy. He takes steps to create a predictable environment for himself and may be overly wedded to systems and routines that provide comfort for him. He has a

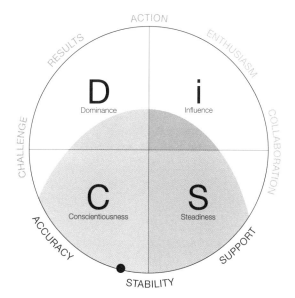

Figure 8.6 Rafael's DiSC Map

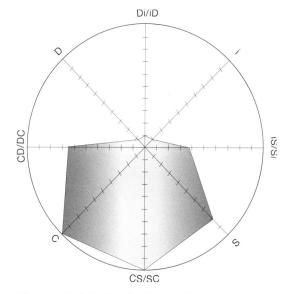

Figure 8.7 Rafael's Umbrella Graph

strong task orientation but is not challenging or argumentative with his colleagues when he disagrees with them. This is largely reflected by his middling placement on the horizontal dimension of the *Everything DiSC* map (skeptical to accepting), but also by his lower placement on the vertical pace dimension (moderate-paced to fast-paced).

Also consistent with his lower placement on the pace dimension is a relatively passive disposition. He is not highly assertive and does not feel comfortable self-promoting. Likewise, he comes across as soft-spoken and avoids the limelight. As a result, his contributions can be overlooked, and he may not come to mind when the organization's leadership is trying to identify its high-potential employees.

Amira: i Style

Amira is a 28-year-old nurse practitioner. She's just started her first job out of school at a large metropolitan hospital and has already made strong connections with most of the people inside her department. Her coworkers find her to be cheerful, warm, and thorough. Her favorite parts of the job are meeting new people, providing support for them, and giving them the medical information that can help relieve their anxiety. Her least favorite part of the job is dealing with a small subset of her coworkers who are cynical, condescending, and sometimes sloppy in their work with patients. Their behavior is deeply unsettling for her, but she does her best to gloss over her objections and remain positive.

Amira's results suggest that she has an i style, with an additional priority on accuracy (see Figure 8.8). In most instances, extra priorities are adjacent to the solid shading within the *Everything DiSC* map. As such, Amira's profile is uncommon, and the conflicting priorities are conceptually more difficult to reconcile compared to a more traditional profile. One theme common among people with this pattern of results is a desire to present a polished appearance. This manifests itself on both a task and interpersonal level. With regard to her work, Amira is attentive to deadlines and ensures that her output is beyond reproach. With regard to relationships, she wants to come across as poised and affable.

Amira has a moderate inclination toward her style. Although she has a clear preference for the i style, the more pronounced characteristics often associated with the i style (e.g., striking up conversations with strangers, being the life of the party) are less likely to be true for her. For instance, although Amira is sociable and has quickly formed relationships with many in her department, she has not necessarily branched out of her department to befriend people with whom she has less frequent contact. The umbrella graph indicates a moderately high score on the C scale (see Figure 8.9), but because she received an extra priority in Accuracy, it is reasonable to assume that she scored high on the Accuracy priority scale in the *Workplace* assessment. The umbrella graph also shows relatively low scores on the D and CD DiSC scales, which may explain why she prefers to

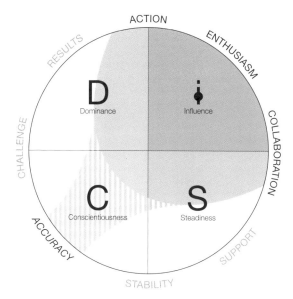

Figure 8.8 Amira's DiSC Map

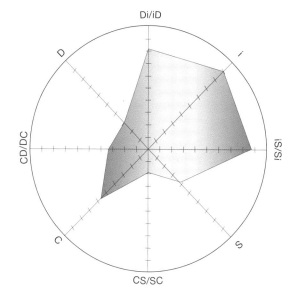

Figure 8.9 Amira's Umbrella Graph

avoid a potentially contentious confrontation with her coworkers, despite being deeply troubled by their behaviors.

James: S Style

James is a 41-year-old manager in a customer service department. For the past 3 years, he has overseen a team of eight employees, before which he was a customer service representative for 12 years. He is highly regarded among his direct reports for his support and flexibility. Further, they respect his wealth of knowledge about the organization's products and processes. Several of his direct reports, however, have expressed frustration at his unwillingness to confront team members that are not pulling their weight. Two employees in particular have stopped answering calls when they are busy and this increases the workload on everyone else. The brunt of the extra work, however, has been picked up by James himself. The director of the department is pleased with the consistency of James' team but notes that he has done little to innovate or advance the group's productivity, even when given a company mandate to do so.

The assessment indicates that James has a fairly typical S style, with a strong inclination (see Figure 8.10). The umbrella graph shows moderate scores on the C and CD scales and low scores on the D, Di, and i scales (see Figure 8.11). James' discomfort with interpersonal tension is reflected in his low CD and D scores, and his discomfort with assertiveness is reflected in his low D and Di scores.

James' willingness to put his own needs aside for the sake of others or for the sake of preserving harmony is typical of the S style. He prefers a calm, peaceful environment

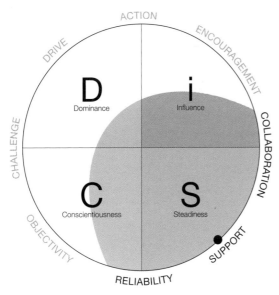

Figure 8.10 James' DiSC Map

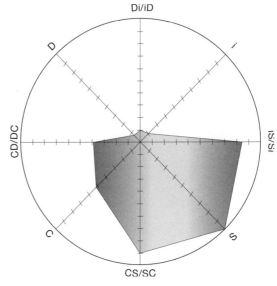

Figure 8.11 James' Umbrella Graph

where everyone gets along. Consistent with this preference, he has little drive to initiate large-scale change in his department or take chances on untested processes. Likewise, he is very reluctant to push his direct reports to work harder or move outside their comfort zones. As a result, the culture on his team is pleasant and low key, but not particularly results-oriented.

Appendix A: DiSC History

The DISC model of behavior was first proposed in 1928 by William Moulton Marston, a physiological psychologist, in a book entitled *Emotions of Normal People.* Like many psychologists of his time, Marston made a deliberate decision to focus only on psychological phenomena that were directly observable and measurable through objective means. His primary interest was in theories of emotions and the physical manifestations of emotional states. From his research, Marston theorized that the behavioral expression of emotions could be categorized into four primary types, stemming from the person's perceptions of self in relationship to his or her environment. These four types were labeled by Marston as Dominance (D), Inducement (I), Submission (S), and Compliance (C). He created a model that integrated these four types of emotional expression into a two-dimensional, two-axis space.

Marston himself had little interest in theoretical concepts of personality or temperament. Thus, he never created a psychological instrument to measure his model. The contemporary understanding of DiSC® maintains some of the core principles advanced by Marston, but the current presentation of the model also incorporates many additions and changes that are informed by advances in psychological measurement and theory.

The history of DISC measurement begins in the 1940s with an industrial psychologist by the name of Walter V. Clarke. Clarke (1956) built a test for use in personnel selection called the Activity Vector Analysis (AVA). He didn't intentionally set out to build an instrument based on the DiSC theory, as his approach was almost purely empirical (i.e., letting the data speak for itself) rather than theoretical (i.e., looking for something specific in the data). Following the "lexical approach" that was popular at that time, Clarke identified a list of adjectives that were commonly used in describing others. He collected information on the adjectives using a checklist format, on which people are asked to check the specific words that describe them. After collecting and analyzing the data on this instrument, he discovered that the four factors produced from the data (aggressive, sociable, stable, and avoidant) sounded a lot like DISC. Clarke concluded that the data could be best explained by Marston's model of human behavior.

He scored the instrument in the following manner. He asked participants to complete the checklist twice, the first time responding by checking "any words I have heard others use to describe me" and the second time responding by checking "any words that I feel honestly describe me." The scores on the four scales, measured twice, were integrated into a single score for each scale ("composite self"), then ipsatized and plotted as a profile. The distance between the highest and lowest plotting points was divided into nine equal intervals regardless of the actual distance between the points. A segment number from 1 to 9 was assigned to each scale. The four segment scores (one for each of the four styles) were then plotted as clusters in three-dimensional space, where distance between the clusters represented a measure of similarity. The clusters that came closest to each other were grouped into a mega-cluster (or pattern). Fifteen such mega-clusters (or patterns) emerged. It was these 15 basic patterns that formed the basis for interpretation of scores.

About 10 years later, a staff member of Walter Clarke Associates developed a version of this assessment for John Cleaver, which they called Self Discription. It began like the AVA as an adjective checklist, but evolved into a 24 tetrad (i.e., four choices), forced-choice instrument. Presumably, the forced choice aspect of the instrument was introduced to minimize the influence of socially desirable responding. Factor analyses of the Self Discription produced two factors that closely approximated the underlying axes of Marston's model, lending considerable empirical support not only to the structure of the model he proposed, but to Clarke's earlier claim that a DISC-based instrument could be created.

In the 1970s, John Geier, a faculty member in the University of Minnesota's Department of Health Sciences, used Self Discription to create the original *Personal Profile System®* (PPS). He formed a company called Performax (which subsequently became Carlson Learning Company, then Inscape Publishing, and is now part of Wiley) that was the first publisher of a DiSC assessment. Geier collected pattern descriptions through clinical interviews with hundreds of people, and by extracting behavioral information from those interviews, he provided richer descriptions of these 15 patterns that had come to be known as the Classical Profile Patterns. In 1994, the items and norms on the PPS were revisited and an updated version of the assessment was created. This assessment contained 28 tetrads and is today called *DiSC® Classic.*

In the early 2000s, researchers associated with Inscape Publishing (now Wiley) began experimenting with ways to represent DiSC with a circumplex model instead of with a line graph model. Here, a person's DiSC style was represented with a dot within the DiSC map. The advantage of this representation was ease of interpretation and application. For instance, users could much more easily see the relationship among the four styles and could plot two people on the same circle. Researchers discovered that this circumplex approach to measuring and presenting DiSC shared substantial overlap with the Interpersonal Circumplex theory (Leary, 1957) in academic psychological research. Drawing on this research and theory, the *Everything DiSC®* series of reports was developed as it exists today.

From Marston up to the present, the understanding of the DiSC model has continued to evolve. In each decade since Marston, new knowledge has been gained about what DiSC represents, and, along the way, new advances are continually applied to the model.

Appendix B: Everything DiSC Sample Demographics

Table B.1 Everything DiSC® Sample Demographics, Percentages

N		760	209	1,340	57,648	811	848
Gender	Male	35.5	61.2	47.9	50.2	48.7	49.9
	Female	38.0	34.4	52.1	47.3	51.3	50.1
	Missing	26.4	4.3	0	2.5	0	0
Age	18–25	6.4	9.1	12.8	9.5	14.7	9.9
	26–35	17.4	32.1	26.2	26.7	16.8	24.9
	36–45	15.4	25.8	27.3	27.9	26.0	18.6
	46–55	22.2	22.5	21.2	22.9	29.3	23.7
	56 or Older	10.4	6.2	12.4	10.3	12.8	22.9
	Missing	28.2	4.3	0	2.5	0	0
Education	High School Graduate or Less	35.0	2.9	11.2	9.8	6.0	22.4
	Associate Degree	20.5	3.3	4.9	4.6	2.1	9.6
	Some College	7.2	19.1	18.7	16.4	23.6	22.5
	College Graduate	8.2	30.6	36.1	35.0	35.1	27.8
	Post-Baccalaureate	1.4	39.7	29.0	31.7	33.2	17.7
	Missing	27.6	4.3	0	2.5	0	0

(continued)

Table B.1 continued.							
N		760	209	1,340	57,648	811	848
Heritage	Asian or Pacific Islander	3.8	4.9	4.3	5.6	1.6	3.2
	Black or African-American	4.7	5.3	4.8	6.0	9.9	8.1
	Caucasian	62.6	76.6	79.6	72.8	78.9	73.3
	Hispanic	5.5	2.4	5.0	4.9	5.8	8.8
	Native American	1.3	0.5	0.7	0.1	1.2	1.1
	Other	1.7	6.0	5.6	8.1	2.6	5.6
	Missing	20.4	4.3	0	2.5	0	0

Table B.2 Everything DiSC Sample Demographics, Percentages		
Gender	Male	50.0
	Female	50.0
Age	18–25	12.8
	26–35	26.7
	36–45	27.2
	46–55	23.2
	56 or Older	10.1
Education	Some High School	1.6
	High School Graduate	13.2
	Technical/Trade School	7.5
	Some College	26.5
	College Graduate	38.8
	Graduate/Professional Degree	12.5
Heritage	Asian	7.0
	African-American	12.2

Table B.2 continued.		
	Caucasian	69.1
	Hispanic	10.2
	Native American	1.5
Employment	Assembly Worker	1.1
	Customer Service	4.0
	Executive	3.5
	Health Care Worker	4.1
	Mechanical/Technical	4.9
	Mid-level Management	15.9
	Professional	21.7
	Sales	5.7
	Secretarial/Clerical	5.5
	Skilled Trades	1.9
	Supervisory	9.6
	Teacher/Educator	1.9
	Warehouse/General Labor	1.3
	Other	18.9

$N = 26,703$

Table B.3 Everything DiSC Assessment Development Sample Demographics, Percentages		
Gender	Male	52
	Female	48
Age	18–25	9
	26–35	24
	36–45	21
	46–55	30
	56 or Older	16

(continued)

Table B.3 continued.		
Education	Some High School	1
	High School Graduate	16
	Technical/Trade School	9
	Some College	28
	College Graduate	32
	Graduate/Professional Degree	14
Heritage	African-American	5
	Asian	5
	Caucasian	80
	Hispanic	6
	Native American	1
	Other	3
Employment	Customer Service	3
	Executive	3
	Healthcare Worker	3
	Mechanical-Technical	2
	Mid-level Management	6
	Professional	10
	Sales	4
	Secretary/Clerical	7
	Skilled Trades	4
	Student	2
	Supervisory	2
	Teacher/Educator	6
	Other	48

$N = 752$

Table B.4 Everything DiSC Sample Demographics, Percentages

N		599	7,200	24,965	3,287	2,270
Gender	Male	44.4	50.5	49.0	60.2	45.8
	Female	47.1	49.5	51.0	39.8	48.8
	Missing	8.5	0	0	0	5.5
Age	18–25	8.2	10.4	9.5	2.7	8.1
	26–35	21.7	27.4	27.8	17.8	26.1
	36–45	19.2	26.9	27.4	33.3	26.6
	46–55	27.4	23.6	23.7	32.8	22.7
	56 or Older	12.9	11.5	11.4	13.4	11.0
	Missing	10.7	0	0	0	5.5
Education	High School Graduate or Less	43.1	7.0	8.1	5.5	9.6
	Associate Degree	26.0	3.7	5.1	3.7	5.3
	Some College	9.0	14.3	15.7	11.9	20.7
	College Graduate	10.2	40.2	38.4	38.6	33.7
	Post-Baccalaureate	1.8	34.8	32.7	40.4	25.3
	Missing	9.8	0	0	0	5.5
Heritage	Asian or Pacific Islander	4.8	5.7	4.6	4.0	3.6
	Black or African-American	5.8	5.8	5.5	5.0	7.4
	Caucasian	77.8	74.2	75.8	82.0	71.6
	Hispanic	6.5	5.4	5.6	3.0	4.7
	Native American	1.5	1.0	0.8	1.0	2.1
	Other	3.6	7.9	7.7	5.0	5.1
	Missing	0	0	0	0	5.5

Table B.5 Everything DiSC Sample Demographics, Percentages

N		39,607	1,047	1,800	3,487	427	699
Gender	Male	47.1	43.4	43.6	63.3	43.8	41.9
	Female	51.6	52.1	50.9	36.0	51.5	52.5
	Missing	1.3	4.5	5.6	0	4.7	5.6
Age	18–25	12.1	14.8	12.4	10.4	7.7	8.4
	26–35	28.2	29.9	29.8	28.2	28.1	26.9
	36–45	27.0	27.1	26.8	26.9	29.5	29.8
	46–55	21.5	17.4	18.4	21.5	21.1	21.5
	56 or Older	9.9	6.3	7.0	12.4	8.9	7.7
	Missing	1.3	4.5	5.6	0	4.7	5.6
Education	High School Graduate or Less	10.9	9.7	10.4	9.3	9.2	10.3
	Associate Degree	4.9	5.4	4.6	4.6	4.4	5.3
	Some College	17.8	23.7	24.8	18.9	28.1	23.6
	College Graduate	34.5	36.7	39.5	47.3	37.0	33.9
	Post-Baccalaureate	30.6	20.1	15.1	19.2	16.6	21.3
	Missing	1.3	4.5	5.6	0	4.7	5.6
Heritage	Asian or Pacific Islander	4.8	3.3	3.6	3.2	2.8	4.2
	Black or African-American	6.2	6.1	9.4	3.7	8.0	8.7
	Caucasian	73.5	74.1	70.4	80.4	74.5	65.8
	Hispanic	5.1	7.4	5.0	5.2	5.9	7.4
	Native American	0.8	.6	0.8	0.7	1.8	4.1
	Other	8.3	4.0	5.2	6.8	2.3	4.2
	Missing	1.3	4.5	5.6	0	4.7	5.6

Table B.6 Everything DiSC Sample Demographics, Percentages

N		10,237	349	777	3,504	483	3,081	8,332
Gender	Male	57.8	57.9	46.3	61.1	40.8	59.9	61.4
	Female	41.4	42.1	53.7	38.2	36.4	40.1	38.2
	Missing	0	0	0	0	22.8	0	.4
Age	18–25	2.7	5.4	1.9	2.7	1.4	2.7	5.7
	26–35	25.5	22.1	21.6	18.9	12.2	17.6	24.0
	36–45	32.1	24.1	26.5	32.7	24.4	32.7	25.2
	46–55	27.0	32.1	29.0	33.5	25.5	33.3	25.9
	56 or Older	11.9	16.3	21.0	11.4	13.7	13.7	18.7
	Missing	0	0	0	0	22.8	0	0
Education	High School Graduate or Less	8.0	45.8	2.6	6.2	4.1	5.3	7.4
	Associate Degree	4.3	28.7	2.1	2.9	2.1	3.5	3.6
	Some College	13.0	9.7	12.1	11.7	9.1	12.2	14.9
	College Graduate	34.9	12.0	42.3	37.0	36.6	39.8	38.9
	Post-Baccalaureate	39.0	2.5	40.9	41.6	25.3	39.1	35.2
	Missing	0	0	0	0	22.8	0	0
Heritage	Asian or Pacific Islander	5.2	4.6	3.5	4.3	1.2	4.0	4.0
	Black or African-American	6.8	6.3	5.1	5.2	3.9	5.1	7.9
	Caucasian	71.3	85.1	85.2	79.1	66.7	87.9	73.3
	Hispanic	5.0	2.4	2.1	3.6	1.9	3.0	5.9
	Native American	0.6	1.4	0.8	0.4	1.0	0	.4
	Other	11.1	0.2	3.3	7.4	2.5	0	8.0
	Missing	0	0	0	0	22.8	0	0

Appendix C: Correlations Among the Everything DiSC Assessment and Other Assessments

Table C.1 Correlation Between the Everything DiSC® Assessment and the 16PF®

| 16PF Scale | DiSC® Scale | | | | | | | |
	Di	i	iS	S	SC	C	CD	D
Warmth	.15	.45	.49	.25	−.30	−.51	−.31	−.01
Reasoning	−.16	−.24	−.18	−.11	.08	.23	.23	.01
Emotional Stability	.21	.31	.38	.17	−.22	−.31	−.33	−.01
Dominance	.54	.28	−.14	−.45	−.63	−.24	.19	.63
Liveliness	.42	.62	.37	.06	−.45	−.55	−.27	.09
Rule-consciousness	−.21	−.03	.18	.23	.11	.07	−.23	−.20
Social Boldness	.52	.70	.35	−.10	−.66	−.60	−.19	.33
Sensitivity	−.17	.01	.15	.18	.10	−.05	−.05	−.19
Vigilance	.07	−.15	−.33	−.27	−.04	.10	.31	.23
Abstractedness	.09	−.07	−.21	−.23	−.02	.01	.24	.15
Privateness	−.21	−.39	−.31	−.04	.31	.33	.17	−.10
Apprehension	−.29	−.26	−.11	.06	.22	.22	.18	−.21
Openness to Change	.36	.19	.00	−.16	−.38	−.23	.08	.24
Self-reliance	−.25	−.47	−.39	−.17	.28	.51	.30	.01

(continued)

Table C.1 continued.

16PF Scale	DiSC Scale							
	Di	i	iS	S	SC	C	CD	D
Perfectionism	.10	.05	.00	.00	−.11	.15	−.12	−.01
Tension	−.05	−.18	−.43	−.45	−.03	.24	.55	.20
Extraversion	.41	.70	.51	.12	−.52	−.67	−.34	.12
Anxiety	−.18	−.31	−.41	−.26	.15	.30	.45	.06
Tough-mindedness	−.16	−.18	−.12	.02	.23	.26	−.04	−.08
Independence	.60	.42	−.04	−.40	−.71	−.38	.14	.60
Self-control	−.18	−.12	.07	.18	.11	.23	−.18	−.17
Realistic	.22	−.05	−.19	−.19	−.08	.09	.03	.20
Investigative	.06	−.23	−.31	−.22	.05	.26	.17	.13
Artistic	.36	.40	.16	−.11	−.45	−.41	.00	.23
Social	.30	.56	.45	.12	−.49	−.57	−.26	.14
Enterprising	.53	.53	.21	−.17	−.65	−.50	−.10	.44
Conventional	.06	.06	.07	.06	−.08	.08	−.18	−.02
Self-esteem	.39	.52	.40	.07	−.46	−.48	−.32	.17
Emotional Adjustment	.24	.32	.33	.15	−.21	−.30	−.36	.04
Social Adjustment	.51	.68	.38	−.06	−.64	−.60	−.24	.32
Emotional Expressivity	.56	.56	.12	−.32	−.69	−.48	.07	.50
Emotional Sensitivity	.27	.45	.42	.14	−.42	−.52	−.23	.10
Emotional Control	.01	−.16	−.18	−.10	.07	.13	.07	.09
Social Expressivity	.55	.74	.41	−.04	−.67	−.66	−.24	.27
Social Sensitivity	−.37	−.26	−.09	.10	.30	.21	.15	−.22
Social Control	.53	.62	.30	−.13	−.67	−.52	−.16	.35
Empathy	.37	.60	.56	.22	−.44	−.57	−.44	.05
Leadership Potential	.47	.60	.40	.04	−.55	−.49	−.33	.20
Creative Potential	.62	.51	.07	−.32	−.72	−.41	.02	.51
Creative Achievement	.37	.19	−.09	−.27	−.35	−.11	.12	.26

N = 552

Table C.2 Correlation Between the Everything DiSC Assessment and the NEO™-PI-3

NEO-PI-3 Scale	DiSC Scale							
	Di	i	iS	S	SC	C	CD	D
Neuroticism	−.31	−.29	−.26	−.12	.26	.31	.28	−.10
Extraversion	.45	.69	.52	.10	−.57	−.63	−.34	.15
Openness to Experience	.27	.10	.06	−.05	−.27	−.10	−.03	.10
Agreeableness	−.40	−.01	.52	.67	.35	−.05	−.48	−.58
Conscientiousness	.26	.09	.00	−.07	−.27	.11	−.11	.10
Anxiety	−.29	−.22	−.18	−.06	.23	.23	.23	−.10
Angry Hostility	.01	−.13	−.46	−.53	−.04	.17	.51	.30
Depression	−.30	−.34	−.30	−.08	.32	.30	.27	−.10
Self-consciousness	−.40	−.48	−.27	.00	.44	.41	.23	−.23
Impulsiveness	−.08	−.08	−.21	−.27	−.01	.05	.35	.14
Vulnerability	−.35	−.21	−.19	−.04	.34	.18	.21	−.14
Warmth	.25	.60	.61	.29	−.41	−.55	−.43	−.03
Gregariousness	.40	.65	.41	.16	−.42	−.59	−.36	.06
Assertiveness	.68	.49	.11	−.30	−.75	−.41	−.04	.55
Activity	.57	.47	.12	−.23	−.57	−.33	−.11	.32
Excitement Seeking	.51	.37	.11	−.09	−.42	−.32	−.13	.19
Positive Emotions	.25	.50	.57	.21	−.35	−.44	−.41	−.06
Fantasy	.15	.05	.04	−.04	−.15	−.11	.05	.06
Aesthetics	.20	.16	.14	.06	−.17	−.15	−.15	−.02
Feelings	.14	.23	.22	.02	−.29	−.20	−.07	.09
Actions	.43	.34	.16	.01	−.34	−.34	−.16	.09
Ideas	.33	.10	−.01	−.15	−.35	−.04	−.01	.23

(continued)

Table C.2 continued.

NEO-PI-3 Scale	DiSC Scale							
	Di	i	iS	S	SC	C	CD	D
Values	.08	.01	.02	.00	−.14	−.04	.06	.02
Trust	.03	.26	.55	.39	−.08	−.27	−.47	−.21
Straightforwardness	−.28	−.03	.27	.39	.24	.05	−.27	−.35
Altruism	.02	.28	.53	.47	−.13	−.27	−.42	−.27
Compliance	−.27	−.01	.47	.65	.41	.00	−.55	−.63
Modesty	−.39	−.21	.09	.31	.37	.16	−.08	−.35
Tender-mindedness	.00	.16	.37	.27	−.12	−.18	−.28	−.12
Competence	.33	.19	.16	.05	−.35	−.07	−.21	.08
Order	.18	.12	.07	.06	−.16	.07	−.17	−.04
Dutifulness	.11	.11	.19	.16	−.17	.00	−.22	−.06
Achievement Striving	.48	.31	.11	−.11	−.44	−.15	−.19	.20
Self-discipline	.30	.23	.18	.05	−.29	−.11	−.26	.08
Deliberation	−.12	−.11	.09	.26	.15	.18	−.22	−.26

$N = 694$

Appendix D: Style Distribution

Table D.1 363 for Leaders Sample Style Distribution

	Frequency	Percent
iD	220	6.7
i	274	8.3
iS	197	6.0
Si	237	7.2
S	229	7.0
SC	157	4.8
CS	228	6.9
C	279	8.5
CD	165	5.0
DC	272	8.3
D	488	14.8
Di	541	16.5
Total	**3,287**	**100.0**

Appendix E: Leadership Correlations

Table E.1 Correlations Between the Everything DiSC® Scales and the Leadership Practice Scales, All Raters

Practice Scales	Di	i	iS	S	SC	C	CD	D
Finding Opportunities	.21	.13	.13	−.01	−.17	−.15	−.09	.05
Stretching the Boundaries	.20	.15	.12	−.03	−.19	−.15	−.08	.10
Promoting Bold Action	.26	.20	.13	−.07	−.24	−.20	−.08	.13
Showing Enthusiasm	.11	.26	.27	.09	−.15	−.23	−.18	−.04
Building Professional Networks	.12	.32	.30	.08	−.16	−.30	−.16	−.05
Rallying People to Achieve Goals	.12	.21	.24	.09	−.14	−.20	−.16	−.03
Being Approachable	−.18	.11	.31	.34	.12	−.14	−.21	−.31
Acknowledging Contributions	−.07	.11	.26	.21	.02	−.12	−.18	−.18

(*continued*)

Table E.1 continued.

Practice Scales	Di	i	iS	S	SC	C	CD	D
Creating a Positive Environment	−.17	.03	.22	.29	.12	−.06	−.17	−.27
Staying Open to Input	−.19	−.01	.19	.29	.14	−.02	−.14	−.27
Showing Diplomacy	−.24	−.02	.23	.37	.19	−.02	−.20	−.34
Facilitating Dialogue	−.13	.03	.20	.25	.09	−.05	−.15	−.22
Maintaining Composure	−.23	−.12	.14	.38	.22	.05	−.17	−.34
Showing Modesty	−.29	−.09	.15	.34	.24	.06	−.14	−.34
Being Fair-minded	−.20	−.08	.11	.27	.16	.05	−.12	−.25
Communicating with Clarity	−.12	−.06	.05	.16	.06	.05	−.07	−.13
Promoting Disciplined Analysis	−.15	−.11	.02	.15	.10	.10	−.05	−.14
Providing a Sense of Stability	−.16	−.05	.08	.20	.11	.05	−.09	−.17
Setting High Expectations	.17	.11	−.01	−.14	−.19	−.05	−.01	.20
Speaking Up About Problems	.09	.00	−.07	−.12	−.12	.01	.07	.14
Improving Methods	−.01	.00	.03	.04	−.02	.03	−.04	−.02
Showing Confidence	.30	.17	−.04	−.27	−.34	−.14	.06	.35
Taking Charge	.24	.12	.02	−.13	−.25	−.12	−.01	.20
Focusing on Results	.21	.13	.06	−.09	−.21	−.10	−.05	.13

$N = 3,287$

Table E.2 Correlations Between the Everything DiSC Scales and the Leadership Practice Scales, Controlling for Leader Quality, All Raters

Practice Scales	Di	i	iS	S	SC	C	CD	D
Finding Opportunities	.38	.10	−.04	−.23	−.25	−.12	.04	.23
Stretching the Boundaries	.41	.14	−.07	−.34	−.34	−.14	.08	.38
Promoting Bold Action	.45	.21	−.05	−.32	−.36	−.20	.07	.36
Showing Enthusiasm	.26	.44	.31	−.06	−.28	−.33	−.17	.08
Building Professional Networks	.18	.37	.23	−.07	−.20	−.33	−.06	.06
Rallying People to Achieve Goals	.30	.35	.26	−.06	−.28	−.31	−.17	.12
Being Approachable	−.22	.13	.33	.36	.16	−.15	−.21	−.36
Acknowledging Contributions	−.09	.13	.28	.17	.05	−.13	−.18	−.18
Creating a Positive Environment	−.31	−.03	.23	.39	.28	.00	−.18	−.41
Staying Open to Input	−.33	−.12	.12	.33	.30	.08	−.09	−.37
Showing Diplomacy	−.41	−.13	.23	.50	.36	.07	−.22	−.50
Facilitating Dialogue	−.26	−.09	.15	.28	.24	.05	−.12	−.31
Maintaining Composure	−.30	−.27	.02	.39	.32	.16	−.11	−.37
Showing Modesty	−.47	−.29	−.02	.34	.46	.25	−.03	−.42
Being Fair-minded	−.37	−.31	−.11	.24	.35	.28	.01	−.28
Communicating with Clarity	−.20	−.22	−.16	.07	.14	.22	.07	−.08
Promoting Disciplined Analysis	−.26	−.37	−.30	.00	.24	.37	.17	−.07
Providing a Sense of Stability	−.32	−.26	−.13	.16	.27	.26	.03	−.18
Setting High Expectations	.22	.02	−.22	−.35	−.19	.04	.15	.38
Speaking Up About Problems	.13	−.13	−.35	−.38	−.13	.14	.30	.35
Improving Methods	.00	−.16	−.27	−.21	.01	.23	.16	.15
Showing Confidence	.35	.11	−.22	−.45	−.36	−.09	.22	.51
Taking Charge	.37	.09	−.17	−.37	−.35	−.09	.15	.44
Focusing on Results	.38	.13	−.13	−.35	−.32	−.06	.09	.37

N = 3,287

Table E.3 Correlations Between the Everything DiSC Scales and the Leadership Practice Scales, Leaders

Practice Scales	Di	i	iS	S	SC	C	CD	D
Finding Opportunities	.52	.26	.13	−.15	−.38	−.27	−.15	.21
Stretching the Boundaries	.51	.25	.11	−.19	−.41	−.27	−.12	.29
Promoting Bold Action	.63	.30	.08	−.24	−.49	−.33	−.09	.35
Showing Enthusiasm	.44	.58	.44	−.05	−.46	−.45	−.33	.13
Building Professional Networks	.35	.59	.41	.02	−.37	−.49	−.31	.08
Rallying People to Achieve Goals	.50	.45	.33	−.07	−.43	−.38	−.31	.18
Being Approachable	−.07	.32	.56	.45	−.03	−.29	−.44	−.32
Acknowledging Contributions	.11	.31	.48	.21	−.15	−.26	−.38	−.13
Creating a Positive Environment	.01	.23	.46	.36	−.03	−.20	−.45	−.24
Staying Open to Input	−.07	.09	.35	.36	.06	−.10	−.37	−.25
Showing Diplomacy	−.19	.09	.44	.58	.14	−.10	−.47	−.42
Facilitating Dialogue	.04	.15	.35	.28	−.03	−.18	−.35	−.18
Maintaining Composure	−.15	−.09	.20	.51	.19	.02	−.37	−.35
Showing Modesty	−.21	−.10	.18	.40	.25	.06	−.30	−.34
Being Fair-minded	−.03	−.02	.11	.24	.06	.03	−.26	−.12
Communicating with Clarity	.05	.01	.05	.13	−.08	.05	−.19	−.02
Promoting Disciplined Analysis	−.02	−.11	−.05	.09	.04	.17	−.11	−.05
Providing a Sense of Stability	−.02	.01	.11	.18	−.01	.07	−.24	−.09
Setting High Expectations	.33	.14	−.02	−.22	−.33	−.11	.00	.32
Speaking Up About Problems	.27	.00	−.12	−.20	−.29	−.02	.10	.27
Improving Methods	.21	.04	−.02	−.08	−.20	.04	−.06	.14
Showing Confidence	.51	.25	−.05	−.37	−.57	−.24	.08	.57
Taking Charge	.54	.23	.03	−.25	−.51	−.25	−.01	.40
Focusing on Results	.50	.23	.03	−.26	−.45	−.17	−.06	.35

$N = 3{,}287$

Table E.4 Correlations Between Leaders' DiSC Scales Scores and the Leadership Practice Scales Scores

Practice Scales	Di	i	iS	S	SC	C	CD	D
Finding Opportunities	.38	.10	−.04	−.23	−.25	−.12	.04	.23
Stretching the Boundaries	.41	.14	−.07	−.34	−.34	−.14	.08	.38
Promoting Bold Action	.45	.21	−.05	−.32	−.36	−.20	.07	.36
Showing Enthusiasm	.26	.44	.31	−.06	−.28	−.33	−.17	.08
Building Professional Networks	.18	.37	.23	−.07	−.20	−.33	−.06	.06
Rallying People to Achieve Goals	.30	.35	.26	−.06	−.28	−.31	−.17	.12
Being Approachable	−.22	.13	.33	.36	.16	−.15	−.21	−.36
Acknowledging Contributions	−.09	.13	.28	.17	.05	−.13	−.18	−.18
Creating a Positive Environment	−.31	−.03	.23	.39	.28	.00	−.18	−.41
Staying Open to Input	−.33	−.12	.12	.33	.30	.08	−.09	−.37
Showing Diplomacy	−.41	−.13	.23	.50	.36	.07	−.22	−.50
Facilitating Dialogue	−.26	−.09	.15	.28	.24	.05	−.12	−.31
Maintaining Composure	−.30	−.27	.02	.39	.32	.16	−.11	−.37
Showing Modesty	−.47	−.29	−.02	.34	.46	.25	−.03	−.42
Being Fair-minded	−.37	−.31	−.11	.24	.35	.28	.01	−.28
Communicating with Clarity	−.20	−.22	−.16	.07	.14	.22	.07	−.08
Promoting Disciplined Analysis	−.26	−.37	−.30	.00	.24	.37	.17	−.07
Providing a Sense of Stability	−.32	−.26	−.13	.16	.27	.26	.03	−.18
Setting High Expectations	.22	.02	−.22	−.35	−.19	.04	.15	.38
Speaking Up About Problems	.13	−.13	−.35	−.38	−.13	.14	.30	.35
Improving Methods	.00	−.16	−.27	−.21	.01	.23	.16	.15
Showing Confidence	.35	.11	−.22	−.45	−.36	−.09	.22	.51
Taking Charge	.37	.09	−.17	−.37	−.35	−.09	.15	.44
Focusing on Results	.38	.13	−.13	−.35	−.32	−.06	.09	.37

N = 3,287

Appendix F: ANOVA Results

Table F.1 ANOVA Results and Effect Sizes of the DiSC® Styles for Each of the 16PF® Scales

16PF Scale	F	Probability	Style	Effect Size	Mean	SD
Warmth	17.68	.00	iD/Di	.28	5.3	1.1
			i	.65	5.9	1.6
			iS/Si	.89	6.4	1.4
			S	.37	5.4	1.7
			SC/CS	−.19	4.4	1.6
			C	−.57	3.7	1.9
			CD/DC	−.26	4.3	1.7
			D	.40	5.5	1.4
Reasoning	4.13	.00	iD/Di	−.41	4.2	1.5
			i	−.10	4.8	1.4
			iS/Si	−.21	4.6	1.7
			S	−.22	4.5	2.0
			SC/CS	−.06	4.8	1.8
			C	.39	5.7	1.9
			CD/DC	.17	5.2	1.7
			D	−.25	4.5	2.0

(continued)

Table F.1 continued.						
16PF Scale	**F**	**Probability**	**Style**	**Effect Size**	**Mean**	**SD**
Emotional Stability	9.08	.00	iD/Di	.45	5.4	1.7
			i	.54	5.5	1.6
			iS/Si	.54	5.6	1.6
			S	.35	5.2	1.6
			SC/CS	−.18	4.3	1.6
			C	−.33	4.1	1.7
			CD/DC	−.23	4.2	1.7
			D	.22	5.0	1.4
Dominance	28.72	.00	iD/Di	.87	6.5	1.5
			i	.18	5.2	1.7
			iS/Si	.03	4.9	1.7
			S	−.33	4.3	1.5
			SC/CS	−.58	3.8	1.5
			C	−.43	4.1	1.5
			CD/DC	.55	5.9	1.7
			D	.85	6.4	1.5
Liveliness	27.45	.00	iD/Di	1.01	6.9	1.2
			i	1.05	7.0	1.5
			iS/Si	.73	6.4	1.5
			S	.23	5.5	1.7
			SC/CS	−.37	4.4	1.5
			C	−.68	3.8	1.6
			CD/DC	−.13	4.8	1.7
			D	.55	6.0	1.5

Table F.1 continued.						
16PF Scale	**F**	**Probability**	**Style**	**Effect Size**	**Mean**	**SD**
Rule-consciousness	4.15	.00	iD/Di	−.21	5.0	2.1
			i	.29	5.9	1.4
			iS/Si	.25	5.8	1.3
			S	.23	5.8	1.6
			SC/CS	.07	5.5	1.5
			C	.15	5.6	1.4
			CD/DC	−.29	4.9	1.8
			D	−.30	4.9	1.7
Social Boldness	38.29	.00	iD/Di	.90	6.7	1.8
			i	.88	6.6	1.5
			iS/Si	.92	6.7	1.6
			S	.13	5.1	1.7
			SC/CS	−.54	3.8	1.6
			C	−.80	3.3	1.4
			CD/DC	.06	5.0	1.8
			D	.81	6.5	1.5
Sensitivity	2.80	.01	iD/Di	−.45	4.6	1.4
			i	.12	5.5	1.8
			iS/Si	.42	6.0	1.3
			S	.10	5.5	1.6
			SC/CS	.07	5.5	1.5
			C	.01	5.4	1.9
			CD/DC	−.14	5.1	1.7
			D	−.25	4.9	1.2

(continued)

Table F.1 continued.

16PF Scale	F	Probability	Style	Effect Size	Mean	SD
Vigilance	4.79	.00	iD/Di	−.06	6.7	1.5
			i	−.30	6.3	1.7
			iS/Si	−.37	6.1	1.7
			S	−.22	6.4	1.7
			SC/CS	−.12	6.6	1.6
			C	.04	6.8	1.6
			CD/DC	.34	7.3	1.7
			D	.15	7.0	1.8
Abstractedness	1.99	.05	iD/Di	.11	5.7	1.4
			i	−.09	5.3	1.5
			iS/Si	−.11	5.3	1.6
			S	−.22	5.1	1.7
			SC/CS	−.07	5.4	1.6
			C	−.06	5.4	1.5
			CD/DC	.21	5.8	1.7
			D	.21	5.8	1.3
Privateness	11.11	.00	iD/Di	−.42	5.4	1.6
			i	−.51	5.3	1.5
			iS/Si	−.66	5.1	1.7
			S	−.20	5.8	1.3
			SC/CS	.25	6.5	1.5
			C	.59	7.0	1.3
			CD/DC	.01	6.1	1.6
			D	−.25	5.7	1.0

Table F.1 continued.						
16PF Scale	***F***	**Probability**	**Style**	**Effect Size**	**Mean**	***SD***
Apprehension	5.21	.00	iD/Di	−.77	4.5	1.4
			i	−.33	5.2	1.6
			iS/Si	−.10	5.6	1.4
			S	−.14	5.5	1.7
			SC/CS	.18	6.1	1.8
			C	.33	6.3	1.5
			CD/DC	.04	5.8	1.6
			D	−.34	5.2	1.3
Openness to Change	7.29	.00	iD/Di	.66	6.0	1.9
			i	.08	5.0	1.3
			iS/Si	.16	5.2	1.5
			S	−.06	4.8	1.5
			SC/CS	−.28	4.4	1.6
			C	−.36	4.3	1.8
			CD/DC	.17	5.2	1.6
			D	.66	6.0	1.4
Self-reliance	13.19	.00	iD/Di	−.70	5.5	1.2
			i	−.60	5.7	1.4
			iS/Si	−.64	5.6	1.8
			S	−.32	6.2	1.8
			SC/CS	.19	7.2	1.6
			C	.53	7.8	1.8
			CD/DC	.19	7.2	1.9
			D	−.21	6.4	2.2

(continued)

Table F.1 continued.

16PF Scale	F	Probability	Style	Effect Size	Mean	SD
Perfectionism	.38	.92	iD/Di	.04	6.0	1.0
			i	.20	6.3	1.7
			iS/Si	−.04	5.9	1.9
			S	−.02	5.9	1.7
			SC/CS	−.05	5.9	1.6
			C	.12	6.2	1.6
			CD/DC	−.02	5.9	1.6
			D	−.02	5.9	1.3
Tension	20.45	.00	iD/Di	−.40	5.0	1.9
			i	−.09	5.5	1.7
			iS/Si	−.76	4.5	1.3
			S	−.49	4.9	1.3
			SC/CS	−.21	5.4	1.4
			C	.33	6.2	1.5
			CD/DC	.58	6.6	1.5
			D	−.04	5.6	1.2
Impression Management	14.69	.00	iD/Di	.19	51.9	28.1
			i	.41	58.4	27.2
			iS/Si	.67	65.9	23.7
			S	.48	60.4	28.7
			SC/CS	.11	49.6	29.4
			C	−.29	38.0	25.5
			CD/DC	−.47	32.6	24.5
			D	−.24	39.3	29.7

Table F.1 continued.

16PF Scale	*F*	Probability	Style	Effect Size	Mean	*SD*
Infrequency	.65	.71	iD/Di	.16	73.5	19.0
			i	.07	71.9	19.8
			iS/Si	−.23	66.7	16.2
			S	.04	71.5	18.2
			SC/CS	.08	72.2	18.2
			C	−.05	69.8	17.4
			CD/DC	−.04	70.0	16.9
			D	.05	71.7	17.9
Acquiescence	3.16	.00	iD/Di	.25	54.3	32.9
			i	−.17	40.6	30.6
			iS/Si	.25	54.3	32.7
			S	−.08	43.5	33.7
			SC/CS	−.24	38.6	32.5
			C	−.13	42.1	30.2
			CD/DC	.16	51.4	31.3
			D	.37	58.1	29.0
Extraversion	39.59	.00	iD/Di	.84	60.9	10.8
			i	1.03	64.3	12.9
			iS/Si	1.01	64.1	15.0
			S	.36	51.7	16.1
			SC/CS	−.42	37.2	14.3
			C	−.83	29.3	15.7
			CD/DC	−.15	42.2	17.2
			D	.56	55.6	14.0

(continued)

Table F.1 continued.						
16PF Scale	**F**	**Probability**	**Style**	**Effect Size**	**Mean**	*SD*
Anxiety	12.78	.00	iD/Di	−.60	52.6	17.9
			i	−.45	55.4	18.8
			iS/Si	−.62	52.3	15.5
			S	−.40	56.4	16.0
			SC/CS	.04	64.5	17.8
			C	.37	70.7	17.4
			CD/DC	.39	71.0	18.3
			D	−.16	60.7	14.4
Tough-mindedness	4.58	.00	iD/Di	−.22	58.3	14.0
			i	−.22	58.2	16.1
			iS/Si	−.50	53.9	12.6
			S	.00	61.6	15.3
			SC/CS	.18	64.4	13.8
			C	.36	67.0	17.0
			CD/DC	−.05	60.9	15.7
			D	−.34	56.3	12.8
Independence	35.51	.00	iD/Di	.98	68.3	18.3
			i	.38	57.5	15.3
			iS/Si	.31	56.1	16.3
			S	−.23	46.4	14.9
			SC/CS	−.62	39.3	14.1
			C	−.64	38.9	12.8
			CD/DC	.48	59.2	16.5
			D	.95	67.8	13.4

Table F.1 continued.						
16PF Scale	**F**	**Probability**	**Style**	**Effect Size**	**Mean**	**SD**
Self-control	3.26	.00	iD/Di	−.29	53.5	11.1
			i	−.03	57.1	14.4
			iS/Si	−.04	57.1	14.7
			S	.09	58.9	14.9
			SC/CS	.14	59.5	13.7
			C	.33	62.3	13.1
			CD/DC	−.20	54.6	15.2
			D	−.32	53.0	11.4
Realistic	3.55	.00	iD/Di	.63	68.7	13.9
			i	−.22	53.6	18.1
			iS/Si	−.44	49.6	15.5
			S	−.07	56.1	18.4
			SC/CS	−.06	56.5	17.8
			C	−.02	57.2	19.6
			CD/DC	.12	59.7	17.6
			D	.26	62.2	13.7
Investigative	4.40	.00	iD/Di	.22	60.4	14.0
			i	−.39	49.6	16.2
			iS/Si	−.48	48.2	14.0
			S	−.26	52.1	18.5
			SC/CS	.02	57.0	17.7
			C	.21	60.3	20.4
			CD/DC	.19	59.9	16.5
			D	.03	57.0	14.4

(continued)

Table F.1 continued.					
16PF Scale	*F*	**Probability**	**Style**	**Effect Size**	**Mean**	*SD*
Artistic	14.70	.00	iD/Di	.51	56.5	15.6
			i	.53	56.8	15.9
			iS/Si	.68	59.1	13.3
			S	.01	48.7	14.7
			SC/CS	−.37	42.8	13.2
			C	−.58	39.5	15.7
			CD/DC	.12	50.4	14.7
			D	.57	57.4	12.0
Social	25.92	.00	iD/Di	.56	57.4	16.6
			i	.74	60.7	17.0
			iS/Si	.96	64.6	13.9
			S	.30	52.8	15.5
			SC/CS	−.38	40.6	14.5
			C	−.68	35.1	16.7
			CD/DC	−.13	45.1	16.3
			D	.66	59.3	13.8
Enterprising	25.36	.00	iD/Di	.94	64.4	17.0
			i	.55	57.5	15.5
			iS/Si	.54	57.3	11.7
			S	.01	47.8	15.8
			SC/CS	−.53	38.4	14.2
			C	−.65	36.2	15.8
			CD/DC	.18	50.9	17.4
			D	.92	64.1	12.8

Table F.1 continued.						
16PF Scale	**F**	**Probability**	**Style**	**Effect Size**	**Mean**	**SD**
Conventional	.41	.90	iD/Di	.12	61.3	11.4
			i	.08	60.7	17.4
			iS/Si	−.09	58.0	16.5
			S	.08	60.7	16.3
			SC/CS	−.02	59.1	15.6
			C	.09	60.8	15.1
			CD/DC	−.07	58.3	16.2
			D	−.03	58.9	14.0
Self-esteem	19.62	.00	iD/Di	.75	60.0	17.1
			i	.71	59.3	13.6
			iS/Si	.74	59.8	13.9
			S	.29	51.7	16.1
			SC/CS	−.37	39.8	16.0
			C	−.56	36.4	16.0
			CD/DC	−.14	44.1	17.9
			D	.61	57.4	12.6
Emotional Adjustment	8.55	.00	iD/Di	.64	58.7	16.9
			i	.48	56.1	16.2
			iS/Si	.42	55.2	14.2
			S	.33	53.6	14.7
			SC/CS	−.14	46.0	16.6
			C	−.37	42.2	14.8
			CD/DC	−.23	44.5	16.4
			D	.24	52.2	12.5

(continued)

Table F.1 continued.

16PF Scale	*F*	Probability	Style	Effect Size	Mean	*SD*
Social Adjustment	35.53	.00	iD/Di	.94	62.6	19.8
			i	.88	61.4	12.7
			iS/Si	.88	61.4	15.9
			S	.17	47.0	18.3
			SC/CS	−.51	33.2	16.1
			C	−.79	27.6	15.2
			CD/DC	.03	44.3	18.2
			D	.74	58.5	14.6
Emotional Expressivity	37.27	.00	iD/Di	.84	63.0	19.4
			i	.60	58.2	17.0
			iS/Si	.48	55.9	17.0
			S	−.11	44.2	16.1
			SC/CS	−.60	34.6	15.0
			C	−.80	30.5	12.3
			CD/DC	.42	54.6	18.7
			D	.89	64.1	14.2
Emotional Sensitivity	18.43	.00	iD/Di	.52	54.4	12.4
			i	.60	55.7	14.8
			iS/Si	.81	59.3	12.3
			S	.28	50.4	15.7
			SC/CS	−.29	40.6	14.4
			C	−.62	35.1	18.0
			CD/DC	−.15	43.1	16.2
			D	.66	56.7	12.4

Table F.1 continued.

16PF Scale	*F*	Probability	Style	Effect Size	Mean	*SD*
Emotional Control	2.01	.05	iD/Di	.09	56.5	16.1
			i	−.12	52.9	16.7
			iS/Si	−.41	47.7	18.3
			S	−.10	53.3	17.7
			SC/CS	.02	55.3	18.0
			C	.25	59.3	15.1
			CD/DC	.04	55.8	18.4
			D	.03	55.6	13.1
Social Expressivity	49.18	.00	iD/Di	1.08	68.3	16.7
			i	1.06	67.9	15.2
			iS/Si	.93	65.2	15.3
			S	.22	50.5	17.2
			SC/CS	−.55	34.5	15.6
			C	−.88	27.7	15.7
			CD/DC	.00	46.0	17.3
			D	.82	63.0	15.6
Social Sensitivity	6.39	.00	iD/Di	−.83	44.8	17.0
			i	−.30	54.6	14.8
			iS/Si	−.18	56.8	15.5
			S	−.07	58.8	18.2
			SC/CS	.22	64.2	19.5
			C	.38	67.0	16.8
			CD/DC	−.02	59.7	18.3
			D	−.43	52.2	15.0

(continued)

16PF Scale	*F*	Probability	Style	Effect Size	Mean	*SD*
Table F.1 continued.						
Social Control	30.78	.00	iD/Di	.93	62.6	21.2
			i	.82	60.4	14.5
			iS/Si	.79	59.8	17.0
			S	.03	44.6	17.6
			SC/CS	−.53	33.3	15.9
			C	−.69	30.1	15.9
			CD/DC	.10	46.1	18.2
			D	.80	60.0	15.2
Empathy	32.22	.00	iD/Di	.90	58.7	14.6
			i	.84	57.5	16.0
			iS/Si	1.02	60.9	13.6
			S	.38	48.8	16.3
			SC/CS	−.30	36.0	15.4
			C	−.64	29.6	16.9
			CD/DC	−.32	35.6	17.2
			D	.56	52.2	12.8
Leadership Potential	25.98	.00	iD/Di	.99	67.0	17.4
			i	.82	63.6	16.4
			iS/Si	.77	62.5	15.9
			S	.24	51.9	18.5
			SC/CS	−.41	39.0	17.0
			C	−.67	33.8	16.6
			CD/DC	−.10	45.1	18.7
			D	.64	60.0	14.9

Table F.1 continued.						
16PF Scale	**F**	**Probability**	**Style**	**Effect Size**	**Mean**	*SD*
Creative Potential	33.53	.00	iD/Di	.95	67.4	18.6
			i	.56	59.6	16.9
			iS/Si	.51	58.6	17.6
			S	−.14	45.4	18.3
			SC/CS	−.61	36.0	16.0
			C	−.67	34.9	15.0
			CD/DC	.34	55.2	17.9
			D	.98	68.2	14.7
Creative Achievement	8.91	.00	iD/Di	.60	66.1	15.0
			i	.36	62.1	14.5
			iS/Si	.10	57.7	14.1
			S	−.18	53.0	18.1
			SC/CS	−.32	50.6	14.9
			C	−.38	49.6	15.2
			CD/DC	.26	60.3	17.1
			D	.56	65.6	17.8

Appendix G: Correlations Among the Work of Leaders and Other Assessments

Table G.1 Correlations Among the Work of Leaders Scales and the Neuroticism Domain and Facets Scales of the NEO™-PI-3

Work of Leaders Scales	NEO-PI-3 Scales						
	Neuroticism	Anxiety	Angry Hostility	Depression	Self-consciousness	Impulsiveness	Vulnerability
Remaining Open	.01	.00	.07	.03	−.01	.16	.02
Prioritizing the Big Picture	−.07	−.06	.03	−.02	−.09	.16	.00
Being Adventurous	−.29	−.29	.02	−.26	−.36	.02	−.29
Speaking Out	−.27	−.24	.06	−.28	−.43	.10	−.33
Seeking Counsel	−.08	−.01	−.19	−.07	−.13	−.06	.02
Exploring Implications	−.08	−.10	−.22	−.13	−.09	−.24	−.13
Explaining Rationale	−.29	−.28	−.15	−.23	−.18	−.27	−.26

(continued)

Table G.1 continued.

Work of Leaders Scales	NEO-PI-3 Scales						
	Neuroticism	Anxiety	Angry Hostility	Depression	Self-consciousness	Impulsiveness	Vulnerability
Structuring Messages	.01	−.02	−.14	−.06	.04	−.20	−.10
Exchanging Perspectives	.08	.13	−.29	.06	.06	−.15	.13
Being Receptive	−.12	−.05	−.49	−.16	−.08	−.27	−.03
Being Expressive	−.19	−.16	.03	−.30	−.44	.10	−.23
Being Encouraging	−.23	−.17	−.42	−.36	−.32	−.16	−.23
Being Driven	−.07	−.09	.35	−.12	−.23	.21	−.22
Initiating Action	−.34	−.31	−.06	−.34	−.44	−.02	−.41
Providing a Plan	.03	.03	−.10	−.05	.00	−.21	−.05
Analyzing In-depth	−.17	−.17	−.14	−.19	−.18	−.21	−.29
Addressing Problems	−.10	−.14	.34	−.07	−.21	.18	−.17
Offering Praise	−.16	−.07	−.41	−.23	−.25	−.22	−.17

Table G.2 Correlations Among the Work of Leaders Scales and the Extroversion Domain and Facets Scales of the NEO-PI-3

Work of Leaders Scales	NEO-PI-3 Scales						
	Extraversion	Warmth	Gregariousness	Assertiveness	Activity	Excitement Seeking	Positive Emotions
Remaining Open	.03	−.06	.00	.04	.07	.14	.04
Prioritizing the Big Picture	.15	.01	.09	.11	.08	.20	.12
Being Adventurous	.44	.23	.34	.56	.48	.51	.24
Speaking Out	.47	.28	.30	.70	.49	.38	.28
Seeking Counsel	.43	.46	.55	.10	.13	.14	.30
Exploring Implications	−.10	.03	−.05	−.06	−.04	−.07	.03
Explaining Rationale	−.15	−.13	−.02	.10	.13	.10	−.13
Structuring Messages	−.15	−.03	−.07	−.06	−.03	−.08	−.03
Exchanging Perspectives	.21	.38	.33	−.28	−.16	−.04	.23
Being Receptive	.29	.46	.31	−.15	−.12	−.04	.40
Being Expressive	.66	.54	.50	.65	.53	.30	.48
Being Encouraging	.60	.65	.46	.25	.22	.13	.68
Being Driven	.28	.03	.14	.61	.55	.34	.05
Initiating Action	.49	.29	.40	.65	.58	.48	.30
Providing a Plan	−.11	.04	−.07	−.06	−.03	−.19	−.05
Analyzing In-depth	−.11	−.09	−.03	.18	.17	.12	−.04
Addressing Problems	.00	−.19	−.08	.41	.29	.19	−.16
Offering Praise	.53	.65	.43	.14	.14	.07	.54

Table G.3 Correlations Among the Work of Leaders Scales and the Openness to Experience Domain and Facets Scales of the NEO-PI-3

	NEO-PI-3 Scales						
Work of Leaders Scales	Openness to Experience	Fantasy	Aesthetics	Feelings	Actions	Ideas	Values
Remaining Open	.43	.41	.32	.15	.25	.26	.22
Prioritizing the Big Picture	.38	.33	.29	.15	.35	.18	.23
Being Adventurous	.29	.18	.19	.12	.44	.31	.16
Speaking Out	.28	.24	.14	.22	.29	.29	.17
Seeking Counsel	.02	−.09	.12	.16	.17	−.01	−.02
Exploring Implications	.02	−.09	.03	.01	−.04	.10	−.01
Explaining Rationale	−.06	−.20	−.17	−.26	.05	.12	.07
Structuring Messages	−.01	−.11	−.04	.02	−.06	.11	−.03
Exchanging Perspectives	−.03	−.10	.13	.17	.04	−.13	−.03
Being Receptive	−.07	−.07	.08	.12	.00	−.14	−.08
Being Expressive	.18	.17	.16	.37	.26	.16	.06
Being Encouraging	.20	.12	.26	.36	.25	.11	.06
Being Driven	.17	.12	.03	.10	.21	.25	.14
Initiating Action	.32	.22	.21	.14	.42	.31	.18
Providing a Plan	−.26	−.26	−.20	−.06	−.28	−.07	−.19
Analyzing In-depth	.32	.10	.13	.06	.14	.47	.18
Addressing Problems	.11	.09	−.05	−.02	.10	.22	.11
Offering Praise	.05	−.01	.14	.28	.13	.01	−.03

Table G.4 Correlations Among the Work of Leaders Scales and the Agreeableness Domain and Facets Scales of the NEO-PI-3

Work of Leaders Scales	NEO-PI-3 Scales						
	Agreeableness	Trust	Straightforwardness	Altruism	Compliance	Modesty	Tender-mindedness
Remaining Open	−.08	−.01	−.14	−.10	−.08	−.11	.14
Prioritizing the Big Picture	−.10	.03	−.22	−.08	−.13	−.07	.12
Being Adventurous	−.38	.05	−.32	.00	−.31	−.34	.01
Speaking Out	−.39	.05	−.26	−.03	−.42	−.35	.05
Seeking Counsel	.29	.38	.08	.23	.24	.02	.26
Exploring Implications	.15	.02	.19	.18	.12	.05	.04
Explaining Rationale	−.19	−.04	−.01	−.11	−.08	−.08	−.22
Structuring Messages	.14	.02	.23	.13	.15	.08	.01
Exchanging Perspectives	.63	.36	.32	.44	.54	.32	.35
Being Receptive	.66	.47	.38	.52	.63	.24	.33
Being Expressive	−.15	.18	−.07	.18	−.25	−.27	.17
Being Encouraging	.47	.51	.28	.52	.32	.07	.45
Being Driven	−.59	−.14	−.34	−.23	−.60	−.35	−.11
Initiating Action	−.32	.15	−.23	.01	−.26	−.31	.08
Providing a Plan	.12	−.01	.23	.16	.13	.03	−.07
Analyzing In-depth	−.14	−.04	−.01	.01	−.13	−.14	.01
Addressing Problems	−.64	−.31	−.38	−.37	−.70	−.30	−.20
Offering Praise	.56	.51	.37	.57	.42	.17	.45

Table G.5 Correlations Among the Work of Leaders Scales and the Conscientiousness Domain and Facets Scales of the NEO-PI-3

	NEO-PI-3 Scales						
Work of Leaders Scales	Conscientiousness	Competence	Order	Dutifulness	Achievement Striving	Self-discipline	Deliberation
Remaining Open	−.27	−.12	−.31	−.30	−.02	−.20	−.27
Prioritizing the Big Picture	−.35	−.12	−.35	−.31	−.03	−.23	−.38
Being Adventurous	.08	.21	.05	.00	.35	.18	−.26
Speaking Out	.14	.28	.05	.04	.40	.20	−.27
Seeking Counsel	−.09	.01	−.01	.02	.04	.01	.04
Exploring Implications	.31	.21	.27	.27	.11	.23	.43
Explaining Rationale	.30	.28	.20	.28	.23	.28	.29
Structuring Messages	.37	.22	.32	.30	.13	.27	.44
Exchanging Perspectives	−.11	−.06	.00	.04	−.14	−.03	.21
Being Receptive	−.03	.11	.09	.16	−.07	.07	.27
Being Expressive	.15	.26	.10	.12	.33	.20	−.20
Being Encouraging	.07	.25	.11	.16	.18	.20	.09
Being Driven	.24	.21	.11	.03	.40	.17	−.28
Initiating Action	.21	.34	.13	.13	.49	.27	−.19
Providing a Plan	.44	.21	.43	.36	.12	.30	.44
Analyzing In-depth	.36	.33	.20	.23	.32	.28	.28
Addressing Problems	.10	.06	−.03	−.06	.20	.10	−.25
Offering Praise	.09	.21	.13	.19	.12	.20	.15

Table G.6 Correlations Among the Work of Leaders Scales and the Scales of the 16PF®

Work of Leaders Scales	Warmth	Reasoning	Emotional Stability	Dominance	Liveliness	Rule-consciousness	Social Boldness	Sensitivity	Vigilance	Abstractedness
							16PF Scales			
Remaining Open	.05	.16	−.04	.11	.09	−.36	.13	.14	−.01	.48
Prioritizing the Big Picture	.17	.04	−.02	.15	.17	−.38	.23	.11	−.02	.44
Being Adventurous	.11	−.07	.15	.50	.41	−.31	.47	−.13	.08	.15
Speaking Out	.27	−.08	.19	.68	.40	−.24	.62	−.12	.04	.15
Seeking Counsel	.45	−.18	.21	−.02	.35	.06	.28	.04	−.30	−.13
Exploring Implications	−.08	−.02	.10	−.07	−.14	.33	−.08	−.05	−.05	−.20
Explaining Rationale	−.23	.10	.20	.17	−.15	.08	−.04	−.30	−.03	−.23
Structuring Messages	−.13	.06	.09	−.07	−.15	.34	−.17	−.02	−.06	−.27
Exchanging Perspectives	.35	−.16	.12	−.40	.19	.22	−.02	.18	−.31	−.18
Being Receptive	.37	−.10	.26	−.44	.23	.31	.08	.18	−.41	−.32
Being Expressive	.45	−.14	.22	.53	.52	−.11	.71	.06	−.08	.02
Being Encouraging	.57	−.18	.41	.01	.42	.18	.45	.20	−.36	−.13
Being Driven	.03	.00	.01	.64	.22	−.28	.39	−.16	.20	.14
Initiating Action	.25	−.11	.25	.56	.45	−.23	.58	−.14	−.06	.14
Providing a Plan	−.12	−.06	.06	−.10	−.15	.42	−.17	−.09	.01	−.41
Analyzing In-depth	−.16	.17	.18	.22	−.06	.09	.01	−.15	.01	−.02
Addressing Problems	−.16	.02	−.04	.62	−.02	−.26	.22	−.24	.31	.25
Offering Praise	.50	−.18	.28	−.12	.32	.25	.35	.10	−.32	−.23

(continued)

Table G.6 continued.

Work of Leaders Scales	16PF Scales									
	Privateness	Apprehension	Openness to Change	Self-reliance	Perfectionism	Tension	Empathy	Leadership Potential	Creative Potential	Creative Achievement
Remaining Open	−.11	−.02	.44	−.06	−.41	−.05	.14	−.09	.23	.36
Prioritizing the Big Picture	−.15	−.07	.46	−.17	−.47	−.10	.24	−.02	.28	.32
Being Adventurous	−.18	−.26	.39	−.19	−.03	−.03	.32	.38	.56	.39
Speaking Out	−.33	−.28	.45	−.20	.02	.08	.40	.47	.74	.42
Seeking Counsel	−.29	−.02	.06	−.65	−.05	−.28	.45	.30	.10	−.16
Exploring Implications	.14	−.02	−.10	.06	.36	−.09	−.03	.07	−.05	−.13
Explaining Rationale	.21	−.26	.01	.06	.27	−.07	−.04	.16	.05	−.10
Structuring Messages	.22	.06	−.19	.07	.41	−.01	−.09	.05	−.13	−.19
Exchanging Perspectives	−.14	.15	−.10	−.45	−.04	−.38	.29	.08	−.25	−.27
Being Receptive	−.11	.03	−.21	−.36	.04	−.47	.40	.21	−.25	−.33
Being Expressive	−.49	−.19	.28	−.33	.09	.05	.50	.54	.67	.32
Being Encouraging	−.36	−.11	.13	−.47	.07	−.41	.65	.46	.26	.00
Being Driven	−.15	−.13	.32	−.02	.11	.39	.07	.27	.59	.37
Initiating Action	−.28	−.28	.47	−.26	.05	−.02	.46	.49	.68	.41
Providing a Plan	.12	.04	−.38	.14	.54	.04	−.17	.07	−.18	−.24
Analyzing In-depth	.12	−.14	.22	.12	.26	−.04	.03	.14	.20	.16
Addressing Problems	−.02	−.24	.32	.16	.00	.31	−.10	.08	.49	.37
Offering Praise	−.37	−.07	.00	−.40	.07	−.44	.52	.38	.10	−.11

Table G.6 continued.

	16PF Scales										
Work of Leaders Scales	Extraversion	Anxiety	Tough-mindedness	Independence	Self-control	Realistic	Investigative	Artistic	Social	Enterprising	Conventional
Remaining Open	.11	.00	−.47	.23	−.54	−.01	.19	.51	.10	.06	−.52
Prioritizing the Big Picture	.23	−.05	−.48	.29	−.59	−.01	.10	.53	.21	.17	−.51
Being Adventurous	.36	−.14	−.21	.57	−.30	.20	.11	.39	.24	.46	−.05
Speaking Out	.46	−.14	−.29	.76	−.24	.13	.01	.48	.44	.65	−.03
Seeking Counsel	.55	−.24	−.12	.04	−.02	−.14	−.27	.13	.39	.23	.04
Exploring Implications	−.13	−.09	.16	−.11	.42	.08	.00	−.19	−.05	−.05	.29
Explaining Rationale	−.18	−.19	.30	.08	.28	.39	.24	−.25	−.21	.09	.35
Structuring Messages	−.19	−.04	.24	−.17	.48	.01	−.02	−.28	−.14	−.10	.36
Exchanging Perspectives	.32	−.18	−.07	−.34	.10	−.25	−.29	−.04	.23	−.11	.03
Being Receptive	.32	−.34	.02	−.38	.22	−.24	−.30	−.09	.25	−.06	.14
Being Expressive	.64	−.16	−.30	.62	−.13	−.10	−.22	.49	.59	.61	.01
Being Encouraging	.60	−.42	−.27	.12	.06	−.23	−.33	.31	.55	.33	.04
Being Driven	.19	.13	−.13	.64	−.17	.13	.06	.28	.19	.47	.03
Initiating Action	.47	−.21	−.27	.65	−.24	.18	.04	.45	.40	.59	−.01
Providing a Plan	−.18	.00	.40	−.22	.63	.01	−.11	−.44	−.14	−.11	.52
Analyzing In-depth	−.13	−.12	.01	.20	.18	.27	.26	.01	−.08	.11	.18
Addressing Problems	−.04	.11	−.08	.60	−.20	.30	.24	.22	.00	.35	−.06
Offering Praise	.51	−.35	−.11	−.02	.16	−.18	−.29	.12	.48	.22	.13

(continued)

Table G.6 continued.

Work of Leaders Scales	Self-esteem	Emotional Adjustment	Social Adjustment	Emotional Expressivity	Emotional Sensitivity	Emotional Control	Social Expressivity	Social Sensitivity	Social Control
				16PF Scales					
Remaining Open	.00	−.04	.14	.23	.21	.01	.18	−.13	.16
Prioritizing the Big Picture	.08	.01	.23	.30	.32	−.01	.27	−.14	.24
Being Adventurous	.33	.19	.46	.55	.25	.04	.52	−.35	.48
Speaking Out	.43	.21	.61	.73	.42	−.03	.63	−.34	.64
Seeking Counsel	.27	.18	.34	.18	.40	−.21	.35	.01	.27
Exploring Implications	.05	.09	−.07	−.24	−.11	.09	−.14	−.03	−.04
Explaining Rationale	.18	.24	.02	−.09	−.19	.32	−.12	−.29	.06
Structuring Messages	.00	.04	−.13	−.29	−.18	.09	−.22	.05	−.10
Exchanging Perspectives	.07	.07	.03	−.20	.24	−.23	.07	.18	−.05
Being Receptive	.20	.22	.12	−.23	.22	−.11	.14	.08	.03
Being Expressive	.45	.20	.68	.74	.50	−.21	.73	−.21	.68
Being Encouraging	.46	.33	.49	.23	.53	−.19	.50	−.12	.43
Being Driven	.19	.01	.36	.59	.17	.00	.37	−.19	.43
Initiating Action	.44	.25	.59	.63	.41	−.01	.62	−.37	.62
Providing a Plan	−.02	.04	−.17	−.27	−.25	.02	−.22	.10	−.17
Analyzing In-depth	.15	.16	.06	−.02	−.04	.22	−.01	−.26	.13
Addressing Problems	.10	.02	.20	.44	.01	.15	.16	−.27	.26
Offering Praise	.35	.26	.36	.13	.41	−.23	.39	−.04	.31

References

Acton, G.S., & Revelle, W. (2002). Interpersonal personality measures show circumplex structure on new psychometric criteria. *Journal of Personality Assessment, 79*(3), 446–471.

Alden, L.E., Wiggins, J.S., & Pincus, A.L. (1990). Construction of circumplex scales for the inventory of interpersonal problems. *Journal of Personality Assessment, 55*(3–4), 521–536.

Bandalos, D.L., & Boehm-Kaufman, M.R. (2008). Four common misconceptions in exploratory factor analysis. In C.E. Lance & R.J. Vandenberg (Eds.), *Statistical and methodological myths and urban legends: Doctrine, verity and fable in the organizational and social sciences* (pp. 61–87). New York: Taylor & Francis.

Benjamin, L.S. (1996). A clinician-friendly version of the interpersonal circumplex: Structural analysis of social behavior (SASB). *Journal of Personality Assessment, 66*(2), 248–266.

Clarke, W.V. (1956). *Manual for the activity vector analysis.* Providence, RI: Walter V. Clarke Associates.

Cohen, J. (1992). A power primer. *Psychological Bulletin, 112*(1), 155–159.

Cole, P., & Tuzinski, K. (2003). *The DiSC indra research report.* Minneapolis, MN: Inscape Publishing.

Conte, H.R., & Plutchik, R. (1981). A circumplex model for interpersonal traits. *Journal of Personality and Social Psychology, 40*(4), 701–711.

Ebel, R.L. (1951). Estimation of the reliability of ratings. *Psychometrika, 16*(1), 407–424.

Forer, B.R. (1949). The fallacy of personal validation: A classroom demonstration of gullibility. *Journal of Abnormal and Social Psychology, 44*(1), 118–123.

Furr, M. (2011). *Scale construction and psychometrics for social and personality psychology.* London, UK: Sage.

Geier, J.G. (1979). *Emotions of normal people by William Moulton Marston: Introduced with an interpretation, references, and a presentation of a new construct-situation perception analysis.* San Francisco, CA: Persona Press, Inc.

Goldberg, L.R. (1981). Language and individual differences: The search for universals in personality lexicons. In L. Wheeler (Ed.), *Review of personality and social psychology: Volume 1* (pp. 141–165). Thousand Oaks, CA: Sage.

Gough, H.G., & Bradley, P. (1996). *CPI manual* (3rd ed.). Palo Alto, CA: Consulting Psychologists Press.

Gray, J.A. (1987). *The psychology of fear and stress* (2nd ed.). New York: Cambridge.

Gurtman, M.B., & Balakrishnan, J.D. (1998). Circular measurement redux: The analysis and interpretation of interpersonal circle profiles. *Clinical Psychology: Science and Practice 5*(3), 344–360.

Guttman, L. (1954). A new approach to factor analysis: The radex. In P.F. Lazarsfeld (Ed.), *Mathematical thinking in the social sciences.* New York: The Free Press.

Hofstee, W.K., de Raad, B., & Goldberg, L.R. (1992). Integrations of the big five and circumplex approaches to trait structure. *Journal of Personality and Social Psychology, 63*(1), 146–163.

Inscape Publishing. (2012). *Research report for adaptive testing assessment.* Minneapolis, MN: Author.

IPAT. (2009). *16PF fifth edition questionnaire manual.* Champaign, IL: Institute for Personality and Ability Testing.

Kendrick, D.T., & Funder, D.C. (1988). Profiting from controversy: Lessons from the person-situation debate. *American Psychologist, 43*(1), 23–34.

Kiesler, D.J. (1987). *The check list of interpersonal transactions—revised (CLOIT-R).* Richmond, VA: Virginia Commonwealth University.

Kiesler, D.J., & Schmidt, J.A. (1991). *The impact message inventory: Form IIA octant scale version.* Richmond, VA: Virginia Commonwealth University.

Kiesler, D.J., & Schmidt, J.A. (2006). *The impact message inventory—circumplex (IMI-C) manual.* Palo Alto, CA: Mind Garden.

Kiesler, D.J., Schmidt, J.A., & Wagner, C.C. (1997). A circumplex inventory of impact messages: An operational bridge between emotion and interpersonal behavior. In R. Plutchik & H. Conte (Eds.), *Circumplex models of personality and emotions.* Washington, DC: American Psychological Association.

Kincaid, J.P., Fishburne, R.P., Rogers, R.L., & Chissom, B.S. (1975). *Derivation of new readability formulas (automated readability index, fog count, and Flesch reading ease formula) for Navy enlisted personnel* (Research Branch Report 8–75). Memphis, TN: Naval Air Station.

Kruskal, J.B., & Wish, M. (1978). *Multidimensional scaling.* Thousand Oaks, CA: Sage.

Laforge, R., & Suczek, R.F. (1955). The interpersonal dimension of personality: III. An interpersonal checklist. *Journal of Personality, 24*(1), 94–112.

Leary, T. (1957). *Interpersonal diagnosis of personality.* New York: Ronald Press.

Locke, K.D. (2000). Circumplex scales of interpersonal values: Reliability, validity, and applicability to interpersonal problems and personality disorders. *Journal of Personality Assessment, 75*(2), 249–267.

Marston, W.M. (1928). *Emotions of normal people.* London: Devonshire Press.

McCrae, R.R., & Costa, P.T. (2010). *NEO inventories: Professional manual.* Lutz, FL: Psychological Assessment Resources.

Messick, S. (1989). Validity. In R.L. Linn (Ed.), *Educational measurement* (3rd ed., pp. 13–103). New York: Macmillan.

Myers, I.B., McCaulley, M.H., Quenk, N.L., & Hammer, A.L. (1998). *MBTI manual: A guide to the development and use of the Myers Briggs type indicator* (3rd ed.). Palo Alto, CA: Consulting Psychologists Press.

Myllyniemi, R. (1997). The interpersonal circle and the emotional undercurrents of human sociability. In R. Plutchik & H. Conte (Eds.), *Circumplex models of personality and emotions.* Washington, DC: American Psychological Association.

Norman, W.T. (1963). Toward an adequate taxonomy of personality attributes: Replicated factor structure in peer nomination personality ratings. *Journal of Abnormal and Social Psychology*, *66*(6), 574–583.

Ojanen, T., Gronroos, M., & Salmivalli, C. (2005). An interpersonal circumplex model of children's social goals: Links with peer reported behavior and sociometric status. *Developmental Psychology*, *41*(5), 699–710.

Prediger, D.J. (1982). Dimensions underlying Holland's hexagon: Missing link between interests and occupations? *Journal of Vocational Behavior*, *21*(3), 259–287.

Soldz, S., Budman, S., Demby, A., & Merry, J. (1993). Representations of personality disorders in a circumplex and five-factor space: Explorations with a clinical sample. *Psychological Assessment*, *5*(1), 41–52.

Streiner, D.L. (2003). Starting at the beginning: An introduction to coefficient alpha and internal consistency. *Journal of Personality Assessment*, *80*(1), 99–103.

Strong, S.R., Hills, H.I., Kilmartin, C.T., DeVries, H., Lanier, K., Nelson, B.N., Strickland, D., & Meyer, C.W. (1988). The dynamic relations among interpersonal behaviors: A test of complementarity and anticomplementarity. *Journal of Personality and Social Psychology*, *54*(5), 798–810.

Sullivan, H.S. (Ed.). (2013). *The interpersonal theory of psychiatry.* New York City: Routledge.

Weiss, D.J. (1974). *Strategies of adaptive ability measurement* (Research Report, 74–75). Minneapolis: University of Minnesota, Department of Psychology, Psychometric Methods Program, Computerized Adaptive Testing Laboratory.

Weiss, D.J. (2004). Computerized adaptive testing for effective and efficient measurement in counseling and education. *Measurement and Evaluation in Counseling and Development*, *37*(2), 70–84.

Wiggins, J.S. (1995). *Interpersonal adjective scales: Professional manual.* Odessa, FL: Psychological Assessment Resources.

Wiggins, J.S., Phillips, N., & Trapnell, P. (1989). Circular reasoning about interpersonal behavior: Evidence concerning some untested assumptions underlying diagnostic classification. *Journal of Personality and Social Psychology*, *56*(2), 296–305.

Wiggins, J.S., Steiger, J.H., & Gaelick, L. (1981). Evaluating circumplexity in personality data. *Multivariate Behavioral Research*, *16*(3), 263–289.

Wiley. (2011). *Personal profile system.* Minneapolis, MN: Author.

Index

Page references followed by *fig* indicate an illustrated figure; followed by *t* indicate a table.